THE
MODERN MOVEMENT
IN ART

by the same author

*

FLEMISH PAINTERS
ENGLISH PAINTING
DUTCH PAINTING
MODERN FRENCH PAINTERS
AN OUTLINE OF ENGLISH PAINTING

Plate A. MATISSE: *The Painter and his Model*

THE
MODERN MOVEMENT
IN ART

R. H. WILENSKI

NEW YORK
THOMAS YOSELOFF INC

First American Edition, 1957
Published by Thomas Yoseloff Inc
New York

Printed in Great Britain

This book is
dedicated
to
GEOFFREY FABER
who
invited me to write it
and
has helped me enormously
by criticizing the first
drafts

CONTENTS

Part I
CHARACTER OF THE MOVEMENT

CONTENTS

Part II
DEGENERATE NINETEENTH-CENTURY ART

Part III
TECHNIQUE OF THE MOVEMENT

10

CONTENTS

Part IV
RELATIVE VALUES

11

ILLUSTRATIONS

COLOUR PLATES

MONOCHROME PLATES
(*between pages* 80 *and* 81)

13

14

PREFACE TO THE 1956 EDITION

This book speaks of art as certain types of action by living men—the types of action which result when the artist asks himself: 'What work shall I do to-day? In what way shall I do it? How will it stand in relation to the products of the cameras? Is it worth while? Can I afford it?' Many people, I know, have found it useful because it approaches the matter in that way; or, to put it differently, the book has been found useful because it is concerned with problems confronting various types of artist at work in their studios, with the relative values of their several approaches to those problems, and with the difference between the permanent intrinsic values imparted to works of art by the artist's action, and the temporary acquired values placed upon them by the appreciation or derision of spectators. And it is, I think, still useful because conditions inside the studios are still much the same, the artists still have to face the same or similar problems, most of the works they are producing are still within the categories I have indicated in this inquiry, and spectators are still prone to assume that the value they themselves present to a work of art is in some way a measure of the work's intrinsic value.

For this new edition I have left the text substantially unaltered because it was written as an integrated argument with strong convictions which I still think right. But I have made some verbal changes and adjustments for the sake of clarity, and I have added some explanatory footnotes and paragraphs on 'Distortion to record disquiet', 'The original artist as salesman' and 'Imaginative illustration' which are clearly indicated as additions.[1]

It would, of course, have been possible to insert some references to recent aspects of the modern movement at appropriate places in the body of the book. But I have preferred to group them as consecutive comments in this Preface.

In the same spirit I have retained the majority of the old black and white illustrations. But I have added about thirty-five new ones and two colour plates; and as my publisher has allowed me a much larger page I have been able to arrange the plates to show some analogies and contrasts. The new colour plates reproduce pictures by Matisse and Paul Klee; the new monochromes show works by Gauguin, Ozenfant and Mondrian among the pioneers of the movement, additional pictures by Matisse, Picasso and Paul Nash, and paintings by

[1] Cf. pp. 155, 178 and 191.

Ivon Hitchens, Ben Nicholson, Victor Pasmore, Cecil Collins, Patrick Heron, Merlyn Evans, Peter Lanyon, William Gear, W. Barns Graham, Soulages, Douglas Hamilton Fraser and Alan Reynolds. The new plates showing sculpture reproduce works by Henry Moore, Giacometti, Frederick McWilliam, Reginald Butler, Bernard Meadows, and Kenneth Armitage.

THE MIDDLE TWENTIES

When this book was written in the middle of the 'twenties, the French Cubist movement led by Picasso, Braque, and Gris (Pl. 15) was some fifteen years old; the English Vorticist movement led by Wyndham Lewis (Pl. 19) was a few years younger; Italian Futurism and the Zurich Dada movement had both run their course; and in Paris Amedée Ozenfant had painted most of his Purist compositions (Pl. 16) and Piet Mondrian had produced some rectilinear pictures in his later manner (Pl. 17).

All these aspects of the modern movement had discarded illusionist naturalistic technique (cf. 'Naturalism and Representation' (i) in Part I and 'Naturalism and Representation' (ii) in Part II) and proclaimed the need for a new pictorial language. This need was felt partly because these artists were very conscious of the difference between their mechanical vision and human perception (cf. 'Human perception' in Part II) and thus recognized the degenerate character of nineteenth-century naturalistic technique, and partly because the influence of the still-camera and the cinema-camera had become a widespread nuisance to artists by encouraging the public in the misconception that the camera's naturalistic vision was the only one appropriate for artists (cf. 'The camera's vision' in Part II). The most clear-headed and adventurous painters had accordingly decided to leave the naturalistic technique entirely to the cameras and to evolve a new non-naturalistic pictorial language symbolizing human perception with which the cameras would be unable to compete. At the same time these artists were in passionate reaction against the Romantic art of the nineteenth century in all its aspects (cf. 'The Romantic heresy' in Part I); and they proclaimed themselves servants of an idea of art summarized in the old dictum 'Architecture is the Mother of the Arts' (cf. 'Architecture as typical art' in Part I).

In this new type of formal classical art it was held as a first principle that the artist must be free, as the architect is free, either to introduce or to exclude the representation of physical objects and concrete things. Thus the Cubists, and

Ozenfant in his Purist works, included such elements while Mondrian excluded them from his later non-representational paintings.[1]

A link between the Cubists, Ozenfant and Mondrian (in his later pictures) was the common acceptance of geometric form as a basis for aesthetic; and in this connection the famous passage about the eternal and absolute beauty of geometric forms in Plato's 'Philebus' was first quoted, I think, by Léonce Rosenberg—an early champion of the movement in pamphlets and a review issued from his gallery *L'Effort Moderne* (founded in Paris in 1918).[2]

In Ozenfant's paintings of the early 'twenties, and in Mondrian's rectilinear pictures, two sets of words, as it were, had been invented for the new technical language of the new formal art, and two separate, though related, sentences had been written with them as new clear symbols of purely formal experience. But Ozenfant, whose Purism had reached a classical perfection in his *Accords*, came soon to the conclusion that he personally could not carry this type of painting further; and there were those who thought that Mondrian also had created something which had reached a finite perfection. Many artists therefore supposed, at that time, that this new language could not be further developed, and they went back to study again the founders of the modern Cubist-Classical movement—Cézanne and Seurat—and to build upon them in some other ways. Thus it came that in the first edition of this book I wrote as a footnote to the section headed 'The Position to-day (December 1926)' in Part III: 'For my own part I must confess that I much regret the shortness of the period spent by artists in these fundamental Cubist experiments. The experiments have been of enormous service to art as I have already indicated; and if original architectural artists for three generations would work exclusively on the Cubist basis we should have, I am convinced, a new architecture and a new architectural art. Unfortunately the extraordinary difficulty of the task, the interruption of the

---

[1] I have used the term 'non-representational' when referring to such art in this book. It is now more usual to refer to it as 'abstract', and some writers use the term 'non-figurative'. The use of the word 'abstract' in that sense is misleading (*a*) because although such works symbolize the formal architectural artist's experience of abstract factors—proportion, balance, recession and so forth—no work of visual art exists till it has in fact been made a *concrete* entity in paint on canvas or in stone or clay, etc.; and (*b*) because the word can also refer to semi-representational works when the forms perceived by the artist have been 'abstracted' from physical objects and concrete things depicted or suggested in those works (as in some pictures by Cézanne and to some extent in the pictures by the Cubists and Ozenfant). I therefore avoided the term in this book. The term 'non-figurative' is less misleading; but as I have not used it in this book I do not use it in this Preface. 'Non-representational', which I stick to, is only misleading in so far as it might be mistaken to mean naturalistic as distinguished from representational; but that interpretation is not likely to occur to the reader in any context where I use 'non-representational' in the sense of 'non-figurative'.

[2] The full text of Plato's passage is quoted in my book 'The Meaning of Modern Sculpture' (Faber) 1932.

1914–1918 war and, in the case of the weaker spirits, the hostility of the public and of rival artists have combined to prevent any general efforts to achieve a new classical art. The attempt is still being made by a few gallant spirits, but there is now, I fear, small hope of any genuine achievement on the Gothic or Renaissance scale.'

THE NEXT TWELVE YEARS

But by 1934 when I re-read the book for the revised edition of 1935, I was able to delete that pessimistic footnote; because in the intervening years the Purist-Functional creed for an architecture with severely geometric aesthetic which Ozenfant and his associate Le Corbusier had expounded in their joint review *L'Esprit Nouveau* from 1920 till 1925, had passed from theory into practice, and the Purist-Functional renaissance of architecture and the applied arts launched by Le Corbusier in France, and Gropius and others elsewhere, had manifestly come to stay.

The painters of the modern movement had meanwhile gone forward with their own particular mission. For their own task was not really to rescue the architects from muddled-headed worship of 'Ye olde' this and that and set them to work in geometrical aesthetic with steel and concrete, glass and chromium; it was indeed to a large extent the painters' doing that, as I have put it elsewhere, 'the dustmen were now carrying to the incinerators pile after pile of obsolete ornaments and trimmings from the architects' studios, the cabinet-makers' workshops and the sewing rooms of dressmakers and milliners'; it was also largely their doing that the interests vested in the manufacture of Georgian replicas for dining rooms and Louis XV replicas for salons, and stuffed birds for hats, and flounces and ribbons for petticoats were roused to indignant protest; but these services were incidental, *par dessus le marché*; and many of the original painters who had left Ozenfant and Mondrian on one side for re-study of Seurat and Cézanne, now also left Le Corbusier and the other architects to their several problems while they themselves experimented, for a couple of decades, with the various marriages between Formal Architectural Painting and Child Brides, Savage Brides and Subconscious Brides referred to in the 'Epilogue to the 1935 Edition' (cf. pp. 46-48) and the 'Addendum to the 1938 Edition' (cf. p. 45).[1]

The singlemindedness of the classical Cubist-Purist painting thus gave way

[1] As the works produced in these three fields are discussed at length, with many illustrations, in my 'Modern French Painters' (Faber) I make no attempt to give details here.

for a time, and in many quarters, to Associationist concepts in tune with the Associationist thought of the period which believed that the League of Nations could organize World Peace and that the new invention of Wireless Telegraphy would radiate Goodwill on Earth. The artists, like others in those years of passionately creative optimism, sought correspondencies across continents and ages; and they were able to find them because museums and publishers collaborated in the process. As I pointed out in 'The Meaning of Modern Sculpture' museums everywhere were being rearranged to show objects of all times and places side by side; carvings by savages were shown beside sophisticated sculpture; drawings by children were hung beside drawings by highly educated artists; and at the same time thousands of photographs of Egyptian, African, Mexican, Mesopotamian, Assyrian and Far Eastern sculpture, and, of course, of European paintings and sculpture of all periods, were widely disseminated in illustrated books. The artists drank eagerly from these varied fountains of strange wines; and many were quickened and inspired by them. But some, perhaps, became a bit intoxicated; and others, like the general public, were sometimes misled by the absence of colour in monochrome reproductions, by the difference in scale between the plates and the objects photographed, and by the obscuring in small reproductions of the symbolic character of classical techniques (cf. 'Naturalism and Representation' (i) in Part I).

ARCHITECTURE AGAIN THE MOTHER OF THE ARTS

But there were nevertheless some clear-headed original formal painters in the early 'thirties who made intensive study of the actual architecture produced by Le Corbusier and the others; and who found themselves as it were re-inspired by this art which had been largely instigated by Cubist and Purist paintings. They saw now that the new architects were preoccupied with transparent as distinguished from opaque form—a pre-occupation which arose quite simply from the nature of the new materials which enabled the architects to build without walls and without ground floors. For in practice the new architects conceived their buildings in terms of steel girders in various conjunctions revealing space between and round them, so that the essence of their structure, its functional skeleton, was aesthetically speaking not an arrangement of walls with holes pierced in them, but a single transparent space punctuated by girders in a contrapuntal pattern. Here, some artists realized, was a new field to be explored by non-representational or semi-representational painters out to symbolize experience of the formal factors—proportion, balance, recession and so forth. The Cubists had taught them to explore the possibilities of symbolizing movement up and down and across the surface of the picture-plane without recession into space behind the actual canvas (cf. 'Architectural form' in Part III); Chirico had shown them the possibilities of perspective used in an emotive way (cf. 'Architectural Perspective' in Part III); but the new skeleton architecture—(which the Crystal Palace and the Eiffel Tower had heralded)—now led them to think of space as an all pervading factor within which forms of varied shape and density, rise and meet and intersect each other in infinitely varied counterpoint. Thus it came that Paul Nash painted his *Aerial Composition* in 1933; and that Mondrian whose *Composition in Red, Yellow and Blue* (Pl. 17) of 1921 had admitted no suggestion of recession behind the actual canvas, spent his last years in adapting his rectilinear inventions into symbols of the interplay of rectangles in three-dimensional space (Pl. 18).[1]

The earlier aspects of the modern movement had their precedents in classical European painting, as indicated in this book (cf. 'Architecture as typical art' in Part I); and there were precedents also for this conscious study of space, as such, in Flemish, Italian and Dutch paintings from the fifteenth century onwards; for, without the figures, the *Last Supper* by Dirk Bouts, painted in 1464, is wholly a spatial configuration; twenty years before that, Squarcione had been lecturing his Paduan pupils on mental travelling through space and teaching pictorial construction by means of a model theatre—such as Poussin was to use again in the seventeenth century; and the precedent can be traced on through Vermeer (cf. 'Original architectural art' in Part I) to Seurat and Cézanne. But the new intensification of this study was born of the technical procedures of the Purist-Functional architects, as just stated; and it was also an aspect of the Associationist concepts of the period, since space was envisaged as a universal constant, always around the artist everywhere, and always inciting him to endless enlargements of experience.

ALEXANDER CALDER

This same concept of universal space as a prime incentive for the artist led the American Alexander Calder to study boughs set swaying and leaves set floating by the wind, trajectories of fountain water and falling fireworks, and the flight of birds and aeroplanes; and, in Paris, in 1931 he made his first *Mobile* to evoke and symbolize these movements, creating thereby a new type of formal

[1] Both these pictures, and others by Mondrian at all periods, are reproduced in colour in the Faber Gallery 'Mondrian', with text by David Lewis.

art, the nearest to music yet achieved, since rhythmic progression is actually, and not only metaphorically, among its constituent factors.

THE INFLUENCE OF GAUGUIN

With the prevalence of Associationist concepts, Gauguin's taste for the exotic and his substitution of dark-skinned Eves for sophisticated white ones, made inevitable appeal to other artists in these years. Gauguin's pictures were therefore much studied after those by Seurat and Cézanne; and in that process some artists became attracted by the free uninhibited organic rhythm in his paintings which had already influenced both Matisse and Braque. As a result, from the turn of the 'twenties to the 'thirties onwards, organic, as distinguished from geometrical aesthetic, was frequently seen in works by painters, draughts-men, sculptors and even architects of the movement. Thus Leon Underwood drew and engraved his *Rhythm of Life* and led a renaissance of English wood-engraving inspired intellectually by Blake but aesthetically by Gauguin's wood-cuts. Gauguin's aesthetic is also discernible in the rhythms extracted from land-scapes with woods and trees, silvery pools and dark hollows by Ivon Hitchens who appeared in 1928 and has since then steadily developed his personal per-ception in a series of sensitive and original works (Pl. 43). Organic aesthetic was also seen from about 1929 in the visceral and amoebic shapes which writhed, wriggled or floated in Joan Miro's compositions. Fernand Léger, a former follower of Ozenfant and devotee of the geometric aesthetic of machine-made things, now turned his attention to free-flying leaf forms; kidney and palette shapes in various conjunctions had become the subject of non-representational pictures by the ex-Vorticist Edward Wadsworth (Pl. 4) by 1932; the apple was now more favoured than the sphere as a type form; free-hand curves, pear and kidney shapes appeared in architects' plans and in their designs for decorative panels; the flowing curves of bent-wood furniture were recommended by designers who had formerly favoured chromium tube frames; and Lubetkin designed the Penguin Pool at the London Zoo in 1935.

HENRY MOORE

But the most impressive emergent from this aesthetic trend was the im-mensely gifted sculptor Henry Moore. After beginning at the end of the 'twen-ties with figures influenced by Egyptian, Sumerian, Mexican and other types of static monumental carvings, Moore has worked consistently, from the early 'thirties onwards, to imbue his figures with compelling organic rhythm; a free flowing uninhibited aesthetic pervades all the figures he has made since then; and this can be seen in the bronze *Family Group* (Pl. 61), which dates from 1947.[1]

PAUL KLEE

In these same Associationist years, the later 'twenties and the early 'thirties, an interest in the work of the Swiss Paul Klee spread from Germany and began to be considerable in Paris where he had not hitherto been much regarded— though he had been there for a while in 1905 (when Rousseau le Douanier exhibited *Le lion ayant faim* and *Une noce à la campagne*) and he had spent a year there in 1912 when he met Picasso and Guillaume Apollinaire, and saw early agoraphobic dream-images by Chirico, and the Salon des Indépendants (which had Chagall's *Marchand de bestiaux* with the foal seen in the belly of the mare) and the first Futurist exhibition (which had Severini's *Pan-Pan* and Balla's *Dog on leash* and Boccioni's ideograph *La rue entre par la fenêtre*).[2]

Klee was already forty-nine in 1928 when he produced his satiric Dada masterpiece *Cat and Bird* (with the bird shown in the mind of the cat), which I refer to in the 'Epilogue to the 1935 Edition'; and his gouache *Flora in an old garden* (Pl. B) had been painted some nine years earlier while the Dada movement was still active. As explained in my 'Modern French Painters', the nihilist anarchic Dada movement was a symbol of the disgusts and disillusions occasioned by Kaiser Wilhelm's war. Klee was in sympathy not only with the Futurists but also with the Dadaists and he exhibited in the Zurich Dada Gallery because he had always desired to operate on a slate wiped clean of all traditional allegiances (as distinguished from the Cubists, Ozenfant, and Chirico

---

[1] I have always found myself ill-at-ease with the little holes or incised circles or triangles suggesting eyes in Moore's figures, for these details seem to me redundant and the works, as a whole, more homogeneous without them. Early in the 'thirties I therefore asked him to explain them. He replied 'If you see a man at the other end of the street, at such a distance that you cannot distinguish his features, you nevertheless feel it, at once, if he is looking at you; if he were a blind man with his face turned in your direction you would not have that feeling; I don't want my statues to be blind.'

[2] Chagall's picture here referred to is reproduced in colour in the Faber Gallery 'Chagall' with text by Michael Ayrton. The influence on Klee of Associationist ideas encountered in Paris— the acceptance of the naif (Rousseau), the disquieting (Chirico) and the irrational (Chagall)—is obvious. But the influence of the ideographic elements in Futurism and of Futurist *technique* was equally important; because the Futurists segmented forms not to achieve an architectural form but to symbolize stages of a movement; thus Balla's dog has twenty legs and the leash is multiple; and Boccioni's *Progressive lines plus dynamic sequences* (*The swifts*) which he was working on in 1912, might now be mistaken for the work of a follower of Klee, if not indeed of Klee himself.

who maintained an allegiance to classical ideas); he had always wanted to recapture, as far as might be, the naif curiosity of a child of five, and in the stage of technique, to make a fresh beginning for each work. Dada, by washing the slate of everything, thus helped him to escape from the technical influences of the past, and, also, as far as might be, from the technical influences of the contemporary School of Paris. Clear-headed, methodical, painstaking, highly educated, witty, tasteful, fanciful and most ingeniously inventive and adaptive in the technical field, he produced at various times nearly nine thousand compositions, mostly on a small scale, in various media, and much enlarged thereby the new symbolic technical language of the modern movement. Though in no sense or degree, I think, a profound philosopher or mystic or complex introvert, as has been by some suggested, he stands as a highly intriguing experimental artist whose procedures I must here examine further in relation to the theory of values submitted in this book.

The fundament of my theory is that the original artist enlarges his experience by his work; and that the work's intrinsic value derives from the artist's will to that enlargement and from his capacity to fulfil that will. The artist's procedures, referred to from various points of view in the various sections of this book, are described as happening in a certain progression, i.e. first an unorganized enlargement of experience obtained by perception actual or imagined, then a mental organization by analysis, synthesis and so on to create the new symbolic form which is the real subject of the work, and finally the organized construction of the concrete object—the drawing, painting, carving or whatever it may be. In some cases the progression may be so swift that the stages are almost simultaneous, in others the stages may be separated by long intervals in time—Stanley Spencer, for example, can carry a huge complicated unpainted painting, with all its details, in his head for years, and need, as mnemonics for the eventual physical painting, no more than indicative drawings made at the time of or soon after the decision to devise a form for some particular experience. But whether swift and continuous, or slow and interrupted, the progression, as I understand it, normally follows that particular order—from initial unorganized experience by actual or imagined perception to the final labour of fashioning the concrete object.

Paul Klee evidently adhered to that order in many of his works. He often started with a satiric or other idea and then evolved ingenious new symbols to express it; at other times he started from visual study of the principles of organic growth, especially of small objects—we are told by people who knew him well that small plants with their roots, grasses, mosses, pine cones, butterfly

23

wings, feathers, fragments of coral, shells and so on were always here and there about his workroom. As a young man he had fallen in love with the Aquarium in Naples and that experience was another starting off point that remained continually with him; and we know from his writings that he sought and found initial stimuli in the revelations of the microscope; some of his pictures had their source in his memories of masks—the masks in Ensor's pictures which he had known since 1907, African masks seen perhaps in Picasso's studio or elsewhere in Paris in 1912, and masks in the ethnographic sections of museums; others again were launched by his study of surfaces and textures—the grains in wood, the weaves in textiles—or by close examination of degrees of transparency and weight in substances and fabrics (little objects made of gauze and twisted wires were also seen about his studio); and finally there were pictures started by the open-minded experiencing of photographs of all kinds of objects (including works of art) as he came across them in illustrated books.[1]

But on other occasions he reversed these normal procedures, and put as it were the cart before the horse, by starting with the concrete stage of making lines and colours on paper or board or canvas. Essentially an intellectual, like Seurat, he had made, like Seurat, intensive study of the aesthetic characters of different types of lines, spots, tones, colours and so forth and of the infinite variety in their possible conjunctions. He went indeed a good deal further than Seurat in this technical study. He often explored the decorative aspect of spaces round his lines and areas of colour—realizing that every line has two sides to it and that both must be considered in a decorative design. He experimented with different primings of his paper or canvas into varied surfaces by the use of complicated media to receive and support the spaces, lines and colours; and above all he studied the varying pace in drawing and degrees of what artists describe as 'tension', i.e. the tautness or fluidity of lines and shapes and the looseness or tightness of their mutual relations. In all these matters he trained his hand to execute to a nicety his mind's dictates; his touch, controlled absolutely, and ordered by his mind to be swift or slow, vague or incisive, heavy or light, often reached a Chinese or Persian delicacy (before it coarsened in the works of his last few years); and though he was never a major architectural composer and often spoiled the aesthetic rhythm by a trick of adding heavy arrow-heads, (obvious ready-made symbols for direction), his taste enabled him

[1] Thus *The God of the Northern woods* might have been born of an encounter with a photo-graph of Gaudier's marble head of Ezra Pound—a carving which stood for years in the front-garden shrubbery of Violet Hunt's house on Campden Hill. Pound's book 'Gaudier Brzeska,' published in 1916 reproduced it. Klee's picture dates from 1922.

Plate B. PAUL KLEE: *Flora in an Old Garden*

to arrive in most cases at a miniature decorative result appropriate to the scale he worked on. His pleasure in this varied technical equipment, and the continual desire of his ingenious mind to enlarge his experience in that field, thus led him, on occasion, to invent for himself a purely technical problem with his lines, dots, spaces, colours and so forth for the sheer fun of setting out to solve it. And when in fact he actually so solved it, the work, by my standard of values, has intrinsic value as an enlargement of his experience in the technical field— though no technical process in itself is accorded intrinsic value in my theory (cf. 'Value of Technique' in Part IV).

We know, however, from Klee himself—as indeed can be suspected in many of his pictures—that he did not always solve the precise problem—the technical experiment—he had embarked on; that he sometimes allowed extraneous experience in the course of the operation to deflect him from his initial purpose; that he sometimes admitted an intrusion of that kind and then added a verbal title which dishonestly suggested that the capture of the particular intruding factor had been the purpose of the action from the outset.

Thus Klee said, in a published lecture, that with the gradual 'growth' of a structure to a new order and form, i.e. an image before the eyes, 'an association of ideas gradually insinuates itself' which may 'tempt' the artist to 'a material interpretation, since any image of complex structure can, with some effort of imagination, be compared with familiar pictures from nature'; that 'nothing need prevent the artist from accepting such association of ideas'; that 'acceptance of this material association may suggest additions which, once the subject is formulated, clearly stand in essential relationship to it'; and that 'if the artist is fortunate, these natural forms may fit into a slight gap in the formal composition, as though they had always belonged there'.

In practice this means that such an artist on occasion may start with setting himself to make an upward rising composition with two swift curving lines, four taut straight ones, and fifty dots in seven colours of three different weights; that half-way through he may see that the image on the paper suggests a mountain village against the sky, and that, turned round sideways, it suggests the sea breaking against a coast with villages and bays; and that he can then decide to increase the resemblance to the one thing or the other and call it 'Sky-Mountain' or 'Mediterranean Coast'. Or that he may start out to create a formal structure with symbols based on alternating visceral and vegetable shapes and that if at some point the lines suggest a female head and shoulders he may put a nose and mouth in and call the whole thing 'Green Devil' or 'Pink Goddess'.

25

In my theory of values such works can have no intrinsic value, because the artist as spectator of his own work in progress, has dishonestly passed it as the perfect solution of his initial problem though that in fact was jettisoned half-way by acceptance of the intruding associated ideas which motived the form thereafter (cf. 'The honest competent artist-spectator' and 'The dishonest artist-spectator' in Part IV).

I am aware, of course, that Klee himself wished us to believe that his subconscious self in contact with deep forces of nature directed his mind and feeling *all through* such productions; that he compared the artist to the trunk of a tree: 'from the root' he said 'the sap flows to the artist, flows through him, flows to his eye . . .'; his work results like 'the crown to a tree'; 'the beauty at the crown is not his own; he is merely a channel.' I know, too, that many artists like to speak of their activity in this way; they like to tell us that their works 'grow' from them (Sickert compared his pictures to his toe nails). But the word 'growth' in this connection is just a metaphor—and metaphors can be insidiously misleading. That the activity which produces any kind of original art 'is an emanation of the human spirit and so mysterious and incomprehensible' is admitted, of course, in this inquiry (cf. 'Genius and the critic' in Part I), and I recognize also that all symbolic techniques involve transformation of the artist's mechanical vision to actual or imagined perception by means of some combinations of sensations, associated ideas, imagination, memories, knowledge, moods and psychological factors which I leave to the psychologists to explain (cf. 'Naturalism and Representation' (i) in Part I). But I insert the word 'deliberate' before the word 'transformation'; and I submit that the artist, like the rest of us, perceives or imagines what he desires to perceive or imagine in order to obtain a satisfaction, and that the concrete work is, throughout, an act of his conscious will (cf. 'Human perception' and 'The Artist's perception' in Part II).

To put it simply, the painter, the draughtsman or the sculptor, in practice does not *grow* his works as he grows his hair or toe nails or even as he may grow anemones or potatoes; he *makes* them—line after line, chip by chip, or clay pellet on clay pellet—(though they may *symbolize* growth as many of Klee's works do when he started from an experience in the normal way (Pl. B)). And here we touch on a point which is a truism for the professional artist though little understood by the layman—especially by trained philosophers or professional psychologists who have not spent years in the physical process of producing pictures, drawings or sculpture. In the normal progression from initial experience to concrete object, a new situation arises the moment the first line or spot is placed on canvas or paper, the first chip made in the stone, or the first clay pellet pressed down upon the armature. Before that point in time the artist's experience has been enlarged in many ways, some evident and some mysterious; but after that point in time there exists a line or a space of colour on paper or canvas, or a block of stone with one chip made in it, and nothing can add anything to those physical factors except a second line, a second colour-spot or a second chip; and a new situation arises again when one line has been made into two lines; and yet another when the two have been made into three and so on to the end. Once the very first line has been made, immediacy (in the dictionary sense of 'that which has no intermediary or intervening member, medium or agent') is no longer possible between the artist and the initial experience which the new object is to be made to symbolize; because the line has itself become an 'intermediary or intervening member, medium or agent'; and as the new object is given more and more shape by more lines or chips, it becomes more and more difficult for the artist to hold on to the initial experience and remember the purpose of the object he is making; and the essentially moral quality of his task, is his will and capacity to keep contact with the initial experience or to recapture it repeatedly and without abatement, despite the fact that his new and immediate experience of the object he is making continuously drives the old experience more and more into the background. As the fashioning of the concrete object is the final organization of the initial actual or imagined experience, the original artist normally comes to understand the initial experience better, and to realize and feel it more completely, in the course of the technical procedures which thus become a further enlargement of the experience; this may result in additions unforeseen at the outset; and such additions, truly born of the initial experience are in fact a part of it. The layman, however, is often misled about this, because artists themselves sometimes speak of such additions as though they were the result of accident or the incidental inspiration of the moment; and some have even ascribed them to the hand working without conscious direction from the mind, an impossible happening in the activity called art as I understand it. In my theory of values the artist who admits a line or chip or colour which he does not know to be born of or intimately related to the first experience, is a man who throws in the sponge; the artist who courts accidents and extraneous additions and exploits them is dishonest; and the artist who makes lines or chips or colours without a conscious goal makes nothing more valuable than the layman's 'doodle' which, as we all know, is not intended to have a particular meaning.

We must also remember here that there is all the difference in the world between an adult layman's aimless 'doodle' which is meaningless (until he thinks it resembles a dog and puts the eye in and adds the tail) and the ideographic drawings made by children (who never doodle) as conscious, secret, symbolic, communication to themselves of their curiosity, desires, or other emotions. The first in my scale of values has no intrinsic value; the second has the high intrinsic value of all original art.[1]

FROM 1937 TO 1945

Paul Klee died in 1940; and by then the creative optimism and the Associationist ideas of the later 'twenties and the early 'thirties were no more. For that optimism and those ideas had been born of the hope that Germany would no longer be a menace to all Europe; and in the later 'thirties that hope gave way to pessimism, and the fear of local danger usurped the place of universal concepts. The stupendous retrospective display of the art of the modern movement in the Paris Exposition of 1937 marked the end of an epoch; and the typical painting of that year was Picasso's *Guernica*.[2]

The climate of the later 'thirties was thus most dispiriting to sensitive and contemplative artists; Paul Nash gave us some mild Surrealist fantasias, Graham Sutherland some romantic obsessive images and arrangements in orange, green and scarlet smouldering through black to symbolize his sense of dramatic growth in hedgerow and field, and a young American Morris Graves produced some delicate ideographs in the tradition of Paul Klee; but many artists lost faith in the value of their action, and some were more than half converted by totalitarian propaganda from the Right and the Left which, hoping to exploit art like other action for its own particular purposes, poured scorn on original and independent artists and assaulted their integrity by arguments summarized in my 'Preface for Artists' in the 1945 Edition (here reprinted on p. 44).

When Adolf Hitler repeated Kaiser Wilhelm's crime and launched the 1939 war, many painters had thus been already conditioned to the notion that service to the professed ideology of a social organization is the proper function of the artist; and many, in the desperate peril of the moment, were happy to receive commissions from the Ministry of Information and to produce the descriptive records asked of them. Some of these invited artists had already

---

[1] Cf. 'Value of technique' in Part IV. Examples of Paul Klee's pictures in various media are reproduced in colour in the Faber Gallery 'Klee' Vol. I and 'Klee' Vol. II with texts respectively by Sir Herbert Read and Andrew Forge; the comments by these writers are very different from my own. The *God of the Northern Wood*, referred to above, is in the second volume.

[2] Reproduced in my 'Modern French Painters'.

made such records in the Kaiser's war; and since the British authorities allowed them, now as before, to combine this official service with personal service to an idea of art, if they wished to do so, the commissions occasioned some original descriptive pictures.

I have referred in this book to a few of the original descriptive paintings by official war artists occasioned by the 1914–1918 war; the reproductions of Eric Kennington's *Kensingtons at Laventie* (Pl. 11) and of Stanley Spencer's *Unveiling a War Memorial* (Pl. 13) are retained in this edition, and I have added to them Paul Nash's passionately symbolic protest *We are making a New World* (Pl. 12) Stanley Spencer's epic chronicle of his experience in that war, which he completed in 1933 for the Burghclere Memorial chapel, is recorded, with plates, in my 'English Painting'. I have not added plates of original descriptive paintings occasioned by the second war; but I must recall that they included a further symbolic protest *Dead Sea (Totes Meer)* by Paul Nash (reproduced in my 'Outline of English Painting') records of shipbuilding at Port Glasgow by Stanley Spencer, and of blast furnaces and bomb-devastated streets by Graham Sutherland, drawings of Londoners sleeping in the Underground tube by Henry Moore, and works by others preserved in the Imperial War Museum.

On the whole, the second series was less significant than the first one perhaps because the artists themselves had suffered less from actual war-service. In the first war Eric Kennington was an infantry private in the Retreat from Mons and felt himself most passionately identified with every single member of the 'poor b——y feet'; Paul Nash, a lover of trees and living landscape, felt his own limbs torn asunder as he looked from the mud-pools in the trenches at the fields churned to barren mounds and the cruelly dismembered trees; Spencer, a hospital orderly in Macedonia, had himself scrubbed floors and tenderly placed cradles round the shattered legs of wounded boys, just as orderlies place them in his Burghclere pictures. But Nash was not a fighter in the second war; Kennington drew portraits of airmen purely as a social duty; Spencer watched his riveters with keen attention and intelligence but without 'inside' experience of the process; and Moore soon began to look upon the snoring charwomen and their children as exciting sculptural groups.

As far as England is concerned, these descriptive pictures occasioned by the second war are nevertheless the most characteristic products of this period. But, since art declines to fit into art history, I must also recall the lyrical pictures which Paul Nash found time to paint here in the 'forties, before his death in 1946. For in this final phase Nash gave us *Pillar and Moon* and a series of personal compositions where flower-clouds, and suns that are also sunflowers, drift softly over landscapes, and giant fungi rise in formal correspondence with the moon (Pl. 46). These final pictures were not Surrealist in the sense that Chirico's first silent and deserted townscapes with emotive recessions were Surrealist, or in the sense that Nash's own pictures of the 'thirties could be called Surrealist; they have indeed an atmosphere of dream-life, but there is no hint in them of nightmare or disquiet; and they are also wholly innocent of the sexual associations aimed at and achieved by the Neo-Surrealists in the 'thirties. In essence these pictures are imaginative illustrations to unwritten lyric poems by the artist, and as such they stand closer to those visions of horses on Hellenic foreshores which Chirico painted in the 'twenties (Pl. 45), and to the lyrical works by Chagall who (though the first Surrealist in the sense that Guillaume Apollinaire invented the word to describe his pictures) has never concerned himself with recording or concocting any species of horror or disquiet.[1]

In Paris, during Hitler's war, the pictures were more horrific. For Picasso was at work there passionately painting ideographic protests—a distorted figure tortured in a concentration camp while a demon-woman twangs her mandoline at him (a study for a colossal *Charnel House*) and other terrifying images which seem to say to us: 'You can beat and slash and batter at life; you can burn, bomb and flood; but within the tortured bodies and the battered faces a pulse still beats to disturb you and an eye still stares to defy your cruelty and your secret fears.' From these productions of the war years I reproduce his *Boy and Birds* (Pl. 47) which can be interpreted either simply as a genre piece with disquieting distortions (cf. 'Architectural and other distortions' in Part III), or as an indicting image of a brutish child-brain about to bash and kill.

FROM 1946 TO THE PRESENT DAY

Since the second war ended most original artists have resumed their status as independent contemplative and creative minds with tasks of their own to accomplish; and the most intelligent and courageous painters have returned to the adventure of formal non-representational or semi-representational painting. But there are also still romantic and descriptive painters who stand outside the movement; and some young men, thrown on their own resources when they left the art schools have quailed before the daily questions—'What work shall I do to-day? In what way shall I do it? How will it stand in relation to the pro-

---

[1] There is no reference in the earlier edition of this book to this special type of lyrical painting; but some comments on the category it belongs to will be found in a paragraph called 'Imaginative illustration' now added to Part IV (cf. p. 191).

ducts of the camera? Is it worth while? Can I afford it?'—and found comfort by responding to new beckonings from those who wish to use them as their servants. Thus paintings serving Socialist or Communist ideas have appeared on the one hand; and, on the other, pictures with religious subjects have become quite frequent, as this period has been marked from the outset by intensive propaganda for religious revivals, and commissions for some churches were forthcoming.

RELIGIOUS ART

Religious art is set aside in this book as resulting from special types of action outside the scope of the inquiry. But I have referred nevertheless to it in several places; and I must repeat here that a work with a nominal religious subject is not necessarily religious painting or sculpture properly so-called. If the artist's concern is basically formal the work is architectural and not religious art; if his basic concern is with the emotive character of the fragments of life depicted, it is romantic art; if his main concern is with the generic character of the physical objects and concrete things depicted or with their social conjunctions or ethical characters, it is descriptive or genre painting. In each of these cases, moreover, the artist may be either original or popular in the senses defined in this book (cf. 'Original art' and 'Popular art' in Part I) and if he is popular in the derivative way, if the initial motive was really to paint something recalling Fra Angelico or El Greco, Matthias Grünewald or Rembrandt, his work, by my standards, is basically void of intrinsic value (cf. 'Value of derivative popular art' in Part IV).

A picture with a religious subject is only in fact religious art when the action of the artist is in fact religious, i.e. when the artist feels that—*whatever the work's appearance*—its existence is justified by service to some religion or as the creation of images embodying his personal concepts of religious ideas. Here again the artist may be original, or popular, or popular-derivative. The religious artist who works within his own or his employer's or other spectator's familiar religious experience, or within his own or their familiar experience of religious art or of art with religious subjects, is the popular or popular-derivative artist in this field. The original artist in this field is the man with a personal religion, or the man who reads his texts with an open mind and enlarges his religious experience by the reading and by the translation of the words into new pictorial or plastic images exactly recording his experience (cf. 'Imaginative illustration' in Part IV). Stanley Spencer when he paints religious subjects is an original religious artist in that sense. We see him as such in the *Resurrection* (*Cookham*) reproduced here (Pl. 14); he is also at times a religious artist when painting descriptive genre scenes—for he has said that when painting the military and hospital panels in the Burghclere chapel he felt them called for and justified as preludes leading to the *Soldiers' Resurrection* (*Macedonia*) on the central wall; and the *Resurrection* (*Port Glasgow*) series was born of his need to associate his new experience in the shipbuilding yards and the streets of Port Glasgow with his concepts of the Day of Resurrection in that place—as he has himself explained when writing of those pictures.[1]

Spencer, however, is not among the artists to whom the recent commissions for churches, referred to above, have been given; his original religious pictures have all been produced on his own initiative; and they have all found homes in public art galleries in London and elsewhere.[2]

SOME NEW ROMANTICS

Among the new Romantic painters many adhering to 'Expressionismus'—the German exaggeration of Van Gogh's art—record their gloom or excitement at the contemplation of unusually battered faces or decaying physical objects in Roualtesque or Soutineish terms; but some still cherish the eighteenth-century Picturesque-Ruin complex and others the nineteenth-century pseudo-Romantic Dignity-of-Labour' notion (cf. 'Degeneration of ideas' in Part I). Most of these new romantics still use the standard Romantic-Expressionist deliberately emotive techniques; some pile up their pigment to the height of an inch and appear to have stirred it like a Christmas pudding; others slap on and flatten their pigment with a palette knife; and others are true to the 'heureuse saleté' of Delacroix's 'brosse ivre' or to 'those strips of metallic paint that catch the light like so many dyed straws' as Sickert said when explaining his dislike of Van Gogh's handling (cf. 'The Romantic heresy', 'Original Romantic Art' and 'Romantic Popular art' in Part I and 'Degeneration of technique' in Part II). But some now paint young women with huge eyes, or dwarfs brandishing dead birds, or lean youths on lonely beaches, or carcasses on cactus leaves, with a slow smooth handling that gives them the ambivalence of hybrid works by Ingres (cf. 'The Daguerreotype and Ingres' in Part II).

A conspicuous original romantic emergent is the later sculpture by Alberto

[1] Cf. 'Stanley Spencer: Resurrection pictures 1954–1950' with notes by the artist and an introduction by R. H. Wilenski in the Faber Gallery, where these pictures, with details, are reproduced in colour.

[2] Essays on the relations between theological art and original religious art in various times and places, and on the present role of museums as homes of religious paintings of both kinds, are called for at this point. But both themes are outside the field of this inquiry.

Giacometti, an Italian-Swiss, mainly resident in Paris, who experimented with various aspects of Cubism and Surrealism in the later 'twenties and 'thirties and 'found himself' as the phrase goes in the later 'forties when he produced the *Pointing man* (Pl. 28) and *The Square* a symbolic composition with one female and four male figures evoking an urban street scene. In a technical sense Giacometti's bronze *Pointing man*, which resembles a clay-modeller's first armature, is a sculptural equivalent of a painting by Matisse. For in the nineteenth century and later art schools, where students were taught to paint naturalistically 'by the tone values' (cf. 'Naturalism and Representation' (i) in Part I and 'Naturalism and Representation' (ii) in Part II) they were often told to begin—if the posed subject was, say, a nude figure before a greenish tapestry—by filling in the figure as a greyish-yellowish-pinkish halftone and putting round it a darker grey-greenish colour for the background, thus 'killing' all the white of the canvas and establishing at once two basic tone relations; but there were always students with a native delight in the vitality of colour, who nevertheless began by suggesting the figure with, say, lines and touches of bright rose-pink and suggesting the background by touches of gay viridian and patches of white canvas left here and there, and such students always regretted the disappearance of this lively colour-pattern when they covered it later with grey tones imitating the tones of the phenomena before them. Matisse 'found himself' as an architectural artist on the day when he decided to leave the bright rose-pink, the white spaces, and the gay viridian touches and build a classic art that way. In the same art school there was always somewhere a romantically-minded student in the sculpture room who felt that the unusual points about the model or the emotive qualities in the gesture which excited him were already 'there' when he had done an hour's work on the initial armature, and who regretted covering this stage with more layers of clay to imitate the flesh and muscles and so forth; and Giacometti 'found himself' as a Romantic artist on the day when he decided to accept his reaction at this first emotive stage and build an original romantic art that way. The resultant success, in each case, was only, of course, obtained by deliberately concentrating mind and feeling on that purpose from the outset of each work, and by treating the very first lines and colours in the one case, and the very first clay pellets in the other, as unalterable statements destined to be visible as operative factors in the final form. The two procedures are thus analogous—though Matisse aimed at and captured a serene gaiety in carefully considered architectural structures, while Giacometti aims at and achieves the creation of mysteriously disquieting fragments.

If I read his recent development correctly Graham Sutherland may eventually evolve as an original Romantic sculptor. But meanwhile Reginald Butler has given us his *Young girl removing her shift* (Pl. 27) an armature covered only to the moment when the artist's romantic perception of the emotive sapling-thinness of the girl had been captured by the pellets pressed upon it; and Kenneth Armitage has given us his *Walking group* (Pl. 29) and *People in the Wind* (Pls. 52 and 53) which are also armatures left faithfully at the very first moment when the pellets had recorded the artist's emotional reaction to particular fragments imagined or perceived in life (cf. 'Architecture and other distortions' in Part III).

SOME NEW DESCRIPTIVE PAINTERS

In the field of Descriptive art some young and serious painters have tried to combine the idea of social service with a doctrine current a hundred years ago—the Realist doctrine of Gustave Courbet and Jean François Millet which declared that the artist must be descriptive and confine himself to recording physical objects and concrete things and genre and social subjects in the daily life around him, and leave to the Romantics all parade of his personal reactions and feelings. Being descriptive painters, these New Realists, as they are called, compete with the still and moving cameras. They are not concerned with the adventures of the modern movement or with the progress of the technical language which that movement is still called on to develop (cf. 'Original descriptive art' and 'Descriptive popular art' in Part I). They are concerned with scientific, social-historical and moral experience in everyday life; their subjects accordingly are landscapes and townscapes, agricultural and industrial genre scenes with labourers and navvies, domestic genre scenes with babies, and domestic still life including kitchen sinks and water closets and laundry hanging on indoor lines; and they use habitually some traditional naturalistic or representational technique—though some use the Van-Gogh-Expressionist emotive handling either (*a*) because they are at heart Romantics, or (*b*) because they react aesthetically to Van Gogh's 'strips of metallic paint that catch the eye like so many dyed straws' or to the heavy mud-like textures favoured by the Expressionists or (*c*) because they are venal and seek contact with the spectators' familiar experience of Van Gogh's technique, or (*d*) because they are just muddle-headed and do not realize that such parade of emotive handling is quite inappropriate in descriptive art.

In my theory of values the work of these New Realists has intrinsic value if the artists are original and in fact communicate to themselves an enlargement of experience born of an impulse to increased comprehension of everyday phenomena or social or moral factors in the everyday world; and I rank the intrinsic value of such original art above the intrinsic value of original Romantic work but below that of original formal Architectural art (cf. 'Value of Original Descriptive Art' and 'Value of Descriptive popular art' in Part IV). But some special merit is claimed for these New Realists by writers who describe them as peculiarly 'involved' with the subjects of their works; and this doctrine of involvement must be examined at this point.

This doctrine comes to us from Paris where the word *'engagement'*—a metaphor from the gear-box of a motor car—is sometimes similarly employed; and Jean Cocteau, protesting against it, has flashed out another metaphor: The artist, he says, is inescapably the 'Cat that Walks by Itself' along the highway; the road is hard, he is splashed with mud and harassed by the glare and roar of passing limousines and motor coaches belonging to other people and serving their concerns, but he has to walk on; only the weaker spirits stop, lose heart and hitch-hike. But Jean Cocteau, I fancy, was assuming that this doctrine of salvation by *'engagement'* is not more than the aftermath of the totalitarian propaganda of the later 'thirties and the war years; and indeed some writers urge the merit of 'involvement' in terms equivalent to the propaganda I have summarized in the 'Preface for Artists' in the 1945 Edition. It is possible however to recognize the essential independence of the artist and still claim as some writers do (*a*) that 'involvement' with their subject is essential for the descriptive artist and (*b*) that 'involvement' is peculiar to such artists. Both claims however are erroneous. For, as regards the first point, though the history of descriptive painting shows many original artists involved in that way—the painters of war pictures in the 1914–1918 war, already referred to, for example —it also shows many such painters intellectually, emotionally and socially detached from the thoughts and feelings of the figures represented and from the social significance of the scenes or objects painted. And as regards the second point, involvement, at the stage of experience, may be part of the action of original artists of all types. Romantics habitually feel themselves intensely *'engagés'* with their chosen emotive fragments; and the formal architectural artists of the modern movement are habitually involved with universal factors—as Braque has put it in his dictum: 'J'ai le souci de me mettre a l'unisson de la nature.'

ORIGINAL FORMAL ARCHITECTURAL ART

It is, indeed, to such involvement with universal factors that the artists of the modern movement have returned since the second war ended in 1945; and as stated above, the most clear-headed and courageous painters are again producing formal non-representational or semi-representational paintings.

This has happened in the first place because they have now found several new ways to carry the adventure further; and secondly because the most intelligent see clearly that the rescue of painting from annihilation by the cameras can only be accomplished in this field.

For the influence of the camera's language, already a widespread nuisance to artists when I wrote this book, is yet more ubiquitous and dangerous now; new lenses and enlargers enable the photographers to record the most subtle effects of light and shade on surfaces; and television, which also speaks the camera's language, is another reinforcement to the enemy. There is also the competition of the camera's subject-matter, as the cinema (now the colour-cinema) provides the world with all, and more than, it asks for in the way of descriptive social records and romantic, dramatic, sentimental and semi-erotic images in illusionist terms. Moreover both the cinema-cameras and the television cameras are directed by men who disseminate impatience of the contemplative preludes to action essential for the artist—his need to stand still on one spot and perceive and meditate his subject before proceeding into action. 'The world' say the film and television men, 'is not of interest unless we see it from a rising or falling lift or aeroplane or a travelling platform'; and they roll or sway the cameras perpetually forwards or backwards, to right and left, down and up (Pl. 2).

This powerful enemy, rejoicing in the rich completeness of his language, triumphant as an image-maker in the whole wide range of his narrative, dramatic and romantic subject-matter, and master of immense distributing resources, continually confronts all painters; and the situation, as I see it, is just this: The art of painting can only conquer in this fight, when the artists have finally abandoned to the camera and television men all the dramatic, sentimental, semi-erotic and descriptive material formerly used by painters, and when they have in fact invented a new and extensive symbolic pictorial technique which they can use to communicate to themselves their formal and other experiences. The fight will be won if the vocabulary and syntax of that new technique are large and flexible enough to symbolize all types of formal order and all aspects of the artists' contemplative reactions; it will be lost if the new language proves itself too rigid or too limited in range (as it was believed to have proved itself in the stage of Ozenfant and Mondrian).

The fight, moreover, can only be won by the most intransigent artists. No compromise with the enemy is possible. There is also no salvation in trying to steal from him; for when painters imitate the cinema's successive images (as the Futurists did) or when they use the camera's language and try to disguise it, when they take photographs and work on or from them in some Cubist or Expressionist or Surrealist idiom to make them appear a bit formal, romantic or disquieting, they are either just venal popular painters (as there is money in such practices just now) or ostriches in characteristic posture; and when Neo-Surrealists make sexually disquieting lynx-eyed records of epidermitous details in illusionist technique they serve only to remind us that the technique evolved by the Van Eycks for the hairs round Adam's nipples in the *Altarpiece of the Mystic Lamb* has been made quite obsolete by proxar lenses and cinema close-ups.[1]

In this new edition I have added some plates which illustrate moves forward in non-representational and semi-representational painting. I show, for example, from the later work of Ben Nicholson, his *March* (Pl. 57) of 1953 which should be compared with his earlier '*Au Chat Botté*' reproduced in my 'English Painting'; for Nicholson has moved from the Cubism of the early picture, through the Purism of Ozenfant and Mondrian, to enlargement of this special type of formal experience; he retains the Cubist concept of the board or canvas frankly accepted as the most distant plane with no recession suggested beyond it; he is also still faithful to geometric aesthetic in the linear structure and to the idiom of the dance of flat cards one above the other; but the formal harmony now symbolized is much more complex and the form itself, made decorative and tasteful by the colour, is more complex too. This *March* is non-representational in the sense that no physical objects or concrete things are represented in three-dimensional terms; but the problem here solved is not only the technical problem of certain relations of lines and shapes and colours, it is also the symbolizing by their means of *all* the aspects of artist's initial experience that evoked the picture; and that experience included the idea of March—the idea of bulbs, of daffodil and crocus, thrusting upward from beneath the surface of the ground.

This idea of pictures symbolizing growth has already been encountered in some aspects of Paul Klee's productions—it pervades indeed his *Flora in an old Garden* reproduced here (Pl. B); it had been used, romantically of course, by Van Gogh in many of his drawings; we find it in a work called *March* by Edward Wadsworth which appeared in the Vorticist 'Blast' in 1914 and should

---

[1] It is arguable that the naturalistic technique of the Dutch seventeenth-century genre painters was made obsolete as soon as the camera was invented (cf. 'Naturalism and Representation' (ii) in Part II); but the Van Eycks' technique in this *Adam*, painted in 1432, was not made obsolete till the modern lenses and the cinema close-up arrived.

be compared with Nicholson's picture; we find it also in landscape compositions by Graham Sutherland; and in new form in *Seeding in Winter* (Pl. 54) by Alan Reynolds a young and exploratory English painter who is moved in some degree by geometrical aesthetic but also delights (like Klee) in small natural forms— ears of corn, seeds and seed pods, leaves and feathers, which he wraps in cellophane and pins into his sketch books and later enlarges as elements in his pictorial concepts.

Geometrical aesthetic is essential guide to John Tunnard whose *Reclamation* is reproduced in my 'English Painting'. But whereas spatial depth is not, as it were, discussed at all in Nicholson's *March*, it is a main concern with Tunnard, as with some artists of the 'thirties already referred to. In Tunnard's picture, which, in 'English Painting', I relate to Poussin's *Burial of Phocion*, we are taken on a flight through the canvas into space, with intervals and directions indicated by ordered planes and angles all abstracted, with the colours, from the initial experience which was possibly occasioned by a beach scene with a sand pool, boats and bollards; and if 'possibly occasioned by a beach scene' (my guess as spectator) is in fact a wrong guess, it is still no false statement on the subject of the picture because that subject is the measured movement from the foreground to the distance and not the particular place and objects which led the artist to perceive or imagine that movement.

Geometric aesthetic, less confidently accepted, is a constituent in some non-representational or almost non-representational paintings made in 1951 and 1952 by the Russian École de Paris artist Nicolas de Staël who died at forty-one in 1955. In those two years de Staël built pictures with rectangular forms—not true squares and oblongs defined by mathematical outlines like Mondrian's pictures of 1921 and 1942 reproduced here (Pls. 17 and 18) or irregular squares of varied sizes filled with transparent colours like Paul Klee's *Blooming* of 1934 (reproduced on the wrapper of the Faber Gallery Paul Klee II)—but rectangular blocks of very thick paint with blurred edges and blunted corners, which suggest, without defining, a visual experience—a host perhaps of large and small motor vehicles approaching in massed formation or a survey of roof-tops; and this implicit visual experience was sometimes defined by a verbal title. De Staël's blunted squares, each one of which operated as a single note, were juxtaposed or placed one upon another like the cards in Flat-pattern Cubist compositions; but the canvas itself was not the evident background as in the Cubist pictures; nor was recession into indefinite distance glimpsed here and there between the particular forms as in some contemporary non-representational pictures; for all the forms were set afloat in an illusion of three-dimensional space a foot or so

deep—like gold-fish in a narrow tank; and the essence of the picture's quality
was the apparent movement back and forward of these blocks of greyish colour,
(with occasional red or pink), within this particular space. De Staël's aesthetic
in these works was at bottom not veritably geometric; it was closer to the
attitude of the Arts and Crafts Movement which believes that a wobbly straight
line is more artistic than a ruled one, and a squareish square more aesthetic than
a true one; and it was also non-classical in spirit because the artist was out to
dramatize geometry, to imbue its lyric austerity with a baroque richness and
to make it luxurious and sensationally emotive by parade of handling and im-
pasto. De Staël, in fact, was basically Romantic and luxurious and never
quite at ease as a non-representational painter; naturalistic skies began to
make his pictures hybrid before 1952 was out; and in his later years, having
made his contribution to the new pictorial language, he took a less arduous
path and painted tasteful, luxurious and almost entirely representational
pictures.

Victor Pasmore's *Spiral motif in black and white: The Snowstorm* (Pl. 56) is
non-representational, but we need no verbal title to discover the experience it
embodies. 'The snow is the snow is the snow'—would surely have been said
of it by Gertrude Stein, for these short-long whirls and squareish eddies are
not symbolic of snow on the ground or on trees or roof tops but of snow in the
air around us, snow making space itself opaque. This *Snowstorm* is thus again
within the space-awareness aspect of the modern movement. But it none-the-
less stands closer to Turner's *Snowstorm* than to Mondrian's *New York City*
(Pl. 18) or to Calder's mobiles; for both Mondrian and Calder are conscious
seekers for Plato's geometric beauty, while both Turner in his later atmospheric
pictures and Pasmore in this picture are aesthetically empiric. The closeness to
Turner ceases, however, when the language of expression starts; for Turner's *ad
hoc* reaction evolved a representational if not indeed a naturalistic idiom to
record the clash of elements, while Pasmore's has evolved a quite new type of
pictorial symbolism, too free for Plato's geometric beauty and too tight for the
free flowing rhythm of organic life and yet combining in a measure some
qualities of each.

This empirical aesthetic, which draws upon some qualities of geometric
beauty and some qualities of free organic rhythm, while declining absolute
exclusive service to either, is also dominant in the attitudes of non-representational painters like the young Frenchman Pierre Soulages (Pl. 58), William
Gear in later works like the *Duet* reproduced here (Pl. 60), Terry Frost who
builds pictures with shapes and rhythms and colour-forms extracted from hill-

sides with stone-walled fields or from fishing-boats packed close in harbour, and W. Barns Graham (Pl. 59). These artists, in symbolizing their perception of related forms in nature retain, on principle, some degree of the particular as distinguished from the universal character of each form perceived; the essential subject, as in the geometric art of Nicholson and Tunnard, is still the formal relation of each form and angle and direction to its neighbour and the relation of all those individual relations to the formal whole, but since the forms are in some degree particularized, since the tree-trunk or bough or wooden paling, the fishing boat, black rock or stretch of sand, the green lawn or hedge, is allowed a measure of its individual shape (and even, on occasion of its texture) there is now no intellectual conversion of the trunk to the perfection of a column, the rock to the perfection of the cube or sphere, or the sand pool or lawn to the square, the circle or the oval. We can note, too, as a further character in such pictures, that the particular forms appearing are mainly massed in unified planes from the forefront of the picture backwards, and that recession even to undefined distance is sometimes permitted in the intervals between these frontal and secondary forms; for these artists try to mate the Cubist principle of the picture plane as a surface to be retained and stressed, with the later Post-Cubist principle of recession, beyond the canvas, into space. Thus it comes that if we turn such pictures sideways or upside-down we may find a space construction wholly different from that conveyed the right way up. The Soulages picture (Pl. 58) for example, turned sideways, has a three-dimensional space-plan with a floor, and what were before the major foreground verticals and diagonals, rising silhouette-wise from nowhere in the forefront of the picture, are now recumbents on the second plane and agents contributing to the flat recession of the floor.

Other most serious efforts, on lines at bottom not dissimilar, are being made by Peter Lanyon (Pl. 66) and Douglas Hamilton Fraser (Pl. 65). For both these artists start with quite empirical aesthetic and no preconceived formal principles. Both are landscape painters; but neither accepts any individual scene or configuration of reeds and river, or rocks and quarries, or beach-sea-sky in a particular effect of light or weather as material in itself to be transmuted to a picture. Both react intellectually and emotionally to certain areas of landscape which they may be said to love as a man loves a particular woman in all her physical aspects and in all her moods; both analyse these many moods and physical aspects and build them to composite totals in their pictures which are thus to some extent descriptive, to some extent romantic and to some extent symbolically formal; and the artists seek a balance between all three modes—a balance so precarious that it can only be achieved by the utmost vigilance each time.

In the event, in some pictures by Lanyon and Fraser, (at the time of writing), the formal qualities appear to be overlaid by or sacrificed to the complexity of the artist's reactions. But (again at the time of writing) Patrick Heron (Pls. 48, 49 and 50) and Merlyn Evans (Pl. 62) both accept the principle of free organic formal rhythm and both work with confidence within it. Evans began with enthusiasm for Chirico and also for the dynamism and geometric aesthetic in the drawings made by Wyndham Lewis and Wadsworth for the first number of the Vorticist 'Blast'; and as late as 1952 he painted a dramatic *Industrial landscape* where fantastic cromlechs, constructed in sharp angles, were disposed upon a plain like the cromlechs in the landscape of the *Garden of Delights* by Hieronymus Bosch; but he has now moved from geometric to organic aesthetic and evolved a more personal technique to express the rhythm and movement he perceives in the world around him. Patrick Heron, as we know from his writings, is an intense admirer of the measured calculation in Braque's painting; but it is nevertheless the miraculous spontaneity and vitality of Picasso's drawing that seem to have inspired the swift flow of his symbolic line and his bold architectural distortions (cf. 'Architectural and other distortions' in Part III). Like Soulages, and some other non-representational painters, he accepts at one and the same time the Cubist assertion of the whole surface of the canvas as a single plane and the later concept which admits recession beyond it into space. His line leaps forward from chair or table in the foreground to the view through the window, and back again to candle or teapot or fish upon the table, and plays within an area so shallow that the landscape is pulled into the room and the chairs and tables are thrust up to the window; and this happens because the artist's purpose is to symbolize his simultaneous awareness of all these separate but related shapes and movements by one continuous rhythm. This purpose is the essence of his gay uninhibited painting—as we know indeed from his written account of his method of work in Cornwall: 'I may swivel my head momentarily away from the open window, with its prospect of the waters of St. Ives Bay, and the thin yellowness which is Lelant sands, and for two seconds, I may absorb visual realities of a very different order, the reddish outline of a near chair cutting up and across the white of a piece of wall, then becoming a silhouette against a patch of alternating dark brown and white stripes and bars (the back of another chair further off, a Windsor); and this, momentarily perceived and registered, becomes an integral part of my apprehension of the reality that surrounds me at this particular moment; and my picture is finished when that moment is exhausted, delimited, revealed as a complete entity, an organic whole which has drawn to itself as much as (but not more than) it can lay hands on. . . .'[1]

In the field of sculpture the formal contributions in recent years have been largely in the nature of plastic equivalents of the new pictorial language evolved by the painters for the painters' purposes. For whereas Barbara Hepworth, the most completely non-representational sculptor in England, has remained true to the concept of sculpture as the carving of blocks of stone or wood planted firmly on the ground, others have moved to a concept of transparent sculpture equipoised in space. The metal cages, for example, which filled the exhibition of projects for the Monument to the Unknown Political Prisoner, had illustrative point in relation to that subject, but they had not been invented for that subject; they already existed as sculptural equivalents of the modern painters' symbols for the architects' girders in transparent space, as sculptural equivalents for Paul Nash's *Aerial Composition* and Mondrian's *New York City* (Pl. 18), and static equivalents of Calder's mobiles. In the same way the organic rhythm in Frederick McWilliam's *Kneeling figure* (Pl. 51) is a sculptural equivalent of the pictorial aesthetic that entered the movement with Gauguin's *Jacob wrestling with the angel* (reproduced in my 'Modern French Painters') and his Tahitian *White horse* landscape (Pl. 41). This rhythm is the basic meaning of this *Kneeling figure* which I reproduce as it appeared by the waterside in a Battersea Park exhibition, because exactly at the moment when I stood before it there, a swan came up from the water to the lawn beside it and twirled its neck and bent it downwards to its wing and up again to show me clearly what the sculpture was about; and I record the episode without suggesting that my resulting pleasure made any contribution to the intrinsic value of McWilliam's work which was of course complete before I reached the waterside and before the swan arrived there to explain it.

Organic rhythm is also the subject of the two sculptures called *Crab* (Pls. 63 and 64) by Bernard Meadows who thus reminds us that the sculptors of the modern movement do not restrict themselves to romantic or descriptive studies of the human figure or to 'abstracting' architectural form therefrom, but are ready to seek and find experience in the whole phenomenal world.

McWilliam's *Father and Daughter* (Pl. 55) is later than his *Kneeling figure* and also more complex in character. The title is romantic; and there are undeniably romantic overtones; but in the calm, serene and ordered rhythm the

---

[1] I have used quotation marks but the text as I give it is really a compression of a longer passage which can be read *in extenso* in the collected edition of Heron's brilliant essays called 'The Changing Forms of Art'.

artist here proclaims allegiance to the classic standards of the early 'twenties when Ozenfant painted his *Accords* and his *Harmony* (Pl. 16) and Picasso the *Portrait* reproduced here (Pl. 22). McWilliam is now making highly interesting experiments with new materials that may lead him to fresh achievements; but I end these notes with my tribute to his *Father and Daughter* because it reminds us that the core of the continuing adventure called the modern movement is still the classical concept and that its basic doctrine can still be summarized as 'Architecture is the Mother of the Arts'.[1]

Cookham Dean
1956

[1] While this Preface was in the press Patrick Heron exhibited a number of almost completely non-representational pictures which may indicate the line of his future development or prove a temporary phase; and Merlyn Evans had a large 'Retrospective' exhibition at the Whitechapel Art Gallery which gave me the occasion to write an Introduction to the catalogue and discuss his works up to date in greater detail.

PREFACE FOR ARTISTS (1945)

In the preface to the first edition I distinguished between the romantic idea of art which assumes that the artist is more important than art and that the artist's emotional personality should dominate his work, and the classical idea which assumes that art is greater than the artist and that the artist is a link between the spectator and some universal order which man, as such, is always seeking to discover. Since that was written another idea of art has been spread about by anti-democratic propagandists who fear both romantic and classical art because both are concerned with aspects of life beyond the range of authoritarian control.

These propagandists are out to destroy the artist's initiative that they may exploit him thereafter for the increase of their own power. To the romantic artist, therefore, they say (in suitably disguised terms): 'The expression by an artist of his personal emotional experience is intolerable individualist pretension; the only tolerable expression of emotion is the expression of mass emotion as and when authority requires it.' To the classical artist they say (again with suitable dissembling): 'The search by an artist for contact with a mysterious universal order is pretentious high falutin; the only order with which the artist or anyone else need concern themselves is the order provided by authoritarian omniscience. It is the business of authority to define the types of art it needs for its wise purposes; and the artist's function is to supply those types and nothing else.'

This propaganda has recently been euphemistically titled 'Art as Public Service' or 'Art for the Nation's Sake'.

After the war the approved euphemism may be 'Art as Reconstruction'.

You have been warned.

London,
1945

ADDENDUM TO THE 1938 EDITION

In the four years that have passed since I wrote the Epilogue to the 1935 edition I have grown more appreciative of the parts played by Gauguin's Synthetism and Ozenfant's Purism; and I have become progressively more conscious of the difference between the Surrealism of Chirico (and, I may add, of Chagall)—which is concerned to make pictures with the character of dream-images and which remains within the framework of the Cubist-Classical-Architectural Renaissance—and the later Surrealism, more properly titled *Neo-Surrealism*, of which Max Ernst was an early and Salvador Dali is a later exponent. *Neo-Surrealism* has set out to explore the whole range of Freudian concepts as material for literature and art; more concerned with non-rational 'subjects' than with form, it is anecdotic and anti-aesthetic; it has no dislike of the photographic image; and it often uses daguerreotypic naturalism and oleographic colour in the mid-nineteenth-century tradition. I have discussed this development at length in my 'Modern French Painters.'[1]

[1] Cf. Index of that book, 'Surrealism' and 'Neo-Surrealism'.

EPILOGUE TO THE 1935 EDITION[1]

In one sense I have too little to add to this book to justify an Epilogue and in another sense I have too much—because since it appeared about seven years ago I have already added to it in several volumes connected with it and based upon it and because to add what I still want to add would fill a few volumes more.

The book is an attempt to tackle at least four separate and very difficult problems. It is firstly a theoretic discussion of certain aspects of the human activity called art; secondly, a theoretic discussion of the difference between intrinsic and acquired values (or as I should now prefer to put it between artist-acquired and spectator-acquired values); thirdly, an attempt to analyse the influence of photographs on pictorial technique; and fourthly an attempt to analyse the characteristics of the artistic developments of the last fifty years (forty when I started on the work) habitually referred to as the Modern Movement in Art. For the reasons given I cannot attempt here to add anything to the sections concerned with the first three problems. But I must make a few comments on what may conveniently be referred to as Post-Cubism, i.e. the creative art which is now developing on the basis of the Cubist-Classical Renaissance discussed in these pages.

The Cubist-Classical Renaissance was fundamentally the exaltation of formal order and planned architectural design against expressions of personal emotion and individualist records of emotive fragments; and the pioneers preached a severe uncompromising doctrine of Classical Discipline against the Romantic Individualism of the nineteenth century.

But there were all along artists who subscribed to the principles of this Cubist-Classical Renaissance but felt that the logical conclusion to which they were driven by Picasso and Braque demanded intolerable sacrifices and repressions; and that the doctrine in its Purist form was too austere, intellectual, and ratiocinative. These artists, both painters and sculptors, sought to redress the balance by finding, as it were, some non-intellectual bride for the Cubist concept of austere architectural ordered form. It was in this spirit that paintings by the genuinely naïf artist Rousseau le Douanier (Pl. 39), and negro sculpture, and psychological experience were all tried as mates for the architectural concept; Child Brides, Savage Brides, and Subconscious Brides were led by the

[1] Written in 1934.

46

Architectural Concept to the altar; and most original art in France and England in recent years has been the product of a union of one of these three kinds.

The unions with Savage Brides have had great influence on contemporary sculpture in ways that I have discussed elsewhere.[1] In painting, where such unions go back to Gauguin, who tried the experiment not only in art but in life, the influence has been less widely apparent. But Picasso had his 'Negro period' in which with characteristic clear-headed courage he drove this double concept to a logical conclusion—and then left it, as usual, for others to exploit as they might please.

The unions with Subconscious Brides have produced the movement now generally known as Surrealism in which Giorgio Chirico was the leading pioneer. Between 1910 and 1914 Chirico painted a series of pictures where formally ordered scenes were imbued with a disquieting quality of a new kind. In these pictures perspective was used as an emotive factor symbolizing the pleasing disquiet which we experience from claustrophobia and agoraphobia in dreams. Chirico followed this with other attempts to make pictures with material of the character of dream-images where fantastic juxtapositions convince, in spite of their incredibility, because they are so clear and definite. He thus created a new form of 'The Sublime' in Burke's sense—an art symbolizing 'pleasing horror' in a new way.

In Chirico's hands Surrealism remained, as far as might be, an architectural art within the main stream of the Cubist-Classical Renaissance. But the Subconscious Bride has led other artists to new forms of subjective Romanticism and to developments of 'Expressionismus'—the central European movement based on the neurotic aspects of the paintings by Van Gogh. Picasso, moreover, has recently made some Surrealist experiments and forced this dual concept, as he has forced so many others, to a logical conclusion where the pleasing horror of Burke's 'Sublime' is converted to horror of a terribly disturbing—sometimes appalling—kind.

A union of the Architectural Concept with the Child Bride lies behind the calligraphic virtuosity of Matisse. This may seem a paradox since Matisse is obviously the most sophisticated and modish of the Cubist-Classical masters. But Matisse has always aimed at the directness and immediacy of the child's vision subjected to architectural invention and control.

These three unions, taken together, will seem, I believe, to our descendants— as the art of Cézanne now seems to us—a transitional gesture attempting to reconcile conflicting principles. From them the creative art of the later twen-

[1] Cf. my 'The Meaning of Modern Sculpture'.

tieth century will no doubt be born. I do not know, of course, what forms that art will take. But I fancy that *Cat and Bird* produced in 1928 by Paul Klee, and the drawing called *Freedom* produced a year or two later by Leon Underwood will seem in 1980 as characteristic of 1930 creative art as Seurat's *Grande Jatte* now seems characteristic of the creative direction in 1884.[1]

[1] Klee's *Flora in an old garden* is reproduced here as Plate B. The *Cat and Bird* is reproduced in the little monograph on Klee, by René Crevel, published by the Librairie Gallimard in 1930. Underwood's drawing is reproduced in my 'English Painting' [1956 note].

PREFACE TO THE FIRST EDITION

The idea behind the modern movement in the arts is a return to the architectural or classical idea. It is fundamentally a reaction not only against the various degenerate forms of nineteenth-century art but also against the romantic movement of the nineteenth century in its purest and most original forms. It is thus, I submit, in line with the general orientation of contemporary thought. Romantic art assumes that the artist is more important than art, and that the artist's emotional personality should dominate his work. Classical art assumes that art is greater than the artist, and that the artist is merely a link between the spectator and some universal order, which man, as such, is always seeking to discover.

The striking difference between the technique of modern artists and that of most nineteenth-century painters is due partly to this new orientation in general aim, partly to a reaction against the camera's degrading influence on nineteenth-century technique, and partly to the realization that for good or evil the camera and the cinema have surpassed the artist in power to record the mechanical vision of his eyes.[1]

I have divided my inquiry into four parts. In Part I, I have tried to indicate what appear to me to be the main types of artistic production in Western Europe when service of the Christian religion was not the *raison d'être* of the work of art's existence and the sole criterion of its value; and to indicate by that classification the general character of the art of the modern movement.

In holding, as I do, that there is such a thing as religious art distinct from other forms of art, I recognize that I run counter to the fashionable aesthetic doctrines of the moment. But, as the reader will discover from my book, I hold that the true character of a work of art is determined at bottom by the artist's attitude and motives, and when the attitude and motive are religious the art produced seems to me to have for that reason a character of its own. I am yet to be convinced by aesthetic critics who tell me that the savage carving an image to scare the devil or bring down rain is engaged in the same kind of activity as the sculptor who looks at a woman who attracts him and makes a statement of her form's attractiveness; I cannot bring myself to believe that the Buddhist sculptor who raises the palm of Buddha's hand because the upraised palm is an emotive religious gesture is doing the same thing as the sculptor who raises the

[1] Cf. 'Human perception', Part II.

palm because the formal relations of a raised palm accord better architecturally with the rest of the figure; or that Fra Angelico painting a pink blue and gold Paradise on his knees was doing the same thing as the young lady who paints a pink blue and gold picture because she thinks pink blue and gold are pretty colours and because she wants to paint pictures that look rather like the Italian paintings of the early Renaissance; or that the artist who painted the Louvre *Pietà* from Villeneuve-les-Avignon, and Matthias Grünewald who painted the Colmar *Crucifixion*, were doing the same thing as a modern architectural artist painting aubergines and onions on a plate.

In my inquiry I make no attempt to discuss religious art. I am not called upon to do so because the modern movement has never been attacked on the ground that it is not religious in character. Such references as occur in the text to certain procedures of religious artists have been inserted solely because I believed that at those special points a comparison with those procedures might help to make my meaning clear.

In Part II, I have described the degeneration of nineteenth-century art in France and England as manifested in confusion of ideas and in degenerate technique. This part, which contains an attempt to analyse the influence of the camera on nineteenth-century pictorial technique, makes no pretence to be a history of nineteenth-century art. It is merely a bird's-eye view of the century's production seen from the angle of the pioneer artists of the modern movement, who decided that both nineteenth-century ideas of art and nineteenth-century technique must be thrown into the dustbin, and that a new art must be created on the basis of the old idea that Architecture is the Mother of the Arts.

In Part III, I have described some of the technical experiments made by the artists of the modern movement; and I have endeavored to explain them.

In Part IV, I have submitted a theory of the relative values of the forms of non-religious art which I have classified in Part I. In so doing I am quite aware I have been guilty of extreme temerity; and I do not for one moment imagine that what I have set down is the whole truth or that all the details of the slim structure I have erected will withstand all the criticism of serious students; but I have been impelled to erect that structure because I feel strongly that some structure on the basis on which it rests can and should be reared; and because, as far as my knowledge goes, no attempt to raise a structure on that particular basis has recently been made.

The basis of the theory of comparative values which I have submitted consists of certain convictions of my own. My first conviction is that, in the case of an original work of art, no reaction on the part of the spectator can constitute a criterion of the work's value, because a work of this character is the secret communication by the artist to himself of an enlargement of his own experience; so that the artist alone can be the perfect judge of the extent to which his work is or is not the perfect fulfilment of his purpose. My second conviction is that, when an original work of art has been honestly and competently passed by the artist as right, it has for that reason an intrinsic value which can never be altered by any reactions on the part of other spectators. My third conviction is that the value acquired by original works of art from the appreciation given to them by spectators (other than the artist) is another kind of value which must be distinguished from the work's intrinsic value. My fourth conviction is that an essential difference between the value of *original* works of art and the value of *popular* works of various kinds is that in the case of popular works the spectator's appreciation can be the true criterion of value when those works have been produced in order to excite that appreciation; whereas in the case of original works of art, as I have said, the spectator's appreciation cannot constitute a true criterion of the work's intrinsic value because the question of the work's effect on spectators other than the artist has not preoccupied the artist at any stage of his procedure.[1]

The theory of values which I have constructed is thus based on my general conviction that the true criticism of an original work of art must consist in an examination of the attitude, motives and procedure of the artist who made it and not in an examination of the emotional or other reactions aroused by the work in spectators other than the artist. This is the case which I have argued in Part IV of this inquiry.

The enemies of the modern movement and also many of its friends have written about it solely by describing their own reactions towards its productions. Mr. Clive Bell[2] for example has stated categorically that we have no right to consider anything a work of art to which we do not react emotionally. I have undertaken this inquiry largely because I am certain (a) that this approach in the case of original art of any kind is fundamentally wrong, and (b) that it is particularly misleading and unhelpful in approaching the works produced by the modern movement which are not romantic but architectural and original in kind.

In thus running counter to the attitude of contemporary aesthetic critics I am, however, supported by a firm belief that the basis of the theory of values I have submitted has always been taken for granted by original artists themselves. All original artists, I am certain, have always worked without reference to their

[1] The exact sense in which I use the words 'original' and 'popular' is defined in the text.
[2] Clive Bell: 'Art'.

work's effect on spectators other than themselves; and they have always assumed that their work has intrinsic value when they themselves have honestly and competently passed it as exactly the thing which they had set out to do. No original artist could go on working but for this assumption, since, as we all know, the reception first afforded to original works of art by other spectators is generally in the nature of apathy, derision or abuse. The basis of the aesthetic critic's attitude on the point of values is a belief that he can react to works of art when he sees them and that his own reaction is the criterion of value of the work of art; or in other words that the artist does not know the value of his own work and that it is valueless till the aesthetic critic has approved it by some 'aesthetic ecstasy' or 'thrill'. My own attitude on the point of values is based on the view that the original artist is *right* in assuming that his work, when honestly and competently passed by himself, has intrinsic value which cannot be altered when the aesthetic critic or some other spectator arrives later on the scene and approves it, disapproves it or ignores it altogether. My attitude is based on the view that the anguish of the original artist who fails to enlarge his experience to the point of symbolic concrete form is anguish resulting from a real failure; and that the original artist's joy when he has achieved his purpose is joy occasioned by a real success.

Parts II and III are historical in character; the technical comments I have made there are based to a large extent on personal experience. I have myself worked in the art schools which I censure; I have myself made experiments in photographically naturalistic and in representational[1] techniques and have found the latter immeasurably more difficult than the former since they involve complex reinforcements to mechanical vision which are not required in photographically naturalistic painting.[2]

Parts I and IV, which go together, are obviously speculative; they have been written with the greatest difficulty; and it may be that in writing them I have bitten off more than I have been able successfully to chew, though I believe the attempt at chewing to have been worth the labour.

It is widely assumed that all the arts and all the forms of each art are the result of the same kind of human activity; or in other words that there is one special kind of activity which produces works of art. The nature of that activity has never been finally or satisfactorily defined.

---

[1] The difference between naturalistic and representational art is discussed in Part I (*f*) and Part II (*b*).

[2] I have also made technical experiments in sculpture. That is to say I have modelled figures and groups in clay for bronze. But the process of carving was obviously so much more difficult that I have never had the courage to attempt it.

I believe that each art and each form of each art is the result of a different activity on the part of the artist; and that some of these activities are almost identical and others are widely different.

Whether this view be right or wrong there can be no question that enormous confusion in our approach to works of art arises from our habit of assuming that the artist who did the work which we may chance to be contemplating to-day, set out to do the same thing as the artist whose work we chanced to contemplate yesterday—particularly when the artist whose work we contemplated yesterday was an artist working in another art. Our comprehension and appreciation of works of art cannot, I am certain, be increased or clarified by the prevailing habit of speaking of one art in terms of another and of assuming that what we hold to be excellent or worthless, essential or incidental, in one art, is necessarily excellent or worthless, essential or incidental, in another.

In this inquiry I am concerned solely with plastic art, by which I mean architecture, sculpture, painting, pottery, and so forth; and the greater part of my comments are concerned with painting. I have not made any comparisons between the activities of the plastic artist and the activities of the musician, the dramatist or the poet; and I earnestly entreat the reader to abstain from such comparisons in his mind when reading this book; but if, as is likely, the habit of such comparisons is so inveterate that he is unable to abstain from it, then I entreat him to keep separate in his mind his experience of his own reactions towards works of plastic art, music, poetry, and the drama, from his experience of the activities of the men who produced those works. If his acquaintance with the activities involved in composing plastic art, music, poetry, and the drama is sufficient to enable him to compare them with what I say about the activities of various kinds of plastic artists, then the comparisons may possibly be of some service; but it is no reflection on the reader to suggest that there are few readers whose experience in creating works in all the arts is sufficient to make such comparisons of any use at all. In other words I entreat the reader (a) not to mix up the activity that produces one art with the activity that produces another; (b) not to mix up the effects upon himself of one art and of another; and (c) not to mix up what he knowns about any kind of artist's activity with the effects upon himself of the work which that kind or any other kind of artist has produced.

The distinction which I have just asked the reader to draw in his mind is of course the distinction between liking or disliking works of art and the power to understand and criticize them. The critic whose method consists in describing the character of his own pleasure or displeasure when confronted with particular works of art is describing not those works but certain aspects of his own psychological constitution. The only critic who can tell us anything about a work of art is the man who has discovered the attitude, motives and procedure of the artist; and that discovery I hold to be the function of artistic criticism.

I acknowledge with thanks the courtesy of the artists whose pictures are reproduced in this book; also the courtesy of Mr. Samuel Courtauld, Mr. Lewis Hoare and others who have supplied me with photographs of works in their collections.

Heston
  December 1926

Part I

CHARACTER OF THE MOVEMENT

A. RELIGIOUS AND NON-RELIGIOUS ART

The phrase 'the modern movement in art' is a term of convenience used by art critics for the outstanding developments in Western European art that have taken place in recent times. In this inquiry I am concerned with the developments in painting and sculpture. I am not concerned with the developments in music or poetry, and I shall avoid comparisons between those arts and the plastic arts because such comparisons seem to me to be more often confusing than helpful.

To fix an exact date for the beginning of the modern movement in painting and sculpture is impossible because the phrase refers not only to actual works produced, but also to an idea of art which lies behind them. As a working date, however, 1884, the year of the foundation of the Salon des Indépendants in Paris, may be taken, I think, as the beginning of the modern reaction against the Romantic idea of art; and we can say therefore that the modern movement has now been in progress for more than sixty years, though scarcely any contribution was made to it by English artists till after 1910.[1]

The movement is based on an idea of art consciously held by the artists. As such, I submit at the outset, it is in line with the main body of Western European art since the middle of the Italian Renaissance, but different in character from religious art of all times and places.

This submission calls perhaps for some explanation, because contemporary critics have told us so often that Art is Art, One and Indivisible, that we have almost begun to believe it. Modern critics tell us that from the most various forms of art they experience the same kind of aesthetic thrill, and they ask us accordingly to credit the various works with a common denominator consisting in the power to give them that thrill. The lamentable confusion in art values which prevails to-day is largely the result of such critics' activities. For when a man says 'This picture gives me a thrill and that does not', he is not talking about the pictures, he is merely talking about himself. When he has confessed to the thrill in fifty different cases we begin to know something about him. But we have not yet begun to know anything about the pictures. When fifty such critics have told us about their thrills before two hundred and fifty pictures, we know quite a lot about the receptivity of contemporary critics. But the pictures still remain unjudged and unexplained.

[1] Except by Whistler, cf. 'Reconstruction in France and England', Part II.

In my view such critics approach the study of works of art from the wrong angle. In this inquiry therefore I shall adopt a different approach. I shall not set down how the works produced by the artists of the modern movement affect my personal receptivity, but I shall try to discover the character and value of the works themselves as compared and contrasted with other kinds of plastic art.

Now I submit, as a first postulate, that art produced in the service of some religion is in a class by itself. The world holds countless temples with countless works of sculpture and painting contributing to the temple's purposes, countless magic images credited in some time or place with the major powers of producing benefits or evils or with the minor power of intercession between believers and a god possessed of major powers of help and harm; it holds also countless carvings and paintings depicting happenings which, from the standpoint of some religion, were known to be dear to the minds of men or were held desirable for men to know. In the case of artists working in the service of a religion there was never any question of what they were doing or why they were doing it. Whether the business in hand was carving a magic image, or a statue of Buddha, or painting scenes from the life of St. Francis, or the story of the Creation, the artist, before he began his work, was provided with a justification for its existence and a criterion of its value.

Works produced with this criterion may still constitute the majority of works of art in the world. But in Western Europe, especially since the middle of the Italian Renaissance, a very large number of works of art have been produced which have not been called forth by the service of a religion. In the case of such works the artists have not had a religious justification for the existence of their labour or a religious criterion of its value.

In the nineteenth century, which was dominated by individualist and romantic ideas, the disappearance of the idea of religious service as the fundamental *raison d'être* for art was looked on by most art critics as an event of great benefit to the European artist. It was assumed that it had greatly increased the range of his outlook and provided him with an enviably unfettered mind. That assumption I believe to be wrong. I believe that the change meant no increase of freedom; that no sooner had the artist shaken off the chains that bound him to the service of religion than he felt the need of other chains to provide security and peace of mind; that, when the justification of his work and the criterion of its value were not provided by the idea of service to religion, he felt bound to seek a justification and a criterion in some idea of service to something else. I am convinced that all the most intelligent artists of Western Europe in recent centuries have been tormented by this search for a justification of their work and a criterion of its value; and that almost all such artists have attempted to solve the problem by some consciously-held idea of art; or in other words that in place of art justified by service to a religion they have sought to evolve an art justified by service to an idea of art itself.

My first point then is that the artists of the modern movement, in basing their art on service to a consciously-held idea of art, are *ipso facto* different from the religious artists of the East and West of all periods, but in line with all the Western European artists of the last five hundred years who have based their work on any type of consciously-held ideas of art; and that the modern movement is the latest attempt to solve the fundamental problem of all intelligent Western European artists since the High Renaissance, the problem, that is, of finding a justification for artistic work and a criterion of its value other than the justification and criterion afforded by the service of some religion.[1]

B. THE SINGLE STRAND

Medieval art in Western Europe was a complex cord composed of many strands. Justified fundamentally in the artist's mind by the idea of service to religion it embraced a number of activities within itself. As Émile Mâle has pointed out, the art of the early Gothic cathedrals, which represented the culmination of medieval art in Western Europe, was the mirror not only of the religious, but also the mirror of the scientific and the moral concepts of the medieval Christian world, of that world's experience of past and contemporary history, and of its perception of architectural form.[2]

One by one, since those cathedrals were built, these constituents have been separated and made distinct in Western European thought. The religious fundament was the first constituent to be withdrawn. Religion first began to be thought of as a thing distinct from art; and the service of religion became an activity of a separate kind. Science, morals, social history, as time passed, followed the path taken by religion. To-day each is in a separate compartment

[1] Our æsthetic critics frequently instance El Greco as a forerunner of the modern movement. As I see it El Greco's magnificent work was essentially religious. The work of artists like Fra Angelico or Sassetta expressed peaceful service to a religion. El Greco's work expressed hysterical service of the same kind. El Greco distorted his figures in a passionate desire to make them appear more saintly and divine. Such an attitude of mind is entirely different from that of an artist distorting in the service of some idea of art. (Cf. 'Architectural and other distortions', Part III). [For another interpretation of El Greco's art cf. the interesting essay by Roger Hinks in Faber Gallery 'El Greco', 1956 note].

[2] Émile Mâle, 'L'Art religieux du XIIIe siècle en France'.

withdrawn from art. Specialists who make their living by specialization have attained to a detailed and elaborate experience in each and all these fields that is quite outside the artist's range. We do not look to the artist to-day for our science, our ethics, or our history any more than for our religion. To-day moreover, we have the camera, the cinematograph and camera-sculpture developed by specialists into instruments of such recording skill that we have learned to look to them for records of our mechanical vision.

Artists at various times have tried desperately to build an art based solely on service to a romantic idea of which the roots can also be discerned in the Gothic cathedrals. The latest and most valiant of these efforts was made in the nineteenth century. The modern movement came into being because leading artists felt that that attempt had failed. The idea behind it, they felt, was inadequate as a substitute for the idea of service to a religion; and they set out to find a justification of their work and a criterion of its value in a different idea of art.

C. ARCHITECTURE AS TYPICAL ART

What then is this idea of art which the artists of the modern movement consciously serve? Stated briefly it is the idea of architecture as typical art. What does this mean? What is architecture? Why do we call it art?

The architect may be said to be at one and the same time a builder and an artist. In his capacity as builder he works theoretically in stone, brick, iron, steel and so forth; as builder he is concerned with the functional aspect of his work, with its practical purpose. But in addition to this theoretical work as builder, which is scientific, the architect has another function the exercise of which produces results so different from the results of the mere builder who is not an architect that men have invented the word 'architecture' to differentiate the one kind of building from the other, and the word 'art' to describe the character of the architect's work.

What exactly do we mean by the word 'art' when we use it to connote the difference between a building that is architecture and a building that is not— when we say that a work of architecture is a work of art and a building is just a building and nothing more?

The answer to the question, difficult in itself, has been made more so by the reckless use of the word 'beauty' as an equally mysterious substitute for the mysterious word 'art'. To be told, as we frequently are, that the difference between architecture and building is that the work of architecture possesses 'beauty' while the mere building does not, is to be told nothing more than that the work of architecture is 'art' and the mere building is not. For the words 'beauty' and 'beautiful' have been and are used in as many senses as there are human beings on this earth; objectively they have now no recognized sense at all; and very little is gained if we substitute for 'art' or 'beauty' the fashionable term of the present moment, i.e. 'significant form' because that term is almost as elastic as the others.

But this much we may say, I think, without wandering into complicated metaphysic and aesthetic. We may say that the words 'proportion', 'balance', 'line', 'colour', 'recession' and so on stand for indefinite, unorganized, and incomplete formal experience in man's mind which it is his nature to desire to make definite, organized, and complete; that the architect as artist makes definite organized complete structures symbolizing and epitomizing special instances of his formal experience; and that it is the creation of such symbols and epitomes which is the typical function of the architect, as artist, as distinguished from his concomitant utilitarian function as builder.

We may say in other words that the architect's business as artist is to contribute to the definition, organization, and completion of his formal experience by creating a concrete object symbolizing his actual or imagined perception[1] of certain lines, balances, recessions and so forth; that if he can do this he is what we call an artist, and that if he cannot he is just a builder and nothing more.

The architect experiences, synthetizes and creates; he experiences proportion, balance, line, recession and so on, he co-ordinates and organizes his experience, and he gives it definite form in a building. He does not look at an isolated fragment and make an isolated imitation of its appearance at some particular point of time and space. He is concerned from first to last with problems of formal relations.

The idea of art on which the modern movement is based is the idea that *this typical function of the architect as artist is the typical function of the sculptor and painter as well.*

This idea of art is not of course new or revolutionary. It is in no sense a break with tradition. It is simply the idea which lies behind all the so-called classical art of the last five centuries. It is the idea of art which was served for example by artists like Raphael in the *School of Athens* (Pl. 3) and by Claude and Poussin in many of their works. It is the idea contained in the cliché 'Architecture is the Mother of the Arts'. It is in fact an idea so well known that we have lost the habit of considering what it means.

[1] Cf. 'The artist's perception', Part II.

61

The first points which I submit then are these:

(1) that the artists of the modern movement, who have based their art not on service to a religion but on service to an idea of art, are in line with all the other European artists since the High Renaissance who have done the same thing;

(2) that the particular idea chosen, the idea of architecture as typical art, is an idea which has been served before by many classical Western European artists since the High Renaissance.

D. CONFLICTING IDEAS

Most of the abuse showered on the modern movement consists of complaints that the works it has produced are (*a*) neither romantic nor descriptive in kind; (*b*) that they are original and not popular in kind; (*c*) that they are not naturalistic in technique; and people who base their estimates of works of art purely on the effects of those works upon themselves, and who make no effort to discover the ideas by which the artists were actuated, complain with vehemence that the works produced by the modern movement are 'abnormal'.[1]

These complaints are made not only by people who approach the movement in the spirit of old gentlemen who once drove horses and now shake their umbrellas at every passing car, but also by people who recognize that the modern movement is the outstanding artistic development of the last sixty years but are nevertheless completely unable to understand or enjoy its productions.

If the productions of the movement are approached from another angle, if instead of saying, 'This bewilders me' the student would say 'What did the artist set out to do?' modern art would not appear abnormal in any way. Because what the spectator means when he calls modern pictures and sculpture 'abnormal' is really that they strike him as abnormal. He means that and nothing more.

Modern works of art strike many people as abnormal simply because they are unlike the painting and sculpture produced in Western Europe in the nineteenth century. The average spectator thinks modern art abnormal because it is unlike the art with which he happens to be most familiar, and which for that reason he regards as normal.

The nineteenth century produced original and popular art of the romantic and descriptive kinds. In spite of attempts by Puvis de Chavannes, it produced

[1] The exact sense in which I use the words 'romantic', 'descriptive', 'original', 'popular', and 'derivative' in this inquiry is defined in the sections which follow.

scarcely any original classical art till the 'eighties when Seurat appeared and Cézanne got into his stride. Ingres was a romantic who attempted a compromise between the two ideals.[1] Stevens was an imitator of Michelangelo. Gérome, Leighton and Poynter were decadent derivative artists who produced nothing but travesties of the classical ideal. The modern movement, based on the severely classical idea of architecture as the mother of the arts, was bound at first to appear abnormal to those who expected works of art to affect them in the ways that original or degenerate nineteenth-century romantic and descriptive art affected them. The movement was bound to seem to such people as much a break with tradition as the romantic art of Delacroix seemed a break to those accustomed to the effects on themselves of original or degenerate works executed in the French classical tradition of which Poussin was the outstanding master.

Those who in the eighteen-thirties thought their own reactions to the *Massacre of Scio* more interesting than the picture itself were never able to appreciate or understand it. Those, on the other hand, who left on one side the picture's effects on themselves and took the trouble to inquire into the idea of art behind it, were not slow to see that the character of Delacroix's picture, in relation to that idea of art, was not abnormal but inevitable. It was possible to understand Delacroix's creed and believe it a heresy. It was not possible to understand it and to regard the *Massacre of Scio* as abnormal or the work of a man anxious to defy the spectator or to pull his leg. In the same way it is possible to maintain that the idea of architecture as the mother of the arts is a misconception of the artist's function, and that the artists of the modern movement are for that reason in a cul-de-sac just as all classical artists have been before them. But it is not possible to recognize the classical architectural basis of the movement and continue to call its productions abnormal or the work of men actuated only by a desire to advertise themselves or annoy the public.

The genuine romantic art of Delacroix was partly a reaction against the degenerate forms of classical art which abounded at the turn of the eighteenth to the nineteenth century; it was partly, that is, a protest against the travesties of the art of Raphael, Claude and Poussin produced by degenerate pseudo-classical artists. It was also partly a protest against the classical architectural idea of art in its purest and most fundamental form.

In the same way the genuine classical art of the modern movement is partly a protest against the degenerate romantic and pseudo-romantic art of the nineteenth century. But it is also partly a reaction against the genuine romantic idea of art as such. To the artists of the modern movement the romantic creed

---

[1] Cf. 'The Daguerreotype and Ingres', Part II.

even at its purest is a heresy. It seems a departure from the strictly classical tradition to which they themselves have now returned. For this reason they deliberately leave out of their works all the features which admirers of romantic art are accustomed to regard as commendable, just as the nineteenth-century romantics deliberately left out all the features which the admirers of classical painting were accustomed to regard as indispensable to art.

To appreciate the conflict between the classical artists of the modern movement and spectators who regard their works as abnormal because they strike them as different from both the original and the degenerate romantic and descriptive works of the nineteenth century, it is necessary to realize exactly how those various types of work are assessed by the modern artists, and why they have felt the need to react from and protest against them.

E. THE ROMANTIC HERESY

The idea of art served by the artists of the romantic movement a hundred years ago was the idea that the artist's function was to discover and record unusually emotive fragments. For the creation of a formal harmony and unity symbolizing a universal harmony and unity, which is and always has been the classical architectural idea of art, the romantic artist substituted the search for some emotive fragment hitherto regarded as without emotive power. The fragments chosen by the romantics were chosen, not for their formal or generic, but for their emotive significance; they were the fragments which had affected the artist's emotions. Whether, judged by standards of Greek or Græco-Roman sculpture or Renaissance painting, the fragment was 'beautiful' or 'ugly' did not affect the issue; if the fragment aroused emotion in the artist it was 'beautiful', and to record it was worth while.

The herald of the romantic movement in the plastic arts was Rembrandt. The French romantics of the early nineteenth century made the romantic elements in his art their point of departure. They made no attempt to achieve contact with an architecture of the universe; all the attempts made by classical art to symbolize such architecture they decried as cold and dead; they were entirely concerned with the emotive significance of individual fragments; they believed moreover that the artist's records of the fragments selected as emotive should be carried out by the artist in a condition of emotion; a passionate painting of the 'meanest flower' meant more to them than Raphael's *School of*

64

Athens or the Parthenon; so did a passionate painting of a beggar or a flayed ox.

To the artists of the modern movement this doctrine seems to have funda-mental weaknesses. For the modern artist's creed, like the creed of all classical architectural artists, postulates a concept in the artist's mind of a formal order or architecture in the universe. That concept may derive from actual perception or purely imaginative perception. The extent to which that perception is emotional is held to vary with each artist and with each artist at different times. The classical architectural creed does not postulate an emotional reaction as the sole jumping-off point which can create a work of formal art. It admits that the perception may be emotional but it admits equally that it may not be emotional. In regard to the subsequent stages the creed denies that a work of architectural art can be produced by what is ordinarily called emotional activity. The initial concept, it holds, may be intellectual or emotional or the result of intellect and emotion working together on some terms; but the subsequent stages of the production of a work of art it regards as the result of a dominant intellectual activity in the course of which the artist's emotion is of the kind experienced by other intellectual workers in the execution of their work.[1]

Now the true romantic artist does not desire intellectual perception of formal order, but emotional perception of emotive fragments; and in the subsequent stages the activity of his mind is directed by his feelings. The dangers of the romantic artist's creed from the classical architectural standpoint are (*a*) that the artist may be led to regard his own emotional reactions to fragments as more important than the cause of them; (*b*) that he may be led thereby to imagine that plastic art is merely the expression of his feelings without examining those feelings and analysing their true character; and (*c*) that from seeking the unusually emotive fragment he may be led to the mental confusion of imagin-ing that all fragments remote in time or space are unusual and so emotive.

In point of fact, the nineteenth-century romantic movement in the plastic arts succumbed to just these dangers, as I shall presently attempt to show. It soon assumed a complacent subjective character. The romantic idea soon became the notion that art was the expression of the artist, which in practice too often meant the unfettered expression of the artist's habitual moods, sensations and taste in female attractiveness. It soon became the notion that a work of art was essentially a thing produced at white heat by an artist expressing his familiar emotional experience. Nineteenth-century romantic art, in a word, soon

[1] Mr. Clive Bell, in my view, quite misrepresents it when he says that the artist's business must be 'the translation into material form of something that the artist has felt *in a spasm of ecstasy*'. Cf. 'The artist's perception', Part II, and 'Criterions of value', Part IV.

degenerated and became partly a series of Confession Albums written by men supremely satisfied with their own familiar sensations, and partly a series of venal appeals to the familiar sensations of other people. Also it soon degenerated when the artists, from seeking and finding unusually emotive fragments in their habitual environment, began to imagine that any fragment was unusual and emotive if it happened to be remote in time or space. Delacroix himself suffered from this confusion at the outset and imagined that Moors and Arab horses were unusual and therefore emotive fragments when really they were only fragments which happened to be unusual in Paris.[1]

In this inquiry I shall examine successively the respective characters of original and popular romantic art, their technical forms in the nineteenth century, and their respective values; and I shall have a word to say also on the ideas behind the Wardour-Street-costume-pseudo-romantic pictures which were so conspicuous in nineteenth-century art in France and England. For the moment my point is that the artists of the modern movement, whose creed is the classical architectural creed, regard the romantic creed as a dangerous heresy because in its purest forms, as well as in its degenerate forms, it conflicts with the notion that architecture is the mother of the arts; and that the productions of the modern movement do not affect the spectator in the same way that romantic works of art affect him because they are not romantic works and are not intended to be such.

What we have then is:

(1) the art produced by the modern movement is not religious in kind; it is art based on a consciously-held idea of art;

(2) that idea of art is the idea of architecture as typical art;

(3) that idea is opposed to the romantic idea of art not only in its degenerate, but also in its purest forms.

F. NATURALISM
AND REPRESENTATION (i)

Many of the attacks on the art of the modern movement, as I have indicated, are really complaints that the works it has produced are not naturalistic in technique. But here again it must be recognized that these works are not

[1] Cf. 'Genius and the critic' in this part and 'Degeneration of ideas', Part II.

intended to be such; though they are in many cases representational—which is something entirely different.

Experience has taught me that the layman finds it difficult to appreciate the fundamental difference between naturalistic and representational technique; and also that he frequently forgets that naturalism and representation are not *types of art* but technical procedures which can be and are employed in many different types of art. I shall attempt a very brief examination of the difference between the two techniques at this part of my inquiry (though Part I is devoted to an examination of different types of art) because, without it, readers who are not clear on the point may find some comments in this part obscure; and I return to discussion of the subject in the section labelled 'Naturalism and Representation' (ii) in Part II.

Nineteenth-century naturalistic painting was a technical procedure in which the artists set out to imitate as closely as possible the appearances of physical objects or concrete things at some particular point of time and space. Such a painter sat down—or stood up—before a physical object or concrete thing and copied in paint on canvas the appearance of that object or thing in some particular place and in some particular effect of light. He used his eye, that is, as far as is humanly possible, as a mechanical lens. If the object moved or the light changed, like a camera he could not continue; he was lost. If the object was stationary, till the light changed he could copy the shapes of the lights and shadows before him, and, if he did it accurately, lo! a nose or apple miraculously appeared.[1]

There is a notion, not confined to the ignorant, that all artists at all times have painted as naturalistically as they could; that the artists of Egypt and ancient Greece, and the artists of medieval Italy would have worked in the technique of a nineteenth-century naturalistic painter had they had the power; that Botticelli would have made his nudes as 'life-like' as the nudes in the Paris *Salon* if he had been a more skilful practitioner; and that the artists of the Far East would have made drawings like photographs had they not been mere ignorant orientals groping feebly in the dark. The Western world is full of people who regard the history of art as a species of progress from Egyptian art to Greek art, from Greek art to the art of the Italian Renaissance, from the Italian Renaissance to Dutch genre and landscape painting in the seventeenth century, and from that plane again to the crowning glory of the nineteenth-century naturalistic Paris *Salon* nude or Royal Academy Lord Mayor or kitten.

[1] Cf. 'The Camera's vision' and 'Human perception', Part II.

This perverted view of art is due partly to the accident that a high proportion of all the naturalistic painting in the world was produced in the nineteenth century, and partly to the accident that the invention of the camera greatly encouraged this technique and gave it two peculiar twists that I shall examine in Part II.[1]

At the end of the century, surrounded by thousands of pictures where this technique had been employed, the average spectator began to think of art as so typically photographically-naturalistic in technique that he was forced to think vaguely of architecture and the various types of classical architectural painting and sculpture as 'something else'; and the works produced by the modern movement have been widely misunderstood because the artists do not employ this particular technique which, in the forms given it by the camera, was only used by nineteenth-century painters, and which, in its normal form, was rarely used by any Old Masters except the Dutch genre painters of the seventeenth century.[2]

Another reason why many people at the end of the nineteenth century fell into the error of regarding photographically naturalistic technique as a type of art, and the only characteristic type, was that this technique, in a form degraded by the camera, was the technique taught habitually in art schools in the later years of that century.

In 'Naturalism and representation' in Part II, I shall examine the vicious systems of 'drawing by the shadows' and 'painting by the tone values' which were taught in these art schools. Here it is only necessary to point out that the art masters favoured this technique because it is nothing more than a facile trick which any intelligent young man or woman can learn in two or three years. Thousands of young men and women in the last fifty years have, in fact, been taught successfully to draw 'by the shadows' and paint 'by the tone values'. After three months' work in such a school any young man or woman who had decided to 'take up art' could take home a set of studies which people (making allowances for a certain lack of assurance) could and did recognize as like the naturalistically drawn and painted pictures in the exhibitions. Students who learned the trick quickly were said to be 'good at art'. Those who were slow were said to be less good. From the artmaster's point of view all that was necessary was to teach the trick sufficiently well in the first term to persuade the parents who were paying the fees that it was worth while paying further fees

---

[1] Cf. 'Past and present' in this part, Part II *passim*, and 'The value of technique', Part IV.

[2] Cf. 'Naturalism and representation' (ii), Part II.

next term. In this they invariably succeeded. Hence the enormous number of 'artists' in the modern world.[1]

Now what is the basis of the technical procedures of the vast majority of the artists of the past who have 'represented' physical objects and concrete things in various relations without using the naturalistic technique?

Put briefly it is a technique achieved not by the mechanical operation of human *vision* but by the complex operation which we call human *perception*.[2]

In this inquiry I shall try later to indicate the main technical procedures of certain kinds of representational artists. But it must be realized at the outset that all representational techniques (as opposed to the naturalistic trick) are deliberately symbolic in character. They range from the obviously symbolic representation of the architect to the less obviously symbolic representation of the original descriptive artist. Between these poles comes on the one hand the classical architectural technique of painters (men like Raphael in the *School of Athens*, Claude, Poussin and the Cubists) who stand close to the architects; and on the other the romantic technique of the romantic artists who stand close to the descriptive artists. All these techniques have this in common: They are all deliberately symbolic, they all involve deliberate transformations of the artist's mechanical vision to perception by means of some combination of sensations, associated ideas, imagination, memories, knowledge, moods, psychological factors, and so on and so forth.[3] *No representational artist ever sets out to record his mechanical vision. Such artists always set out to symbolize their perception.* Technically speaking, the representational artist's work is a structure symbolizing a certain general perception, and the details in that work, when they represent physical objects and concrete things in various relations, are symbols for the artist's perception of such fragments and their mutual relations.[4]

It is the recognition of the symbolic character of all representational art that is the clue to its comprehension. Once it is recognized that Michelangelo when representing the hair on his athletes by architecturally disposed curving lines was deliberately using a method of representation as symbolic as the Egyptian's deliberately symbolic outline for an eye, or as Brancusi's deliberately symbolic representation of a fish, there is no difficulty in recognizing that all three

---

[1] At the present day, outside the modern movement, the main mass of painters still use the degraded naturalistic nineteenth-century technique, and this trick is still taught in art schools. Many people to-day for these reasons still fall into the same errors in assessing it. Cf. 'Naturalism and representation' (ii), Part II, and Part II *passim*.

[2] Cf. 'Human perception', Part II.

[3] Cf. 'Human perception' and 'The artist's perception' in Part II.

[4] The Artist's perception, Part II.

symbolic methods and a thousand others are one kind of technical activity and that naturalistic copying of passing effects of light and shade is another.

It is the deliberately symbolic character of architectural representation that gives it what is known as 'style'. All architectural art has style; painting which is naturalistic in technique is always devoid of 'style'.[1]

Finally it must be noted at this stage that the difficulty encountered by so many people to-day in distinguishing naturalistic technique from representational technique has been increased by the dissemination of photographic reproductions of pictures. For such reproductions reduce the scale so much that the symbolic character of the representational technique is lost. A photographic reproduction of Raphael's *School of Athens* (Pl. 3) can demonstrate the architectural character of the composition; it can demonstrate its character as an architectural construction as symbolic as the most symbolic composition by an artist of the modern movement; but Raphael's symbolic representational symbolism, determined by his perception distinguished from his mechanical vision, is not visible when a life-size figure in a painting is reduced to the size of a small finger nail. Photographic reproductions have rendered considerable services to students of the arts, but they have done much to blind us to the fundamental difference between naturalistic and representational technique.

What we have then now is:

(1) the art produced by the modern movement is in line with all the types of Western European art which have been based on service to a consciously-held idea of art;

(2) the idea of art which it serves is the idea of architecture as typical art;

(3) that idea of art has been served in the past by countless classical artists;

(4) it is an idea opposed to the romantic idea of art;

(5) it is an idea opposed to nineteenth-century naturalistic technique;

---

[1] Writers on art use the word 'style' in several senses. Some use it as a substitute for the words 'type of art'. Others use it as a substitute for the word 'technique'. The word is used in the second way, for example, when an artist's name on the frame of a picture of unknown authorship is said to be a 'style ascription' (i.e. a guess made on the basis of technical characters in the picture); and it is often used in the second way when writers, speaking of 'the style of a period', or the 'Cubist style' mean thereby a conglomeration of technical characters invented by some original artists (cf. 'Original Art' in this Part) lumped together with imitations of those characters by other types of artist (cf. 'Derivative Popular Art', Part I and 'Value of Technique', Part IV). I have not used the word in either of those ways in this book. In the few places where it occurs I have used it in the sense of a *quality* which resides in all kinds of deliberately symbolic technique but which does not reside in naturalistic technique or in the language of the still camera, the cinema-camera or the television camera. This use of the word is common among artists; it is what they mean when they say that a work 'has style'; and I have used it thus and not attempted to define it further (cf. 'Technique of Sargent' in Part II). [1956 note.]

(6) it is an idea which makes use of deliberately symbolic representational technique;

(7) deliberately symbolic representation, determined by the artist's perception as distinguished from his mechanical vision, gives a work of art the quality called 'style';

(8) the use of deliberately symbolic representational technique is not an invention of the modern movement; some form of it has been used by all representational artists in the past;

(9) the naturalistic trick has hardly ever been used in the past except by the Dutch painters of the seventeenth century and by the nineteenth-century painters whose technique was further degraded by the influence of photographs.[1]

G. POPULAR ART

Much abuse of the modern movement amounts to a complaint that the works it has produced are original and not popular.

When I speak of popular art, I do not mean work which happens to be admired by a number of people; I mean art which is popular in kind.

As a rule we use the word 'popular' in a quite unscientific sense. We speak of a work of art as 'popular' when we mean that we know that a certain number of people like it. What number of admirers is necessary to bring the work into the 'popular' category we do not trouble to inquire; nor do we stay to remember that the 'popularity' of a work in this sense may be largely the result of accident or circumstances. Of two painters painting precisely similar pictures the work of one with a gift for self-advertisement may be liked by thousands, while that of the other who happens to live quietly in the country and not exhibit may remain unknown. This is an instance of opportunity affecting 'popularity' in the ordinary sense of the word. Every reader will be able to think of many others, and in so doing will realize, I think, that when we call a picture 'popular' in that unscientific sense we are not saying anything precise about the picture or describing its essential character, but merely saying that the picture, as a material object, has in fact had certain effects on a certain body of spectators; and the reader will, I think, agree that the important thing to discover is not the *effect* of a picture, which may be the result of incidental and accidental

[1] Cf. 'The camera's influence', Part II.

factors, but the *essential character* of a picture that is likely to make it widely admired if opportunity or accident chance to make it widely known.

Now popular art, in my sense, is art produced by a man who works *within his own or other people's familiar experience.*

In some cases he does this because he is a man of low mental energy and is content to remain within his own familiar experience. But in most cases the popular artist deliberately remains within the experience of other people in order to please them and attract their money.

Popular artists in most cases do what they do, and do it in the way they do it, because they believe other people are likely to be pleased with it or pay them money for it, or because they know that other people are doing the same thing or have done it before. They work within the familiar experience of some section of the contemporary public, within the familiar experience of actual or possible patrons, of art critics or of other artists living or dead; and their work is generally either derivative, descriptive, or romantic in character.

Derivative popular art is produced by men working within their own or what they believe to be the average 'artistic' spectator's familiar experience of art.

Descriptive popular art is produced by men working within their own or what they believe to be the average spectator's familiar experience of everyday life.

Romantic popular art is produced by men working within their own or what they believe to be other people's familiar experience of emotive fragments.

The vast majority of works of art produced in the nineteenth century were of one of these three kinds; and the same is true of the vast majority of works produced to-day. I have said above that much of the abuse showered on the modern movement amounts to nothing but a complaint that the work it has produced is not popular in kind. That complaint is quite beside the point because the art of the modern movement is not intended to be popular in kind. It is essentially original, and originality is a character which is the exact antithesis of popularity in art.

The antithesis between original art and popular art is so important for the appreciation of the art we are studying that I must now examine various forms of original art; and then contrast them with various forms of popular art.

H. ORIGINAL ART

In my last section I pointed out that we habitually speak of a work of art as popular when we mean in a vague way that we know the work to be liked by a number of people; and I submitted that the term should more usefully be employed of works which are popular in kind, of works, that is, which are popular as a result of the attitude, motives and procedure of the artist. I submitted, in fact, that the popularity of a work of art is an intrinsic, and not a relative, characteristic.

In the same way we habitually speak of original works of art when we mean that we do not happen to have seen any pictures or sculpture of that kind before. The word 'original' in this sense is merely a more friendly substitute for the hostile spectator's 'abnormal'. It is based on the same false approach to the problem. For it assumes that the character of an original work of art results from its effect upon ourselves.

We are so familiar with the works of the old masters that the one term we never apply to any such works is the term 'original'. Yet many of the old masters were essentially original in their attitude, motives and procedure. Ignoring this character of their work we often underestimate the work of the great original artists of the past and overestimate their imitators.

We can never arrive at the originality or non-originality of a work of art by using the word 'original' in the sense of unfamiliar to ourselves. In studying past or contemporary art we must regard originality, like popularity, as an intrinsic not a relative characteristic.

I submit, accordingly, that the originality of a work of art consists in the attitude, motives and procedure of the man who made it; that *if the artist sets out to enlarge his experience by his work, and in fact does so, his work is original.*

Work which is original in this sense remains original for ever, though a million people may have learned to regard it as familiar. It remains equally an original work if it happens to lie buried in the desert.

There are, I am confident, several kinds of original artists, each enlarging a different kind of experience in a different way. To speculate on the means whereby each type of artist effects the enlargement that constitutes the originality of his art is the task of the aesthetician and the psychologist, and is outside the scope of this inquiry. I am about to indicate the three most important kinds of original artist and to stress the differences in the character of the experiences which they enlarge and the differences in their motives and technical procedures. But I shall not attempt to consider the springs of originality in plastic art, though I venture to suggest that the original artist's perception may be actual or imagined, which no one, I fancy, will oppose.[1]

[1] Cf. 'Human perception' and 'The artist's perception', Part II, and 'Architectural form', Part III.

I. ORIGINAL ROMANTIC ART

I must now touch on two forms of original art which the artists of the modern movement have rejected; and then pass to a consideration of original architectural art which is the form of art which the artists of the movement set out to achieve.

The romantic artist, as I have indicated in the consideration of the romantic heresy, is a man who sets out to perceive unusually emotive fragments. He runs a danger of degenerating into a man exclusively concerned with the expression of his own familiar erotic, sensational or sentimental experience—of degenerating, that is, into what I shall describe later as the disinterested romantic popular artist. He runs a second danger of degenerating into what I shall call later the venal romantic popular artist, and a third danger of degenerating into what I shall call later either the disinterested or the venal producer of derivative romantic art. Nearly all romantic artists are of one of these three degenerate kinds. But original romantics, though rare, have obviously existed in the past and obviously exist to-day.

The original romantic artist is the man who regards as fit material for his art only such emotive fragments as have in fact enlarged his own emotional experience. Such an artist will not be content with discovering a fragment that causes an emotional reaction on himself. He will analyse that reaction and find out whether it is in fact a reaction within his familiar experience or an enlargement. In the first case he will reject it, in the second he will make it the initial experience for a work of art.

The later stages of the original romantic's procedure obey laws of their own. It is useless for such an artist to proceed in the architectural manner, because the initial impulse of his work was not architectural but romantic. An architectural picture on a romantic foundation is a contradiction in terms. The result must either be bad architecture or bad romance,[1] because the basic idea behind the original romantic impulse is the stressing of the newly discovered emotive fragment. The original romantic artist does not set out to construct a picture or a piece of sculpture but to stress a romantic discovery. If he attempts to work by the architectural procedure he departs from his initial purpose. In an original romantic work the only constituent that is vital is the unusually emotive fragment the perception of which as an enlargement of his emotional experience

---

[1] Unless, of course, the artist is a genius, cf. 'Genius and the critic' in this part and 'The value of genius', Part IV.

was the initial impulse of the work. Everything else in the work is merely setting, a kind of chorus designed to assist and show off a *prima donna's* voice.

Thus it comes that a romantic picture containing one or more figures is generally a picture of one or more figures with a background; the architectural picture with one or more figures is a pictorial construction of which all the parts are equally important because the subject of the picture is the relation of those parts.[1] In carrying his initial enlargement of experience to the stage of a concrete work of art the original romantic artist usually works round a point of focus, and never loses that focus at any stage; to retain its predominance he resorts to various manœuvres; Rembrandt often used a spotlight effect, and many other romantic painters have used, and use, exaggeration and distortion to this end.[2]

In sculpture the original romantic artist resorts to analogous procedures to stress the newly discovered emotive aspect of his chosen fragments. Verrocchio stressed the beetling brows and glaring eyes of his *Colleoni* (Pl. 26) and the lean angularity of his boyish *David*. Rodin, the most original romantic sculptor of the last century, stressed the cadaverous aspect of his *Vieille Heaulmière*.[3]

The original romantic's central fragments are frequently what the man in the street considers 'ugly'; because, as I have indicated in considering the romantic heresy, such artists regard all unusually emotive fragments, which have enlarged their own erotic, sentimental, sensational or emotional experience, as 'beautiful'. The man in the street frequently describes the original romantic artist's work as caricature. This is a perfectly sound description. All caricatures are not original romantic art, because popular artists in making caricatures do not enlarge their experience of emotive fragments but remain within their familiar experience in this field. But all original romantic works are to some extent caricatures; the point of each and all of them being the stress of some unusually emotive fragment. This notion of unusually emotive, as opposed to formal, beauty has been served by all original romantic artists. Rembrandt, Delacroix, Daumier, Degas, Guys, Rodin, Van Gogh, Epstein, Rouveyre and Augustus John are examples.[4] The technique of such art I shall discuss in Part II,

[1] Cf. 'Original architectural art' in this part and Part II *passim*.
[2] Cf. 'Degeneration of technique', Part II, and 'Architectural distortion' in Part III.
[3] Cf. 'Degeneration of technique', Part II. Also my 'The Meaning of Modern Sculpture'. [1935 note.]
[4] Rembrandt was the first original romantic artist after modern society arrived with the Dutch revolution; he was also a pioneer of what I shall describe in Part II as the nineteenth-century romantic's emotive handling. But there were numerous romantic European artists before him, mainly in the northern countries. Indeed as a generalization we can say that northern art when not descriptive is romantic and that architectural art has been mainly produced by Mediterranean peoples among whom, of course, the French are included.

and the value of such art and other forms of original art I shall discuss in Part IV. For the moment I have merely tried to indicate the character of the original romantic artist's initial impulse and motives.

J. ORIGINAL DESCRIPTIVE ART

Certain types of descriptive artists are also original. The original romantic artist enlarges his erotic, sentimental, sensational or emotional experience; the original descriptive artist his scientific, social-historical or moral experience.

Original artists of this kind have been extremely rare since Gothic times. Nearly all the descriptive artists of the last five hundred years have been, or are, not original but popular in kind. The original descriptive artist tends moreover to become rarer and rarer because this is the kind of artist who has suffered most from the labours of specialists to which I referred in the section called 'The single strand'. The original romantic artist's experience is not generic but exceptional; he deals with the unusual, with abnormalities and extremes. For this reason specialists who are concerned with the main mass of normal examples leave to the romantic artist the exceptions that prove their rules. But the experience of the original descriptive artist is generic, not exceptional in its character; and for that reason specialists are not content to allow the original descriptive artist the same monopoly of his type of experience that they still allow to the original artist of the romantic class.

In the last five hundred years, in fact, specialists in the various sciences, social history, morals and so on have usurped more and more the field of the original descriptive artist. It was easy for the original artist in Gothic times to enlarge his experience in the various fields covered by descriptive art; he embarked, moreover, on his task with enthusiasm because original descriptive art was part of the advanced art movement of the time, part of the new thought which was urging man to look at the everyday world about him and learn more about it.

By the time we get to Leonardo da Vinci the task was already much harder. Leonardo's powerful mind enlarged his experience in a score of scientific fields. He enlarged his experience of geology, botany, anatomy, medicine, aviation, town-planning, engineering, mechanics, life-destruction, life-preservation, and so forth. He was so absorbed in all these enlargements of his scientific experience that he found relatively little time to co-ordinate his enlargements into works of

76

art. As has been truly observed he was an original man of science who occasionally produced an original work of art. Specialists in Leonardo's day had not yet monopolized the original descriptive artist's experience to any extent comparable with modern conditions; but Leonardo's mind was so remarkable that, as an artist, he had to compete with a dozen specialists within himself.

To-day the descriptive artist's familiar experience in his own fields consists inevitably of an immense mass of data provided by the specialists. Before he can effect an enlargement he has to get beyond his encyclopaedic experience derived from specialists. He has to be certain that the work of art which he contemplates is really an enlargement of all his familiar experience of the generic character of physical objects and concrete things, or of social history, or of ethics. In our own day the original descriptive artist has also to make certain that his descriptions of physical objects and concrete things really enlarge his familiar experience derived from photographs.

Most descriptive artists, in our day, find the task, not unnaturally, beyond their powers; and most descriptive artists for that reason do not attempt to enlarge their familiar experience of everyday life, but work within it and are thus popular, not original, in kind.[1]

The original descriptive artist's procedure, when he has effected the difficult initial enlargement of his experience, differs both from that of the original architectural and the original romantic artist. For such an artist is not concerned with constructing an architectural picture nor with stressing the unusually emotive character of a fragment. He is concerned with expressing enlarged experience of everyday life. The form and character of his picture is not with such an artist a matter of interest in itself. Original descriptive artists invent a style and technique peculiarly suited to their experience; or they make use of the style and technique that comes most easily to their hand.

The outstanding character of the original descriptive artist's initial impulse is thus, in a word, the enlargement of some aspect of his everyday experience; this becomes each year more difficult as the artist's familiar experience is increased by the labours of specialists and the productions of machines; and the character of such an artist's *technical* procedure in translating his initial impulse into concrete form may be original or derivative provided that it serves its purpose.

[1] I have referred to the original descriptive art produced in England by the 1914–1918 war in 'The position to-day', Part III.

K. ORIGINAL ARCHITECTURAL ART

The leading artists of the modern movement are original in kind. They do not produce original romantic art which they mistrust for reasons which I have explained in the section called 'The romantic heresy', and they do not produce original descriptive art which they regard as a form of art rendered impossibly difficult by specialists and machines. They strive to create original architectural art the nature of which I have already tried to indicate in 'Architecture as typical art'.

The experience enlarged by the original architectural artist is formal experience; it is the experience of the architect already examined. Artists of this calibre have to achieve a triple enlargement of experience. First comes some fresh experience of proportion, line, balance, recessions and so forth achieved by actual or imagined perception; then comes the enlargement involved in the mental analysis and synthesis of that experience and in the invention of homogeneous formal symbolism; and then comes the actual execution, which is a third enlargement and gives concrete existence to the first two enlargements and provides for them 'a local habitation and a name'.

All original architectural artists have achieved this triple task; and all the artists of the modern movement are pledged to attempt it. As I have already indicated, Raphael in his pictures in the Camera della Segnatura, Poussin and Claude are examples of such original architectural or classical artists in the past. It must not, however, be assumed that the original architectural artist's attitude, motives and procedure have always resulted, or result to-day, or will result in the future in works that bear any resemblance at first glance to the works of those particular masters. I have selected those artists as examples of this type because the architectural character of their work is very evident. But any subject matter can be the material for architectural art provided that the experience which the artist set out to enlarge in his work is formal in kind, or in other words provided that the enlargement of architectural experience, and not the nominal subject, is the real subject of the picture.

Vermeer of Delft, for example, is an artist of the same architectural character as Poussin or a modern Cubist, not an artist of the same kind as most of the other Dutch painters of interiors. For in the case of an interior by Vermeer the formal elements, the relation of lines, proportions, lights and shades, colours, recessions and so on are the real subject of the picture; the catalogue subject of a picture by Vermeer is merely a peg upon which the artist has hung

78

the enlargement of his formal or architectural experience. Vermeer's *Lady standing at the Virginals* is a formal arrangement from which no detail can be removed without destroying the whole architectural structure. The idea contained in the title is not the subject of the picture. If the passage in that picture which we now believe to represent virginals were discovered to be the form of a Dutch seventeenth-century coffin, and the picture were to be re-labelled *Lady standing by a Coffin*, the subject of the picture would remain the same; but if Vermeer had left out the chair in the foreground the subject of the picture would be entirely different, because the picture would then be a symbol for a different architectural experience. The original architectural artist thus enlarges his formal experience, analyses and synthetizes that enlargement in his mind, and executes the synthesis with his hand. The nominal subject may be anything from the *School of Athens* to a *Portrait of my Grandmother*, or *Aubergines and Onions on a Plate*, because the nominal subject is not the real subject.[1]

The representational style in such art may be anything from Vermeer's technique, which can easily be mistaken for naturalism, to Michelangelo's stylistic bravura or the severe geometrical style of the Cubist, because the only essential of such an artist's representational style is that it should completely symbolize the particular enlargement of formal experience which is the real subject of the work, and be homogeneous and consistent within itself; and the execution may exhibit anything from the extreme of manual dexterity and assurance to complete absence of facility.[2]

Let me try to point out the difference between the original romantic, descriptive and architectural artists by an example. Let us suppose that we have a thatched cottage, an oak tree and a country lane, and that we have asked an artist of each type to paint us a picture of the 'subject'. The original romantic will give us a painting stressing some unusually emotive aspect of the cottage, the oak and the lane, considered as emotive fragments. The original descriptive artist's cottage, oak tree and lane will be a typical cottage, a typical oak tree and a typical lane. The original architectural artist's picture will be an architectural arrangement symbolizing some actual or imagined perception of the formal relations of the cottage, the tree and the lane to one another; that arrangement will be compounded of representational symbols for the artist's

---

[1] The nominal subject may be a religious subject, but in that case the work is still architectural not religious art. On the other hand if the religious subject is the *real* subject the work is religious art whatever architectural qualities it may include. I have discussed Vermeer's art in some detail in my 'Dutch Painting' (Faber). [1935 note.]

[2] Renoir produced architectural art when his hand was paralysed and the brush was strapped to his wrist.

perception of the formal relation of the parts to each whole—the formal relation of the verticals of the wall to the dome of the roof, of the curving parallels of the lane to the cylinder of the tree trunk, of one colour to another, and so on and so forth; his picture, in a word, will be a series of symbols of formal relations perceived or imagined.[1]

My experience of the reception accorded by many spectators to the examples of original architectural art produced by artists of the modern movement leads me to believe that it is not so much the formal character of such artists' experience as the fact that the works are *enlargements* of the artists' formal experience, the fact, that is to say, that they are original and not popular in kind that arouses so much hostility towards them; and as those who are most zealous in abuse of the original art of the movement habitually exhibit appreciation of all art that is popular in kind, I shall now try to indicate what they actually receive from the artists whom they prefer.

L. ROMANTIC POPULAR ART

Romantic popular art is produced by a man working within his own, or what he believes to be other people's familiar experience of emotive fragments.

In practice such art generally consists of society portraits of pretty women and handsome men painted as records of familiar emotive fragments; pictures of nudes and draped figures painted in the same way; landscapes where the central fragment that forms the point of focus is emotive in some familiar dramatic or sentimental way; dramatic 'subject' pictures where the central fragments are emotive in a familiar erotic or sentimental way; caricatures where the fragment stressed is within the artist's familiar experience of emotive fragments, or within what he believes to be other people's familiar experience in that field; and so on and so forth.

Romantic popular art, in a word, is generally fashionable, sentimental, sensational, or erotic, and frequently, of course, a combination of two or three of these characteristics; and pictures of pretty women constitute by far the greater part of its productions.

The technique of such artists is frequently derivative, an ape-like imitation of some way of painting which happens to be appreciated at the time.[2] But

---

[1] Cf. 'The artist's perception', Part II, and 'Architectural form', Part III.
[2] Cf. 'Degeneration of technique', Part II.

1. *Photograph of race-horses*

2. *Photograph of television cameras at work*

3. Raphael: *The School of Athens*

4. Edward Wadsworth: *St Tropez*

5. Cézanne: *The Aqueduct*

6. Paul Nash: *The Pool*

7. Seurat: *The Bathers*

8. Mark Gertler: *The Coster Family*

9. Seurat: *Woman with a Powder Puff*

10. Keith Baynes: *Still Life*

11. Eric Kennington: *Kensingtons at Laventie*

12. Paul Nash: *We are making a New World*

13. Stanley Spencer: *Unveiling a War Memorial*

14. Stanley Spencer: *The Resurrection (Cookham)*

16. Ozenfant: *Harmony*

15. Gris: *Composition*

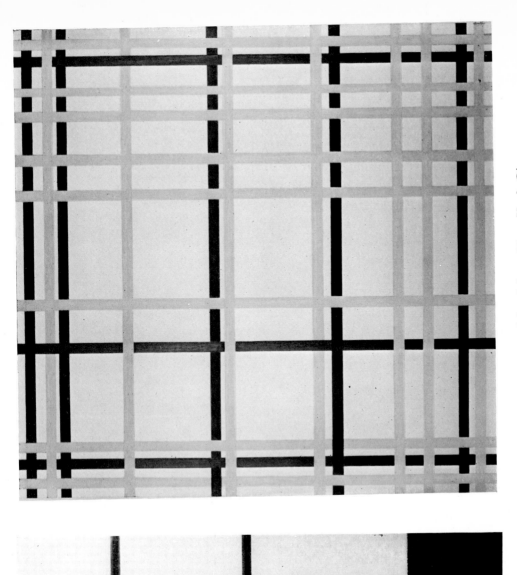

18. Mondrian: *New York City*

17. Mondrian: *Composition in Red, Yellow and Blue*

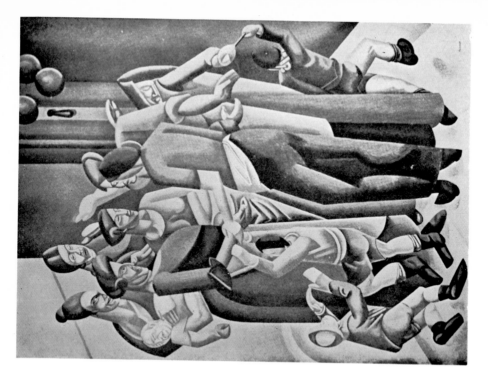

20. William Roberts: *Brass Balls*

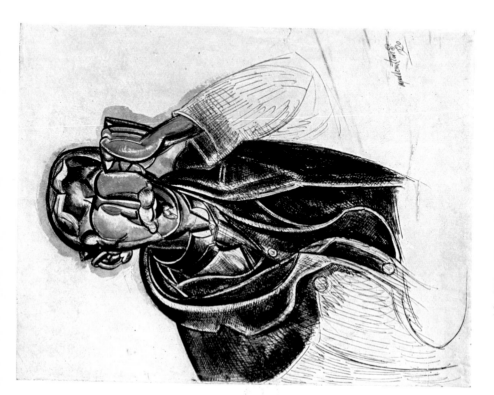

19. Wyndham Lewis: *Drawing*

22. Picasso: *Portrait*

21. Metzinger: *Girl with a Bird*

23. Frank Dobson: *Lydia Lopokova*   24. Pollaiuolo: *The Young Warrior*

25. Jacob Epstein: *Anita* (Detail)   26. Verrocchio: *Colleoni Monument* (Detail)

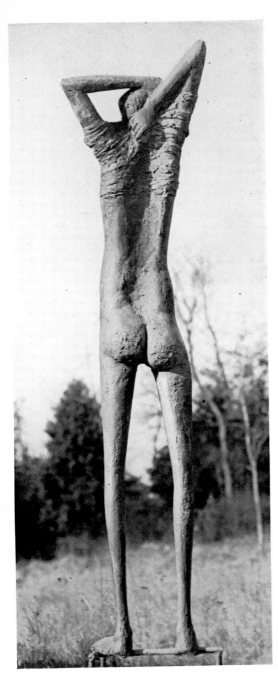

27. Reginald Butler: *Young Girl removing her Shift*

28. Giacometti: *Pointing Man*

29. Kenneth Armitage: *Walking Group*

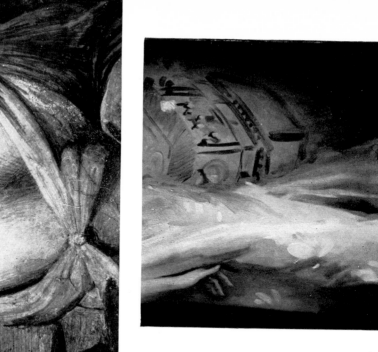

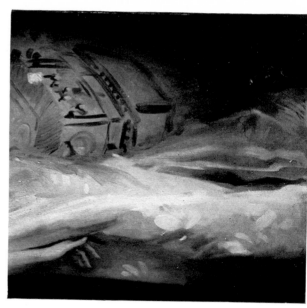

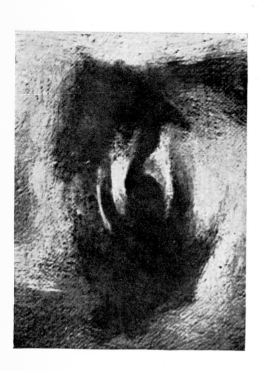

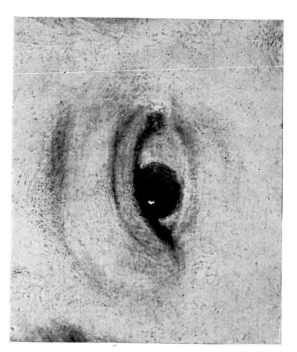

31. Raphael: *Parnassus* (Detail)

33. Sargent: *Eva and Peter Wertheim* (Detail)

30. Sargent: *Henry James* (Detail)

32. Rubens: *Marie de Médicis* (Detail)

55. *Photograph* (Detail)

57. Corot: *Le Concert Champêtre* (Detail)

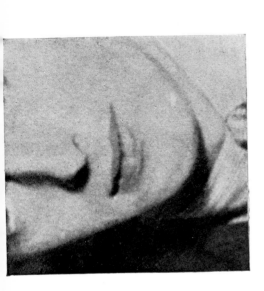

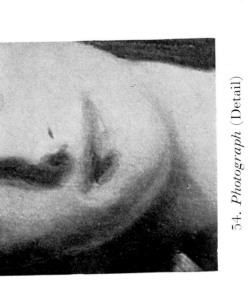

54. *Photograph* (Detail)

56. Sargent: *Ena and Betty Wertheimer* (Detail)

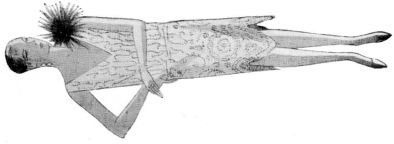

58. *Fashionable-emotive drawings*

frequently also the technique is naturalistic. The romantic popular artist is generally a man incapable of the intellectual effort required for symbolic representation, or is crafty enough to avoid asking the spectator to make the intellectual effort required to read a symbolic language. He simply gets the pretty women dressed or undressed or partially dressed, or draped, or partially draped, in his studio and copies her appearance on the studio throne in some particular light by copying the lights and shadows.[1]

In the case, however, of society portraits the romantic popular artist does sometimes, and indeed frequently, use symbolic representational style. He invents or borrows a formula for recording fashionable effects which are emotive because they are fashionable. If a pigeon breast and a small waist are emotive, because in fashion, such an artist evolves or borrows an hour-glass formula for his figures; if luxuriant hair is held to be attractive he evolves or borrows a formula for incredibly luxuriant hair; if a boyish silhouette for women is regarded as emotive by the fashion of the moment he evolves or borrows an arbitrary boyish silhouette with coiffure trimmed to incredible smoothness and perfection. If rouged complexions are much admired, the rose madder glows in artificial glory on each cheek; if face-powder and lip-salve are emotive-fashionable, then flake-white cheeks appear on each canvas and mouths are painted pure vermilion. Always the women's eyes are made a good deal larger than they are in nature because, it would seem, large eyes in pictures of pretty women are always regarded as an emotive-fashionable feature. These exaggerations and distortions by the society portrait painters are exaggerated on magazine covers in still more deliberate distortion; and it is, for example, a recognized rule among artists who work for that particular market that the width of each eye in a 'pretty girl's head must be exactly double the width of the mouth.[2]

Fashionable emotive distortions are also, of course, the stock-in-trade of fashion-plate draughtsmen who must rank as romantic popular artists (Pl. 38).[3]

A certain amount of romantic popular art is produced by men who are disinterested and find in such painting a safe outlet for snobbish, erotic, sensational or sentimental inclinations, men, in fact, who paint pictures in the same spirit that other men read social gossip and react emotionally to titles, or go to a drama to get mildly thrilled, or to a revue to look at legs, or moon in an arm-

[1] Cf. 'Naturalism and representation' (ii), Part II.

[2] Women who paint their faces are engaged of course in the same procedure as the romantic popular artist. They are creating deliberate distortions of the form of their faces to make the fragments more emotive.

[3] But fashion-plate draughtsmen are now a disappearing species because photographs, emotively distorted on negative or print, have been found more effective in persuading women that they can 'really look like that.' [1956 note.]

chair in the twilight, or listen to an organ because it gives them a sensation in the spine.

But most romantic popular artists are not disinterested but venal. They produce their work with the deliberate intention of making money by contact with other people's familiar snobbish, erotic, sensational or sentimental experience.

Such is the character of the work which romantic popular artists actually supply to their admirers. The original artists of the modern movement regard original romantic art, as we have seen, with distrust and disfavour. They regard all the various productions of romantic popular artists with disgust.

M. DERIVATIVE POPULAR ART

All derivative art is popular in kind. It is produced by a man working within his own familiar experience of art or within what he believes to be certain other people's familiar experience of art.

This form of art thus includes all imitations of other works whether the model followed is the work of some original old master or some original artist living or just dead. It includes all imitations of formal architectural works, of romantic works, of descriptive works and of other derivative works.

It also includes all those pathetic imitations of their own earlier work which are so frequently produced by artists in middle and old age. In such cases, when the early work was popular, the artist who repeats himself is of course merely multiplying his popular attitude with each work. When the early work was original the artist who repeats it ceases thereby to be original because he is no longer enlarging his experience but either remaining lazily within it or working to achieve contact with the familiar experience of people who liked his early work. The artist who makes imitations of his own original early work and ceases thereby to be an original artist and becomes thereby a derivative popular artist has, however, very often material consolation in modern England; for he is likely to be made a Royal Academician and he is pretty certain to acquire a substantial balance at the bank.

A certain amount of derivative art is produced by men who are disinterested but of such low mental energy that they feel no desire to enlarge their experience of art by artistic creation and are quite content to imitate some existing work in the spirit of a man imitating bird-calls for his own amusement.

But derivative art is not usually eccentricity of this kind; it is much more frequently produced for money, and it is generally called into existence in the following way. Original art, being in the nature of an enlargement of experience, is never appreciated by many people on its first appearance. But a generation or so later, when the necessary adjustments to the enlargements of experience for which the works stand have automatically been made, the same original works find admirers on every hand. Popular artists of the derivative kind exploit this situation and produce works which, to eyes with no special training, look remarkably like the art to which a general adjustment has recently been made. Thus it comes that what each generation of the public regards as the original art of its day is generally in fact derivative popular art imitating the original art of a generation or so before.[1]

At the present time, for example, Impressionist and Post-Impressionist pictures are part of the general 'artistic' public's idea of 'art'; and any derivative painter who makes imitations of such pictures can now find patrons by the score. Similarly a man who imitates the works of some original old master can always sell his concoctions when the old master's experience is sufficiently well known to have become a part and parcel of the average patron's idea of 'art'; and he can, of course, sell still more readily imitations of pictures by comtemporary painters whose attitude in the first place was not original but popular in the sense that it established contact with the spectator's familiar experience of everyday life or his familiar experience of 'art'. Also it must be remembered that the modern movement has been developing since 1885. In the years that have passed since then a plentiful crop of derivative popular artists imitating the original modern artists has arisen. To-day there are almost as many derivative popular painters imitating the works of Cézanne, Picasso and Matisse as there are derivative popular painters imitating the works of Botticelli, Constable, Reynolds, the Impressionists and the Post-Impressionists. The character of all imitations, whether the works imitated are architectural, romantic, descriptive or themselves derivative, is, of course, the same.

Such is the character of the work which derivative popular artists actually supply to their admirers. No derivative artist can, of course, in any circumstances be original. To the original artists of the modern movement all derivative artists, whether disinterested or venal, seem men whose activity degrades the name of art.

---

[1] This is particularly the case in England. Cf. 'Reconstruction in France and England', Part II, and 'Popular cubism', Part III.

N. DESCRIPTIVE POPULAR ART

Descriptive popular artists, like derivative artists, are people of two kinds. They are either disinterested men of low mental energy who are quite content to work within their own familiar experience of everyday life, or else they are men who are out to please other people and attract their money, and do so by working within what they know to be other people's familiar experience of everyday life.

Descriptive popular art generally takes the form of portraits, animal studies, interiors, topographic landscapes, genre scenes of high or low life, historical pictures, didactic pictures and so on, when the artist in producing such things is either a man making records of his familiar experience of the generic character of physical objects and concrete things, or of his familiar experience of the social-historical aspects of everyday life, or of his familiar experience of morals or ethics. Such an artist may make his records because he enjoys the recording (as other men play golf or tennis because they enjoy playing golf or tennis), and he is then a disinterested descriptive popular artist; or he may make them with a view to pleasing other people and attracting their money by achieving contact with their familiar experience in these fields, in which case he is a venal descriptive popular artist.

Descriptive popular art tends to be either naturalistic or derivative in technique because the disinterested popular artist of this calibre who is content to record his own familiar experience is usually a man of low mental energy and incapable of symbolic representation, while the venal artist of this calibre desires his records to be easily recognized by the public which he has set out to please and attract. The astute venal descriptive popular artist, like the astute romantic popular artist, does not ask his public to make a mental effort. He gives his average spectator what he believes that spectator would have produced in his, the artist's, place. He does not ask him to enlarge his experience or give him an opportunity to do so. His technique is either designed to achieve contact with the spectator's mechanical vision or else to achieve contact with the spectator's familiar experience of artistic technique.

The disinterested descriptive popular artist is rare. Few men of this calibre record entirely without reference to their work's effects on other people. But there are, however, a few eccentrics who can afford to spend their days in recording in paint their familiar experience of everyday life and do so, just as there are men who can afford to spend their days playing golf and do that. But the great majority of such artists are venal; they deliberately work to please the average spectator; they set out to flatter the spectator and attract his money by providing him with the pleasure of finding in a picture a confirmation of his own familiar experience of everyday life. The vast majority of descriptive popular artists, like the vast majority of derivative artists, are simply manufacturers of wares for an existing market.

Such is the character of the work which descriptive popular artists actually supply to their admirers. The original artists of the modern movement regard the original descriptive artist, as we have seen, as a man whose task has been rendered impossibly difficult by the labours of specialists and the production of machines; they regard the descriptive popular artist as a footler or a tradesman.

O. PAST AND PRESENT

Most people who keep their eyes open have, I believe, some suspicion of the fundamental difference between the activities of the original architectural romantic and descriptive artists on the one hand, and those of derivative and other popular artists on the other. But they are inclined to imagine that in past periods original artists were the rule and popular artists the exception—though in our own day the proportions are obviously reversed.

Both kinds of art have doubtless existed in all times and places. There have always everywhere been hundreds of popular artists to every ten with the desire and the ability to create original art.

Derivative popular art, for example, has always everywhere existed. The men who designed the prototypes of the Egyptian magic funeral monuments were imitated by thousands of other Egyptian artists for two or three thousand years.[1] Every original Greek sculptor had a hundred Greek and Græco-Roman imitators in antiquity who have been imitated again by thousands of imitators from the Renaissance to the present day. Every original Italian master had scores of derivative popular imitators whom we label as his 'school'.

Descriptive popular art has also existed everywhere at all times. We have the genre sculpture in Egyptian tombs to remind us that there was a popular naturalistic art in Egypt side by side with the formal religious funeral art and the formal dynastic art which were Egypt's outstanding contributions to the world's heritage of art. We have the Greek vase paintings to make it clear that

[1] Cf. 'Architectural and other distortions', Part III.

Greece had descriptive popular draughtsmen; there were legions of descriptive popular painters in Holland and elsewhere in the seventeenth century; and legions of popular engravers in the Renaissance and later centuries.

Romantic popular art has also existed everywhere at all times. Every age and place had artists who worked within their own familiar erotic, emotional and sentimental experience as a pastime, or with the venal motive of achieving contact with other people's familiar experience of the same kinds.

There is thus nothing abnormal in the abundance of popular art in Western Europe at the present time. Derivative artists who indulged themselves in the eccentric hobby of imitating some original work of art, or did so to please and get money from the people who had learned to admire that original art, descriptive artists who worked within their own or other people's familiar experience of everyday life, and romantic artists who worked within their own or the public's familiar experience of fashionable, sentimental, sensational, or erotic emotive fragments have always been numerous. The original artist of any kind has always been everywhere a rare bird, and of the three kinds I have indicated the original architectural artist has always been the rarest.

Popular artists have always been more numerous than original artists (a) because it is easier to remain within experience than to enlarge it, and (b) because it is easier to work in naturalistic or derivative technique than to invent a technique to symbolize an enlargement of experience.

It must, however, be noted that popular art in the last hundred and fifty years has received great encouragement from the system of large public annual exhibitions in great capitals. At first the works shown in such exhibitions were not influenced to any extent by the opinion of the visitors. But gradually the visitor who paid his shilling began to imagine that for this shilling he was paying a piper and had a right to call the tune; and gradually the artists began to accept this attitude and to work for approbation by the crowd.[1]

Popular artists were also much encouraged when the system of engraving popular pictures became extended by the cheaper system of the photographic print. A way of converting the crowd's approbation to some advantage was thus discovered by the artist whose picture had 'made a hit' at the exhibition; for he could get a publisher to pay him handsomely for the reproduction rights.

Popular art has further been encouraged in modern times by museums of art when the directors and trustees of such museums conceive their function to be rather the flattering than the education of their visitors.[2]

[1] Cf. my 'French Painting' (Medici) where I have discussed the history of the Paris *Salons*. [1935 note.]

[2] Cf. 'The question of survival', Part IV.

As a result of these special encouragements there have probably been even more popular artists of all kinds in Western Europe in the last hundred years than, relatively speaking, before in any time or place. To-day it is estimated that a hundred thousand pictures are painted in Paris every year; and nearly as many are certainly painted every year in England. All Western European countries and several parts of the American Continent turn out similar quantities of pictures. Perhaps two per cent of this colossal production is original romantic art; perhaps two per cent is original architectural art; less than one per cent is original descriptive art; the remaining ninety-five per cent and a fraction is popular art including popular advertising, magazine illustration, etc., which, as I shall try to show in Part IV of this inquiry, has no intrinsic value but merely a different and variable kind of value acquired from the appreciation of spectators and which, if it has no acquired value, is without value of any sort or kind.

P. GENIUS AND THE CRITIC

The classifications I have made in this first part of my inquiry are an attempt to provide a rough working guide for those who desire, as I do, to arrive at greater comprehension of works of art and not merely to enjoy them or enjoy the pleasure of disliking them. The classifications have been established as an attempt to answer myself when I say before a picture: 'What is it?' instead of 'Do I like it or dislike it?'

I know well that the critic can only speak about one thing at a time, and that he therefore delights in classification and analysis which help him to have one thing at a time to speak about; whereas the artist can speak of more than one thing at a time, and frequently does so. I recognize, that is to say, that there are artists whose attitude, motives and procedure extend beyond the barriers I have indicated, and that fully to describe the characters of such artists' work the classifications I have indicated must be made to overlap.

But we must remember that in many cases when overlapping occurs it is caused by the muddle-headedness of the artist who has not discovered what in fact he set out to do, or who has begun to do one thing and finished by doing another; and sometimes such overlapping is due to the dishonesty of the artist who has deliberately deserted a hard path for an easy one half-way through his work.[1]

Then, again, an artist may belong to different categories at different times of

[1] Cf. 'The dishonest artist-spectator', Part IV.

his life as the result either of degeneration or of an increase in clear thinking and artistic development—though instances of the artist moving from the original to the popular class are much more common than instances of the opposite change. Also at one period of his life an artist may be romantic and at another descriptive or architectural.

I recognize also that the genius can combine attitudes which logically speaking, are irreconcilable, and that the greatest artists have almost invariably done so. It is a truism that the genius establishes his own laws and breaks them himself at every turn. For this reason the procedure of the genius, who knows exactly what he wants to do, often appears to resemble the procedure of an ordinary muddle-headed artist.

The work of a genius like Delacroix, for example, is extremely complex. Delacroix's romantic creed was compounded of true romantic elements and other elements that were accidental. His use of *moyen-âge-Renaissance* subjects was partly due to the accident that these subjects had been officially encouraged by the Restoration, and partly to the facts that he had reacted to the romantic poetry of Byron and that pioneers of the romantic movement in literature had exalted Gothic against classical architecture. For the rest his use of *moyen-âge-Renaissance* motifs and Oriental motifs was based on the confused notion that fragments which were remote in space or time were unusually emotive by reason of their remoteness.[1]

In the work of many pioneer artists there is an element of protest and an element of propaganda. Derivative artists who imitate the original pioneer artist's work habitually imitate just these incidental elements and generally miss the original master's main artistic achievement, which can only be discovered when the elements of protest and propaganda have been thought away. Delacroix's use of Gothic and Oriental motifs was partly a protest against the classical motifs used in pseudo-architectural art of the Davidian school, partly propaganda for the new romantic appreciation of Gothic art, and partly propaganda for the pseudo-romantic notion of the unusually emotive character of remote fragments. These incidental elements in Delacroix's art did not destroy the artist's original romantic achievement because Delacroix was a genius. But the derivative pygmies who followed him were swamped by them as I shall try to indicate in Part II.

Delacroix, moreover, advanced from romantic to architectural art as he got older; and he contrived in a magic way to harmonize the two standpoints— again an achievement reserved for genius.

[1] Cf. 'Degeneration of ideas', Part II.

In the same way a genius like Rubens combined the architectural with the descriptive attitude, and his art, like the art of Delacroix, was a storehouse of incidental elements which were plundered by his followers.

I should be led, in fact, to submit as a definition of genius 'the power to combine more than one kind of artistic activity in a single homogeneous work of art' were it not that this would rule out Raphael, who was undoubtedly a genius and yet produced works like the *School of Athens* which are purely classical in kind. I therefore attempt no definition of the character of genius, merely repeating (*a*) that the attitude, motives and procedure of the genius may seem as confused as those of an ordinary muddle-headed artist; and (*b*) that they may be absolutely simple; and adding to these points (*c*) that the quality of genius has nothing to do with a precocious facility in some artistic technique (for which talent is the proper word) and (*d*) that the genius is so rare in art history that we can never read that history aright by studying exclusively those conspicuous figures and attempting to set up standards from their work.[1]

This is my excuse for the cold-blooded classification I have attempted. I know that when all is said and done the activity which produces any kind of original art is an emanation of the human spirit and so mysterious and incomprehensible. But all pictures and sculpture are not original art; and human spirits are good and bad, complex and simple, delicate and coarse, disinterested and venal, lively and obtuse, developed and atrophied. The difference between the works produced by these different spirits is worth examination. But there is no man living who could truly and completely set them down, and I know well that my classifications are only the beginning of the story.

One must, however, begin somewhere and by some method; and I believe that the beginning I have suggested may prove helpful at a time and in a place where the main habit of art critics is to say: 'Art is Art; I know it, when I see it, because it gives me an aesthetic thrill.'

Q. RECAPITULATION

What I submit then in Part I is briefly this:

(1) The modern movement is based not on service to religion but on service to a consciously-held idea of art.

There is nothing abnormal in this because most Western European art

[1] Cf. 'The value of technique' and 'The value of genius', Part IV.

since the High Renaissance has been based on service to some consciously-held idea of art.

(2) The basic idea in this case is the idea that architecture is typical art.

There is nothing abnormal in this because that idea has been held by all the classical artists since the High Renaissance.

(3) The modern movement is opposed to the romantic idea of art.

There is nothing abnormal in this because architectural artists have been opposed at all times to the romantic idea.

(4) The movement does not make use of the naturalistic technique.

There is nothing abnormal in this because most architectural artists of all times and places have used a symbolic representational, and not an imitative naturalistic, technique.

(5) The works produced by the movement are original and not popular in kind.

There is nothing abnormal in this because original as well as popular works of art have been produced at all times and in all places.

(6) The original works of the movement are few in number compared with the multitude of popular works of various kinds produced by artists outside the movement.

There is nothing abnormal in this because popular works have always everywhere been numerous, and their production has been encouraged in modern times by large public exhibitions and the enterprise of printsellers.

(7) The genius overrides all classifications.

Part II

DEGENERATE NINETEENTH-CENTURY ART

A. DEGENERATION OF IDEAS OF ART

In this part of my inquiry I shall try to indicate the various kinds of art which surrounded the early artists of the modern movement when they decided that a return to the classical architectural basis was essential, not only as a means of escape from the prevailing degeneration of ideas of art, but also as a means of escape from the prevailing degeneration in pictorial technique.

In the section called 'Conflicting ideas' in Part I, I reminded the reader that the nineteenth century produced original and popular art, of both the romantic and the descriptive kinds, but that it produced scarcely any original classical art. It would be flogging dead horses to examine here the obvious degeneracy of pseudo-classical derivative popular artists like Flaxman and the followers of David at the beginning of the century, and of Gérome and Leighton later on. The derivative character of their concoctions is now recognized on every hand. When the pioneers of the movement looked upon these absurdities their obvious course was to say: 'This at any rate must go'; and those who realized the essential character of original art were not likely to find much inspiration from Stevens' imitations of the work of Michelangelo. It was not thus, they knew, that Raphael's *School of Athens* or the art of Poussin had been created. Most nineteenth-century artists who called themselves 'classical' forgot that architecture is the basis of all true classical art; they believed classical art to be a matter of Græco-Roman costumes and of 'purity of line'.[1] The artists who founded the modern movement were better educated. They could distinguish the romantic and descriptive forms of Greek art from its classical or architectural forms and they could recognize popular Greek art as such when they came across it. In their return to the classical architectural basis they could derive no assistance from the pseudo-classical standards of the Wardour-Street-Græco-Roman confectioners except the negative assistance provided by the knowledge that that path, at any rate, could lead to nothing but further confusion between classical and pseudo-classical ideas of art and to further degeneration of academic derivative technique.

When they looked on the romantic art of the nineteenth century the degeneration was even more obvious. In France they saw a handful of original romantic artists—Delacroix, Rodin, Daumier, Renoir,[2] Degas, Guys and so on;

---

[1] My view of Ingres' position is stated in 'The Daguerreotype and Ingres', in this part.
[2] Renoir's later architectural work is referred to under 'Architectural form' in Part III.

in England they saw Constable, the Pre-Raphaelites in their early youth, and a few others; and all about them they saw thousands of pseudo-romantic derivative popular pictures by muddle-headed and venal followers of these men.

Let us look for a moment at the stream of degenerate, pseudo-romantic art deriving from the work of Delacroix.

In 'Genius and the critic' in Part I, I have stressed the extremely complex character of Delacroix's achievement. I pointed out that his art contained elements of protest and propaganda, and that his voyage to Africa was partly due to a confused romantic notion that Moors and Arab steeds were unusual and so emotive fragments, whereas in fact they were only unusual and so emotive in Paris.

These elements and the *moyen-âge* motifs in the romantic art of Delacroix which may be called its impurities, were picked up by the derivative popular artists who worked to achieve contact with the public's familiar experience of those elements in his art.

Thus Delacroix painted *The Death of Marino Faliero*. Then Delaroche, the prince of his addle-pated imitators, followed with *The Death of Queen Elizabeth*, *The Death of Cardinal Mazarin*, *The Death of President Duranti*, *The Execution of Lady Jane Grey*, *The Assassination of the Duc de Guise*, and so on. Delaroche never had the faintest notion of the original romantic principle behind Delacroix's art, of his genuine search for unusually emotive fragments, nor yet of the architectural elements in Delacroix's pictures to which I have referred in my comments on his genius. Delaroche also completely misunderstood the principle behind Delacroix's impetuous technique. He imagined that he was going one better than Delacroix by painting similar subjects with more archæological detail, failing to realize that to Delacroix the *moyen-âge-Renaissance* subject was merely a peg upon which to hang his original romantic art.[1]

Delacroix's work was not widely known in England. But Delaroche's imitations had great influence on this country. He was the painter of *The Princes in the Tower*, and many English nineteenth-century artists crossed the Channel to become his pupils. Delaroche's derivative popular parodies of the original romantic art of Delacroix were in fact the source of the nineteenth-century English artists' notion that *moyen-âge-Renaissance-tableaux-vivants* were romantic art. Before that, it is true, Shakespearian illustrations were already a feature of the English Royal Academy exhibitions. But the origin of

[1] I have discussed the genesis and development of this 'mediævalism' in my 'French Painting' (Medici). [1935 note.]

those pictures was mainly the accident that Alderman Boydell, the printseller, in the late eighteenth century had conceived the idea that engravings after paintings of Shakespearian scenes by famous artists might be popular and might be sold in large numbers, and that he had accordingly commissioned all the best-known artists of his day to paint them.[1] The tradition of illustrations in oil paint in the Royal Academy was thus already established, but it was greatly reinforced by the new idea from Paris which represented the painting of *moyen-âge-Renaissance* subjects as the very latest romantic development of art.

The Pre-Raphaelite brotherhood was founded as an attempt to recapture what Hunt described as 'the freedom from corruption, pride and disease' which the young artists felt to be characteristic of Benozzo Gozzoli's art when they looked at a book of engravings from his pictures. They started out with rigid resolves to be original romantic artists; and they did in fact produce six or eight original romantic pictures. But the Delacroix-Delaroche *moyen-âge* elements in their art were simply a pseudo-romantic confusion.[2]

The public soon learned to think of Wardour-Street costumes in a picture as the hall-mark of romantic art; any kind of picture with a title relating to Queen Eleanor or *La Belle Dame sans Merci* or to any event which happened or purported to happen a long time ago or a great distance away was held to be romantic art. This ridiculous confusion found voice in an article by Watts-Dunton in the *Encyclopaedia Britannica* where all these degenerate costume pictures by addle-pated derivative artists were described as evidence of a great 'Renascence of Wonder' in England. Watts-Dunton was writing of Rossetti; if he had used the phrase of Rossetti's later romantic work exclusively (which in fact he disliked) it might be justified as a flamboyant description of the original romantic point of view; but in fact he meant it to apply to the whole mass of English pseudo-romantic costume illustration.

The pseudo-romantic notion that fragments remote in time or place are unusual and so emotive was reinforced here by the notion that the production of such pictures was a protest against the ugliness of industrialism. This confusion was followed by the idea, to which I am about to refer, which regarded fragments associated in the mind with industrialism as romantic.

But the *moyen-âge-Renaissance* illustration was not the only degenerate

---

[1] Northcote relates that when Boydell invited Reynolds to paint *The Witches in Macbeth* Reynolds refused, thinking it degrading to work for a printseller; but when Boydell had discreetly sent him £500 on account of £1,000, he relented and painted the picture.

[2] Ruskin warned the Pre-Raphaelites against 'medievalism' at the very beginning. Cf. my 'John Ruskin' (Faber). [1935 note.]

stream that came from Delacroix. For Delacroix seeking unusually emotive fragments went to Africa and painted on his return a number of Moorish subjects. This was the signal for an outburst of what the French called 'Oriental-ism' in painting. Decamps, who had begun as an imitator of David, then painted that horrible picture in the Wallace Collection called *Le Supplice des Crochets;* and Chasseriau, who had gone to Rome and begun as a classical architectural artist, now deserted Raphael (and also Ingres whom he at one time imitated) and began to ape the 'Orientalism' of Delacroix. A regular epidemic of 'Oriental' pictures followed in which Moors, Arab steeds with blood-red nostrils, 'belles juives' and 'odalisques' at their toilette attended by negresses were the recognized component parts. The fever persisted in France well into the second half of the century (we find its influence in Manet's *Olympia*) and it also produced a crop of similar pseudo-romantic derivative popular pictures in English art.[1]

Another stream of pseudo-romantic derivative popular art in both France and England came out of the romantic-realist art of Jean François Millet. The derivative artists who followed Millet picked up from his work a confused pseudo-romantic 'dignity of labour' notion which produced thousands of derivative popular works of art. It is to this notion that we owe the Juno-esque peasants by Jules Breton,[2] the posturing bronze miners of Constantin Meunier, and the navvies in picturesquely torn shirts by English painters. From the pseudo-romantic notion of the picturesque peasant and the picturesque navvy the nineteenth-century artists proceeded to a more original romantic notion of the picturesque factory, the picturesque warship and the picturesque railway-station. It was not till Cubism arrived that machines, warships and so on were architecturally perceived.

In England there was also a derivative popular stream that came out of Constable's original romantic landscape. We are so accustomed to thousands of imitations of Constable's pictures that we are apt to forget that Constable was a truly original artist. In his days brown trees and pink skies were recognized by popular artists as familiar emotive fragments. Sir George Beaumont, the *arbiter elegantiorum* of the period, said that a picture, like a violin, should be a rich golden-brown colour. When Constable enlarged his experience by finding other

---

[1] Chasseriau's portrait of Ali Hamed, Caliph of Constantinople, was a sensation in the Paris *Salon* of 1846. Théophile Gautier, writing of the Caliph's visit to the Paris opera when the romantic movement was at its height, describes his eyes as '*yeux de gazelle et de lion, mornes et flamboyants; yeux qui ont fait frissonner tant de belles Parisiennes au fond de leurs loges*'. Chasseriau had clearly chosen first-rate emotive fragments.

[2] '*Elles sont trop jolies pour rester au village*' was Millet's comment on Breton's debasement of his art.

aspects of landscape emotive he was profoundly original. But the swarm of derivative popular artists who came after him merely copied his pictures with lazy and addled minds.

Finally, here in England there were the popular sentimental, romantic anecdotic pictures which were painted to attract attention in the Academy, and to be reproduced. Their character was that which I have described in Part I under 'Romantic popular art'. The men who produced them sought to establish contact with the spectator's familiar erotic, sentimental or emotional experience, and if the picture proved a success in the Academy they succeeded in their aim.

The course of nineteenth-century descriptive art was rather different. It was born derivative, and it was produced by venal popular artists working to attract and please the new bourgeoisie created by the Revolution. To achieve this the artists looked back to the Dutch genre painting of the seventeenth century, most of which had been produced in circumstances that were much the same.

When Holland threw off the Spanish yoke and started on a new life at the beginning of the seventeenth century, modern bourgeois society arrived. Holland soon became rich, a country of self-made men of property, the sons and grandsons of men who had driven out the Spaniard and smashed thousands of works of art in churches and cathedrals. The new Dutch bourgeois called for a new art. But it was not to be an art in the Southern tradition which Rubens had once more brought from Italy. It was to be a Dutch art. Also, the artists were to remark, it was not to be a romantic art stressing warts and wrinkles like the art of Marinus van Reymerswael. What was required was an art making generic records of the solid peaceful worthiness of the new Dutch bourgeois, his wife, his house, his servants, his meadows and his dog. To meet this situation the descriptive popular artist arose in Holland. There are those who believe that the Dutch painters were disinterested. I doubt it. The new bourgeoisie had not been going long enough when the new art was created for it to have been produced by young men of independent means. Rich Dutch aunts had not yet died in sufficient numbers to have created a class of leisured cultured nephews. The new bourgeois was rich but he was still a farmer or a tradesman. If he allowed his son to become a painter he had to make his living by his work. If he could not sell his pictures he was, I am certain, immediately apprenticed to another trade. The main mass of the Dutch art of the seventeenth century was produced by venal descriptive popular artists who set out to please farmers and tradesmen; the artists were men of no education; they sold their pictures, literally, in the open market-place; and they painted the kind of picture that people in the market-place could understand.[1]

Conditions in France at the beginning of the nineteenth century were similar. Descriptive popular art, the kind of art which is always demanded by a new middle-class after a revolution, was the art demanded by the new French bourgeoisie at the beginning of the nineteenth century; and venal popular artists set out to provide for this new and profitable market. But the nineteenth-century venal descriptive popular artists at the outset were also derivative, since all they could think of as a means of pleasing the new patron was to provide him with imitations of the Dutch pictures which were already part of his experience of art.

French popular landscape at the beginning of the century, when it was not romantic landscape derived from Constable, was 'realist' landscape derived from Hobbema and Ruysdael; Charles Jacques added a flock of sheep—the first of those thousands of flocks of sheep which wander through nineteenth-century descriptive popular pictures. Troyon decided to copy Paul Potter, and cattle began to parade round the exhibition walls. From the first decades of the century to the very end of it French descriptive popular painters continued to attract and please the bourgeois and extract his money by providing him with imitations of Dutch popular genre, portrait and landscape painting, and thus to achieve contact with his familiar experience of everyday life and with his familiar experience of art.

In England the new bourgeoisie born of the industrial revolution was established earlier, and descriptive popular art imitating the Dutch pictures arrived a little earlier too. When an ambitious venal young Scotsman, named David Wilkie, came to make money by his brush in London, at the very beginning of the century, he surveyed the situation, put a picture by Teniers on his easel and painted *The Blind Fiddler* which set the derivative ball rolling in England. The Norwich school came straight out of Hobbema. Next came Landseer with a degraded version of the Paul Potter tradition;[2] then the influence of the pseudo-Dutch-French painters crossed the Channel and flocks of Jacques sheep invaded the Academy, where, lost in snowstorms, we can still see them wandering to this day. Finally we had here the venal descriptive popular illustrations of everyday life of the Frith variety which were painted to attract attention in the Academy and to be reproduced.

---

[1] I have already referred to Rembrandt as an original romantic and Vermeer as an origina architectural artist; and there were of course other exceptions, but the general situation I am convinced was as I suggest in this passage. Cf. my 'Dutch Painting' (Faber). [1935 note.]

[2] Landseer mixed a romantic popular attitude with his derivative descriptive art. He treated his animal's eyes as emotive romantic fragments.

Put briefly then, the works produced in the nineteenth century consisted mainly of (*a*) derivative pseudo-classical popular parodies of classical art; (*b*) derivative pseudo-romantic popular parodies of the original romantic art of Delacroix mainly via Delaroche; (*c*) derivative pseudo-romantic popular parodies of the original art of Constable and Millet; (*d*) romantic popular sentimental anecdotic pictures painted to be reproduced; (*e*) romantic popular portraits; (*f*) derivative descriptive popular parodies of Dutch (or Flemish) seventeenth-century descriptive popular genre, portrait, and landscape art; and (*g*) descriptive popular illustrations of everyday life painted to be reproduced.

Such was the main character of the art with which Seurat and Cézanne in France and Whistler in England were surrounded.[1] I must now examine the technical degeneration and confusions which accompanied this degeneration and confusion of ideas.

B. DEGENERATION OF TECHNIQUE

I. DERIVATIVE DEGENERATION

The technique of original classical architectural art must of necessity vary with every artist and with every work.[2] In the nineteenth century this type of art is found, if at all, only in the works of Puvis de Chavannes. But Puvis always had the greatest difficulty in co-ordinating the parts of his plan to one another, and his freedom of creation was hampered by the same confusion that reigned in the minds of nineteenth-century pseudo-classical artists; he imagined that the way to create architecturally was to imitate the productions of the Greeks. Apart from Puvis, if he can truly be classed as an original classical artist, it may be that there was no other nineteenth-century painter in France or England who was fundamentally both architectural and original in kind till we get to Seurat and Cézanne in France and Whistler in England.

Puvis' technique was based on a rather vague architectural notion that mural decoration should be kept flat and that a simple way of achieving this was to paint in pale colours. This technical theory was reinforced by the example of the fresco painters of Italy whose pictures appear pale to-day, partly owing to the

---

[1] The relation of the art which surrounded Seurat and Cézanne to that which surrounded the later pioneers in England is referred to in 'Reconstruction in France and England' in this part.

[2] Cf. Part III *passim*.

absorbent nature of the ground they worked on and partly because they have faded.[1]

In the work of most nineteenth-century pseudo-classical popular artists the drawing was derived from Greek vase-painting or Greek or Græco-Roman statues, and the colour was derived from Italian frescoes, without any understanding of the principles of classical art. Certain of the artists combined the pseudo-classical idea of art with naturalistic technique; they dressed studio models in Wardour-Street chitons and togas, stood them on the throne, copied their appearance in the studio light, and 'faked up' a background from an engraving or photograph of a Greek building. The result they described as a 'classical' picture, and on Show Sundays they would suggest to their visitors that they had done the same kind of thing as the artists who produced the Parthenon.

The technique of original romantic art in the nineteenth century was more interesting and important. When the first original romantic pictures made their appearance the French critics described Delacroix's *Le massacre de Scio* as '*le massacre de la peinture*'; just as Ruskin spoke contemptuously of Constable's 'spotting and splashing'. Such critics' wrath was roused by the deliberate freedom of the original romantic artists' technique. It was the artists' deliberate disdain of smooth polished execution, it was what Delacroix called the '*heureuse saleté*' created by his '*brosse ivre*', and it was Constable's 'snow' flung riotously about his pictures that made the critics of seventy and a hundred years ago speak and write about the new romantic painting in much the same terms that certain critics speak and write about the new classical painting of to-day.

The new technical idea served by the romantic artists was the idea that the actual handling in a work of art should be expressive of the artist's emotional condition when he worked. No attempt was made to conceal the series of touches which built up their work, on the contrary, the touches were left deliberately visible as witnesses of the divine fury or divine languor or the virile vigour of the artist's emotional state; and thus the nineteenth-century romantics started the notion that an artist's actual handling should be emotive in itself.[2]

It was for this reason, of course, that all nineteenth-century sculpture was modelled by the artist in clay and transferred afterwards mechanically by other hands to bronze or marble. The romantic sculptor could reveal his very thumbmarks and the little strips of clay with which he built up his model. With a chisel and a hard surface he felt himself constrained. This type of romantic

---

[1] Many Italian frescoes have been frequently restored and some have been largely repainted; but the restorers usually adhere to the tradition of pale colours. [1956 note.]

[2] For this they had the authority of Rembrandt, who before them had defied the smooth polished handling of the classical tradition and had made his actual handling emotive in itself.

emotive handling in sculpture is seen in the work of Rodin, and we can see it also in the work of Epstein (Pl. 25), the leading original romantic sculptor in England in our day.[1]

The deliberately free, spontaneous and emotive technique of the early nineteenth-century romantics was made still more free, spontaneous and emotive by the first Impressionists with their vibrant touches of 'broken' colour. Seurat, when he founded the modern movement, invented Pointillisme which put this handling under rigid control. Later artists of the movement abandoned all varieties of romantic emotive technique. But the tradition of original romantic emotive technique has only been abandoned with great difficulty. Its use by Van Gogh was characteristic because Van Gogh was not a classical but a romantic artist. Its use by more recent painters of the modern movement seems to me to be due simply to an inability to recognize that in classical architectural art such parade of the artists' emotional condition is meaningless and out of place.[2]

Another aspect of the original romantic artist's technique I have described in the section dealing with the character of original romantic art in Part I, where I pointed out that a romantic picture usually consists of a central emotive fragment or a number of emotive fragments surrounded with a background which serves as a setting to attract attention to the point of focus. There also I pointed out that such romantic artists often use exaggerated light effects to stress their emotive fragments, as Rembrandt did, and that they frequently, for the same purpose, use distortion, so that their work is often described, and rightly described, as caricature. It is usual in writing of Rossetti to describe those studies of women with distorted necks and exaggerated lips which he produced in his later years as his weakest work. This I hold to be an error. Those works are surely original romantic art in an extremely characteristic form. They are as original and romantic as Botticelli's *Venus*, where the artist used gold leaf to stress the high lights in the golden hair—a picture by the way which Rossetti, as he never went to Italy, never saw.[3] Distortions and exaggerations of this kind

---

[1] Epstein started as a classical architectural sculptor, and when carving, as in his Strand statues, his Wilde Memorial, *Rima* and so forth, he is faithful to the architectural principle. When he gives his romantic temperament full play he models in clay and uses the 'rough surface' of romantic emotive technique. Cf. my 'The Meaning of Modern Sculpture' (Index, 'Epstein'). [1935 note.]

[2] This applies also to some young non-representational formal architectural painters in France and England to-day. [1956 note.]

[3] Two reservations are called for here. (1) Rossetti's finest work I hold to be the sketch for his religious picture *The Annunciation* (if such a thing exists) on which cf. my note in 'The dishonest artist-spectator', Part IV. His other early works imitated Gothic manuscripts and the *moyen-âge-Renaissance* costume pictures by Madox Brown (who had studied with Wappers, one of Delacroix's pupils). (2) Botticelli was of course a genius. He could and did combine classical architectural and romantic elements in his art.

have been characteristic of original romantics of all times and places.[1] They have no relation to architectural distortions, which I shall consider later, nor, of course, have they any relation to distortions in religious art with which I am not here concerned.[2]

Also we must note that the original romantic artist uses colours and colour as emotive factors to stress his point of focus. Sometimes such an artist finds the limitation of the palette to two or three colours an aid to the romantic stress which he is seeking. This was the case with Rembrandt. Sometimes the central fragment or fragments are portrayed in strong colours. Sometimes again the point of focus is kept relatively colourless and the full gamut is used behind as a brilliant setting to the sombre emotive point. The original romantic artist, moreover, in using individual colours, has regard to their emotive significance deriving from associated ideas. Van Gogh's letters make it clear that he painted a man's yellow hair and a blue background in a celebrated portrait in this way, and Delacroix's use of red as an emotive colour must be obvious to everyone.[3]

These technical characteristics of the original romantic art of the nineteenth century were all debased in derivative and pseudo-romantic popular art. The original romantic's spontaneous emotive technique was debased by imitators who had no real understanding of its character and purpose and believed that free, spotty, vigorous and spontaneous handling was a merit in itself. Eventually any other method of painting was described as intolerable and 'tight', and everyone familiar with the pictures which fill the French official *salons* and with those produced by the legions of followers of Sargent and the Glasgow Impressionists which fill the English Royal Academy, the Royal Oil Institute, the Royal Society of British Artists and other such exhibitions to-day, is familiar by the same token with thousands of pictures whose only claim to attention is a degenerate parody of the original romantic artist's emotive handling. The original romantics' use of a central point of focus led likewise to the production of thousands of pictures which were merely hack records of fragments surrounded with slush as a background setting. The original romantics' stress by means of light effects was debased to theatrical lighting which had no romantic

---

[1] We are so accustomed to Millais' *Carpenter's Shop* that we cannot now see in it the original romantic distortions by means of which Millais stressed the fragments that he had perceived as emotive. But they were so obvious to Dickens that he described the boy Jesus in this picture as 'wry-necked', his Mother's throat as 'dislocated', the Mother generally as a figure that would stand out for ugliness in 'the vilest cabaret in France or the lowest ginshop in England', and the whole picture as 'repulsive' and 'revolting'.

[2] The early Christian religious artists deliberately distorted their figures to make them seem more saintly and divine. They *de-humanized* their figures because they were not representing human but saintly or divine personages. Cf. 'Architectural and other distortions', Part III.

[3] Cf. 'Human perception' in this part and 'Architectural colour', Part III.

purpose or other reason for its existence. The original romantics' use of individual colours as emotive agents was debased to a haphazard use of individual colours without any purpose of romantic stress; and the true romantic use of distortion was debased in romantic popular portraiture in the curious fashionable-emotive distortions which I have noted in discussing the character of these productions in Part I, and in magazine covers and other forms of 'commercial' popular art where these distortions were and are exaggerated to astonishing degrees.

On the other hand we must note one type of degeneration in nineteenth-century romantic technique that was due to a cowardice or venal instinct in romantic popular artists which prevented them from stressing their emotive fragments by emotive colours or distortions. Such degenerate romantic artists often employed purely naturalistic technique; they chose their emotive fragment, a naked woman, or a pretty girl in a pretty frock, or whatever it might be, and copied the lights and shades on the fragment as it appeared in the studio at the moment when the model climbed upon the throne.

Thousands of romantic popular artists in the nineteenth century were too timid to stress their emotive fragments, or too anxious to please their patrons by a technique which they could understand, to use anything approaching the original romantic's methods; and they fell back first on a naturalistic technique which they imitated from the Dutch pictures, and, later, on a naturalistic technique derived from the camera.[1]

The technique of the pseudo-romantic popular costume-picture makers also bore no relation to the technique of original romantic art. When derivative it was derived from all sorts of painters of all times. It was derivative-romantic, derivative-classical, and even derivative-naturalistic. A technique imitating the naturalistic technique of Dutch genre pictures was in fact used with extraordinary inappropriateness by such artists in many of those pictures produced to meet the 'artistic' public's familiar experience of remote emotive fragments which Watts-Dunton described in the passage already referred to as the 'Renascence of Wonder'. Illustrations intended to be emotive by reason of the remoteness of their subject from daily life were put together from naturalistic studies of models posing in studios in Wardour-Street costumes. There was no limit to the addle-pated confusion of the pseudo-romantics; and Watts-Dunton, in raptures over such works, wrote solemnly that the artists reached 'that world of wonder and mystery and spiritual beauty which the old masters knew and could have painted had not lack of science combined with

---

[1] Cf. next section, 'The camera's influence'.

slavery to monkish traditions of asceticism crippled their strength', or in other words that the early Italian religious artists would have painted in naturalistic technique if they had been technically more efficient and had not been faithful servants of their religion.[1]

In nineteenth-century descriptive art in France and England the technique was also in part derivative and in part naturalistic. The original descriptive artist's technique is most appropriately representational since his business is the creation of a record symbolizing an enlargement of his scientific experience of the generic character of physical objects or concrete things, or an enlargement of his social-historical or moral experience of everyday life. But there were so few original descriptive artists in the nineteenth century that no original descriptive technique was evolved.[2]

Descriptive art in both France and England, as I have already indicated, was born derivative. It was founded in France by descriptive popular artists imitating the Dutch and Flemish genre paintings and landscapes, and in England by Wilkie and the Norwich school doing the same thing. The derivative descriptive popular artists, who came after, occasionally used technique derived from other forms of art, but for the most part they stuck to the naturalistic technique derived from the Dutch pictures, till the new variation of that technique due to the influence of the camera arrived.

The naturalistic technique is merely a matter of taking pains in a mechanical task, and in both France and England the first derivative descriptive popular artists took certain pains in their naturalistic procedure. But those who came later discovered that the visitors to the *Salon* and the Royal Academy were solely concerned with the descriptive popular subjects of their works; provided that a certain standard of naturalistic technique was achieved (a standard which could in fact be achieved by any industrious student at the art schools in three years or less) the visitors to the Academy were able to recognize such derivative descriptive work as within their own familiar experience of everyday life and of art; and the printsellers naturally cared nothing at all for the technical aspect of the painting if the subject was one which would sell well when reproduced. The naturalistic technique of these nineteenth-century descriptive popular pictures became for this reason poorer and poorer and less and less thorough as the century advanced.[3]

This degeneration of naturalistic technique went hand in hand with an

---

[1] Cf. 'Architectural colour', Part III; and 'Architectural and other distortions', Part III.
[2] Cf. 'Naturalism and representation' in Part I and in this part.
[3] Cf. 'Naturalism and representation' (ii) in this part.

104

enormous increase in the size of the pictures. In England, as the artist's aim was solely to attract attention in the Academy, he made his pictures larger and larger every year till kitchens and cows and anecdotic episodes became, as a matter of course, life-size. In Paris, as the *Salon* was much larger and there were also many more galleries in the building, the inflation of the size of these miserably-painted pictures became even more fantastic. Landscapes with life-size trees, rail-way-stations with life-size engines, life-size rooms with a couple of dozen life-size inhabitants, battle-pieces with life-size horses and guns became the order of the day.

Every nineteenth-century artist of this calibre in both countries had in his studio a number of these monstrosities, which had been to the *Salon* or the Academy, and had or had not succeeded in 'making a sensation' or in tempting a printseller to reproduce them; when the artists died, their heirs generally offered them to public galleries, which explains why we see so many of them in these institutions to this day.[1]

This form of degenerate naturalistic technique appeared in a vast number of descriptive popular pictures in the nineteenth century. But a still greater number of pictures was produced in the second half of the century, in two varieties of naturalism, which were brought about by the influence of the camera.

One of these twists given to naturalism by the camera, which degraded pictorial technique to unimaginable depths, is so important in this inquiry that I must examine it at length; and I must begin by a general examination of the camera's vision as compared with human perception and the artist's perception, because one twist was caused by a mistaken notion of that vision, and the other by a correct understanding of it and a mistaken desire to imitate and rival its achievements.

II. THE CAMERA'S INFLUENCE

(i) *The camera's vision*

Certain of the camera's limitations are now universally admitted. To-day everyone recognizes that the camera cannot comment; that it cannot select; and that the variation between the shortest time and the longest time which it can behold its 'subject' is, in daylight, extremely limited. There are still, how-ever, many people who imagine that the camera can record the forms of physical objects and concrete things and the formal relations of such objects and things to one another.

[1] Curators nowadays tend to remove these huge 'white elephants' from the main galleries and put them in corridors or cellars. Whenever possible they lend them to any other public institution that will take them.

Both these last activities are in point of fact as far beyond the camera's powers as the other activities just mentioned. The camera records degrees of light, obstructions to light, reflections of light and relations of light and shade. It cannot record a house, a tree or a man. It can only record the momentary effects and degrees of light as affected by such physical objects or concrete things. Its records, moreover, are determined by two accidental physical factors—its own physical position at the moment of exposure, and the angle and degree of the light obstructed by or reflected by the objects before it.

The cottage recorded by the camera at ten in the morning is a different cottage from that recorded by the same camera in the same position at four in the afternoon, because the lights and shades—which constitute the camera's records—have entirely changed. Also, the cottage recorded at four in the afternoon by a camera on the top of a step-ladder is a different cottage from that recorded at the same moment by a camera placed beneath it on the ground—because the physical positions of the cameras are different.

The camera produces records which fall within our familiar experience of degrees of light, obstructions to light, reflections of light and relations of light and shade because the human eye considered as a lens records in very much the same way as the lens of a camera; and it was because the camera's records corresponded largely to the purely mechanical part of the average human vision that, when photographs first appeared, the average human being recognized them as records of his own familiar experience and called them for that reason 'true'.

Left to itself the camera can and does give delightfully gay records of light and the effects of light; and also, it must be noted, those records are never purely fragmentary in character since they are always inevitably records of *relations* of lights and shade, and so records of one aspect of formal order or architecture in the universe, the aspect manifested in, or thought of, as relations of light and shade. But the camera cannot record any relation of physical objects or concrete things, one to another, except the apparent relation caused by momentary effects of light and shade.[1]

---

[1] To this statement it may be objected that we recognize in a photograph the camera's record of our house and the camera's record of the formal relation of our house to the tree behind and so on, and that therefore the camera must be said to record forms and relations of forms. But this objection is a confusion between the camera's record and the *effect* of that record on ourselves. The camera makes statements of effects of light. We call these statements a house, and a house in front of a tree, by the use of associated ideas. We can go many steps further by the use of associated ideas. We can recognize in the photograph our gardener's cottage and the new Crittall windows which we had installed. But the camera knows nothing of gardeners or of Messrs. Crittall; we know these things and add them to the camera's records just as we know about the form of the cottage and its formal relation to the tree and add that knowledge to the camera's record. Cf. 'Naturalism and representation' (ii) in this part.

Finally it must be noted (*a*) that the camera's eye can see relations of colours in so far as they are relations of light and shade; but (*b*) that as far as we know at present the camera's vision of individual colours does not yet correspond to our own.[1]

The so-called 'artistic' photographers of the present day do not realize the character or significance of the camera's records. They are so incurably stupid that they will not leave the camera to do its business; they want it to do more than it can and only succeed in making it do less. 'Artistic' photographers fake and fiddle with their negatives and prints and produce hybrid abominations that are not true photographs and not works of art. Such photographers nowadays generally try to make the camera's records resemble romantic popular art; they stress familiar emotive details in their 'touching up'. If the photograph is a landscape they stress familiar dramatic or sentimental 'notes' in imitation of romantic popular landscapes; and frequently they destroy the photograph's gay clear statement, and still further limit the photograph's limited range of colour by a deliberate and horrible smeariness that they call 'mystery'—which is, of course, only a variant of the old confused pseudo-romantic notion that a fragment is unusual and so emotive because it happens to be far away.[2] If the photograph is a portrait these 'artistic' photographers imitate romantic popular portraits and stress the fashionable-emotive or erotic-emotive details—and they always enlarge the eyes.[3]

'Artistic' photographers are all derivative; and like derivative popular artists they are of two kinds. They are either disinterested or venal. In the first case they are addle-pated, in the second they are tradesmen working to achieve contact with the average 'artistic' spectator's familiar experience of romantic popular art. In both cases they refuse to accept the camera's records, preferring to distort them into hybrid imitations of various forms of art.

What I submit then on this point of the camera's true vision is this:

(*a*) the camera can and does record degrees of light, obstructions to light, and reflections of light;

[1] Cf. 'Human perception' and 'The artist's perception' in this part, and 'Architectural colour' in Part III.

[2] Many 'artistic' photographers imitate the pictures of Corot's middle period, which, as I shall show alter in 'Technique of Corot and the Impressionists', were produced by Corot when he began to imitate photographs. A singular example of a vicious circle (cf. Pls. 35 and 37.)

[3] Frequently, of course, their women sitters arrive with their eyes enlarged and their lips accentuated by procedures which, as I have noted earlier, are the same in character as those of the romantic popular portrait painter and are now seen to be the same as those of the 'artistic' photographer. If the women do not stress the emotive fragments in their faces before they sit to the camera the 'artistic' photographer has to do it later on the negative or print. In film studios, I am told, the performers always have to do the work themselves, as the subsequent 'emotivizing' of the records by hand would be an impossibly long procedure.

(*b*) it cannot record the forms of physical objects or concrete things;

(*c*) it cannot select;

(*d*) it cannot comment;

(*e*) it can and does record relations of light and shade;

(*f*) but it cannot record any relations of physical objects or concrete things one to another except their apparent relation caused by momentary effects of light and shade;

(*g*) the camera can see relations of colour in so far as they are relations of light and shade;

(*h*) the camera's vision of individual colours does not yet correspond to our own;

(*i*) 'artistic' photographers are neither photographers nor artists; their concoctions are hybrid atrocities which destroy the camera's gay clear records by addle-pated or venal attempts to disguise them as romantic popular and other forms of art.

(*ii*) *Human perception*

Stated very briefly the difference between the camera and the human eye may be said to be that the camera has merely vision while the human eye habitually perceives.

Human perception consists (*a*) in a mechanical physiological vision and (*b*) in reinforcements to that vision which the camera lacks.[1]

Our mechanical vision, like the camera's, is obviously influenced by physical conditions. It is influenced by our physical position; by degrees and angles of light. Like the camera we can scarcely see anything in the dark; and if there is an obstruction before us we cannot see through it.[2]

So far, obviously, our mechanical vision is much the same as the camera's vision; and we can, I think, speaking generally, find a further common denominator in the two mechanical visions (as opposed to perception); for the human eye has the power to register mechanically light, degrees of light, obstructions to light, reflections of light, and relations of light and shade.

---

[1] I make no claims to any special physiological knowledge of the mechanical human vision. The comments on that vision in this section are based (*a*) on my own experience as a person with sight which oculists and opticians describe as 'average normal' and (*b*) on many years' experience as a painter in the course of which I have made special efforts to distinguish my mechanical vision from my vision reinforced to perception.

[2] I am told that a camera left in a dark room all night does make some sort of a record.

108

It must be admitted, I think, that our mechanical vision is not quite so mechanical as that of the camera. It has a certain elasticity of its own. We have two eyes to the camera's one, and though the process of focusing is almost automatic, we see mechanically not one vision but two, which we continually fuse. This in itself constitutes an elasticity in our vision which is foreign to the camera; and, it may be remarked in passing, this elastic automatic focusing is possibly the explanation of our sense of the third dimension which is usually held to appertain to our perception, to derive, that is, from our experience of tactile sensations, or in other words to derive from our knowledge of the solidity of physical objects and concrete things which we have acquired by having at some time or other touched them or others like them. Also our eye has a certain sensitiveness that would seem to make possible an almost direct communication between it and our sensations. But it is easy to exaggerate this sensitiveness and the directness of this communication by confusing our vision with our perception; because the human eye is physiologically, I am told, most intimately and elaborately connected with the brain.[1]

But, speaking very generally, we can, I think, say that average normal human sight mechanically registers light, obstructions to light, relations of light and so on in much the same way as the camera.

Now what is our mechanical vision of relations of colours and of individual colours?

I have suggested that the camera's eye can see relations of colours in so far as they are relations of light and shade, and that the camera's vision of individual colours does not yet correspond to our own.

The human eye, I fancy, registers mechanically relations of colour in much the same way as the camera does. It registers such relations mechanically, that is to say, in so far as they are relations of light and shade. But the human eye also mechanically registers individual colours (though the colourman's names red, blue, and so on, are not added till our vision is reinforced by the brain); and it does this in a way that is different from the camera's registrations of individual colours.

If we look at a picture or a wall painted in different colours our eye does, I

---

[1] In the very general survey which I am attempting here it is not, of course, necessary to consider variations from average normal sight. We can ignore all those chronic variations which we call defective vision and also all the temporary variations caused by temporary physiological causes.

The ear, I am told, is much less intimately and elaborately connected with the brain. This is one of the reasons why comparisons between our reactions to music and our reactions to pictures are so dangerous. Music makes a much more direct assault upon our sensations through the ear than art can make upon them through the eye. Cf. 'Architectural colour', Part III.

think, mechanically register the individual local colours, but it has much more difficulty in registering mechanically the *relations* of the colours because they are not to the same extent relations of light and shade as the relations of colours are in 'nature'. The camera suffers from the same limitations in respect to such relations of colours on a flat surface, and it is also, at present, unable to register individual local colours in a way that corresponds to the human vision. The camera confronted with a picture can only register the variations of colours on its surface in so far as they are relations of light and shade. But its registration of the individual colours is peculiar to itself. Light blue, white and grey in a picture seem much the same to the camera; so do red and black, or orange and dark grey. It is for this reason that photographers when 'taking' a painted picture use a special device to 'correct' the camera's vision of individual local colours, to bring it, that is to say, nearer to the mechanical vision of the average normal human eye.

It must, however, be observed that our eyes' mechanical registration of individual colours does not operate to the same extent in all conditions. The nearer we are to an object the more intense is our mechanical registration of its individual local colours. As things recede farther into the distance our eye mechanically registers less and less the individual local colours and more and more the light and shade and the relations of colours as part of light and shade.

I shall further discuss the questions connected with the relations of our mechanical vision to the camera's vision in the sections which immediately follow. For the moment all I submit is:

(1) that speaking very generally the mechanical action of the normal human eye is much like that of the camera in the registration of light, degrees of light, obstructions to light, reflections of light, relations of light and shade, and relations of colours in so far as they are part of light and shade;

(2) but that our eye mechanically registers individual colours in a way that is not, at present, the normal procedure of the camera;

(3) that this last characteristic of our mechanical vision does not apply to individual colours seen at a distance.

Or in other words, I submit that when we look with half-closed eyes we mechanically see much what the camera sees except that in the foreground we see individual colours in a characteristic way; and that when we wear dark glasses we mechanically see a world like the camera's records which we know as photographs.

Now that which we see by the mechanical operation of our eyes is converted to perception by reinforcements of various kinds. These reinforcements are physiological and psychological; intellectual and emotional; conscious and un-conscious. Associated ideas, imagination, memories, knowledge, sensations, moods, desires and fears and other ingredients which are the concern of psychologists, all play their parts in forming these reinforcements. The exact constitution of these reinforcements varies with every individual and with every separate perception by every individual man.

The fundamental fact about our perception is simply this. *By the aid of our reinforcements we perceive as far as possible what we desire to perceive, and ignore, as far as possible, what we do not desire to perceive.*

We continually seek satisfactions. Men of high mental energy obtain them by enlargement of their experience, and the reinforcements they call up to convert vision to perception are selected to this end. Men of low mental energy obtain some satisfaction by re-experiencing experience which is already theirs; and the ingredients of their perception are selected for that purpose. Men of exception-ally degenerate mentality adopt an active obstinate psychological attitude of hostility to keep enlargement of experience from their doors; the perception of such men, whom we call Philistines, is controlled, limited and given its char-acter by the Philistine's cowardly conviction that the satisfactions he already enjoys will be dangerously jeopardized if he permits any enlargement of his experience to take place.[1]

For the special purpose of this inquiry we need some rough grouping of the reinforcements which we can call upon to help us convert our vision to the kind of perception we desire to achieve. I submit that for our purpose we can divide the reinforcements into those which help us to perceive formal relations, i.e. architectural order; those which help us to perceive emotive fragments; and those which help us to perceive the generic character of physical objects and concrete things, and to achieve social-historical and moral experience through perception.

Further than that, at this point, for our special purpose it is, not, I fancy, necessary to advance.

What I submit then on this point of our perception is:

(*a*) that the reinforcements which we can call upon to convert our vision to perception are numerous and diverse in character;

(*b*) that we make our selection among them to help ourselves perceive what we wish to perceive;

(*c*) that what we wish to perceive depends on the character of the satisfaction which we are attempting at the time.

[1] Cf. 'The Philistine and original art' in Part IV.

111

(iii) *The artist's perception*

From the last section, and the earlier classifications I have made, the reader will be prepared for the comments on the artist's perception which I now submit.

There is, I am convinced, no single grouping of the reinforcements to our vision which is solely characteristic of the artist's perception as such. Different artists, I am certain, perceive with different groups of reinforcements and each group is parallel to that used in similar perception by other normal men. The artist is not different from other mortals; his special powers are special merely in degree.

The classical architectural artist's perception is achieved by the reinforcements which enable normal men to convert their vision to perception of formal relations, i.e. architectural order. The romantic artist's perception is achieved by the reinforcements which enable normal men to perceive emotive fragments. The descriptive artist's perception is achieved by the reinforcements which enable normal men to perceive the generic character of physical objects and concrete things, and to achieve social-historical and moral experience through perception.

When we say, 'The artist paints what he sees', we are talking nonsense unless what we mean by an artist is the man who makes studies in the naturalistic technique which is an activity achieved by a deliberate degrading of human perception to its foundation of mechanical vision.

What we should say, I submit, is, 'The artist paints what he *perceives*'; for here we have a formula so general that it embraces the three main kinds of artistic perception and all the countless variations within each kind.

We all mechanically see things in much the same way; and the artist mechanically sees them much as we do. But each individual human being and each individual artist perceives differently; and the particular character of each individual's perceptions and of each artist's perceptions varies with each act of perception, though the general character of each individual's perception and the general character of each artist's perception is dictated by that which the individual or the artist desires to perceive; because the artist's perception, like our own, is a search for a satisfaction. After many years the artist tends to see almost mechanically what he has frequently perceived. When he adopts the attitude that any enlargement of that habitual perception is unnecessary he is, of course, just a Philistine. It is the degenerate artist-Philistines of this kind, producing

112

derivative popular art in imitation of their own earlier productions, who are the bitterest enemies of original art.

When we say that 'the artist paints what he perceives', we must recognize of course that, in the case of original artists, perception may be *actual or imagined*. Here again there is, I am certain, no special type of imagination peculiarly characteristic of the artist. The original classical architectural artist's imagination is the normal human imagination of architectural order, the original romantic artist's imagination is the normal human romantic imagination; the original descriptive artist's imagination is the normal human descriptive imagination. The difference in all cases is simply one of the degree. The artist is simply a man who has the power to realize his actual or imagined perception (of any calibre) to the point of inventing and producing symbolic concrete form to express it.[1]

(iv) Technique of the Pre-Raphaelites: the Daguerreotype and Ruskin

We can now look in more detail at the part played by the camera in degrading nineteenth-century technique.

It is difficult to fix a definite year as the point when photography began to influence Western European painting. Daguerre was awarded his pension by the French Government and took out his patent in England in 1839, and the calotype followed soon after; the 'fifties saw the development of collodion processes; collodion emulsion was invented in 1864, gelatine emulsion in 1871; by the 'eighties the use of the gelatine-coated plate was general; and the first commercial half-tone process dates from 1882. Speaking generally, from 1850 onwards the camera's influence can everywhere be seen.

The camera in one aspect was an element in the industrial revolution. It was a labour-saving device which, like all labour-saving devices, made certain calculations irrelevant and rendered certain standards of judgment out of date. It was, moreover, not only a labour-saving device, but also a parlour game, and something more important than either—a lens that made records which corresponded very largely to the records made by the average mechanical human vision as distinguished from perception.

Photography on its first appearance in this country was advertised as 'a useful and elegant invention'. But it was not for its usefulness or its elegance that the world acclaimed it. The sensation caused by its appearance was due to

[1] Cf. 'Architectural form' in Part III and 'Imaginative illustrations' in Part IV.

the mistaken notion that a photograph was a record of physical objects and concrete things of the same kind as would normally be made of the same physical objects and concrete things by an artist of exceptional skill. 'The camera cannot lie' became a nineteenth-century slogan because in the beginning people thought that the only difference between a photograph registering the camera's vision and a picture registering an artist's perception was that the picture could record physical objects and concrete things in what was called at the time 'the proper colours of nature', whereas the photograph could only record them in a monochromatic scale. At the beginning people failed to recognize (a) that the camera recorded not physical objects and concrete things but only one aspect of such objects and things, i.e. their effects in light at the moment of exposure of the lens, and (b) that this aspect, though all or nearly all that which is apprehended mechanically by human sight, is only the beginning of that which is apprehended by human perception.

Ruskin's view of the camera's vision was based at the outset on these misconceptions. He saw daguerreotypes for the first time in 1845 in Venice where he was drawing palaces; and he wrote to his father as follows:

'Daguerreotypes taken by this vivid sunlight are glorious things . . . every chip of stone and stain is there . . . it is a noble invention . . . anyone who has worked and blundered and stammered as I have done for four days and then sees the thing he has been trying to do so long in vain done perfectly and faultlessly in half a minute won't abuse it afterwards.' A little later we find him saying: 'Photography misses certain of the utmost subtleties of natural effect'—(he was thinking, of course, of Turner's perception of effects of light)—'while it renders subtleties of form which no human hand could achieve'—a description which is the exact opposite of the truth, since the camera cannot take cognizance of *forms* or record them, while it can and does record, and record exclusively, *effects of light*. In his old age Ruskin saw his error and began to warn students to keep clear of the study of effects of light which he pointed out then had been encouraged by the camera and to urge them to concentrate instead on the study of generic forms. But before that change arrived his misconception of the camera's vision had had immense results on his own attitude to painting and, owing to his influence, on English art.

Many young artists in England in the 'fifties, sharing Ruskin's enthusiasm for the new invention and failing to see the meaning in his rhetoric, imagined that the camera had set a standard of completeness in detailed records of the forms of physical objects and concrete things which it was the artist's duty to attempt to rival; and the first result of the photograph in England was an effort

114

on the part of such artists to achieve a minute naturalism to rival early photographs—which were much 'sharper' than the 'muzzy' productions of modern 'photographic art'.[1]

Thus English artists, as I have already noted, were led in the middle of the nineteenth century to naturalistic technique, partly by the example of the Dutch pictures and partly by an attempt to rival the camera's vision, the character of which they misunderstood.

The camera is bound to record all the effects of light which it sees before it. By misreading Ruskin, the young English artists of the 'fifties mistook this limitation for the power of recording completely in every detail the generic forms of physical objects and concrete things. Desiring to rival this supposed achievement of the camera they set out to evolve a naturalistic technique in the execution of which they imposed on themselves the camera's limitation which prevents it from selecting. Thus Hunt when forming the Pre-Raphaelite brotherhood read the first volumes of *Modern Painters* and was impressed with Ruskin's 'go to Nature in all singleness of heart, . . . rejecting nothing, selecting nothing and scorning nothing' intended only as advice to beginners.[2]

This represents the first twist given to nineteenth-century naturalism by the camera. The influence of daguerreotypes and of early 'sharp' photographs was responsible for a passionate pursuit of an 'all-in' technique based on mechanical vision which the English artists of the 'fifties regarded as a moral justification of their art.

Everyone is familiar with the stereoscopic paintings which resulted from this attempt to degrade normal selective commenting perception to a mechanical 'all-in' description of forms rivalling what was supposed to be the vision of the camera. Dyce's *Pegwell Bay* in the Tate Gallery is a case where the artist was clearly influenced also by the monotonous tone and metallic colour of daguerreotypes where the metal always permeated through the transparent image on the surface. The technique of the Pre-Raphaelites in their early pictures was based on the misconceptions I have indicated. Ruskin praised the pictures which Hunt, Millais and John Brett painted in the 'fifties; and work based on these misconceptions continued to be produced here in large quantities right up to the 'nineties—and such work is still occasionally produced to-day by 'Gem-room' exhibitors in the Royal Academy.[3]

In their earliest days the Pre-Raphaelites were original romantic artists. For

---

[1] But the 'sharpness' now of photographs taken with modern 'proxar' and other lenses and of cinema 'close-ups' far surpasses the 'sharpness' of the early photographs. (Cf. Preface to the 1956 edition.) [1956 note.]

[2] Cf. my 'John Ruskin'. [1935 note.]

[3] And by Neo-Surrealists. Cf. Addendum to the 1938 edition. [1938 note.]

this reason the Philistines abused their pictures in the way the Philistines always abuse such art—by calling them 'hideous'; and they considered the artists' technique hideous also. But in 1862 Martineau painted the descriptive popular picture called *The Last Day in the Old Home*, now in the Tate Gallery, and used the 'all-in' descriptive naturalistic technique. By that time the technique was no longer new. That fact and the popular appeal of the subject won the battle for the 'all-in' technique; and the Philistine's notion of a well-painted picture became the notion of a picture 'with a lot of detail'. J. F. Lewis met this demand with his Oriental interiors; Tissot came across from Paris and made money by pictures painted in the same technique; and Leader appeared to supply the same thing in landscape.

There is a notion that the Pre-Raphaelites' technique was modelled on the technique of the Italian painters before the time of Raphael. This, I fancy, is an error. The Pre-Raphaelite brotherhood was founded by Rossetti, Millais and Hunt in the autumn of 1848. None of these artists was acquainted at that time with the painting of the early Italian artists. None of them had been to Italy, and in the National Gallery at that time there was not a single picture by an Italian artist before the time of Raphael. It is doubtful if any of them had ever seen an Italian Pre-Raphaelite picture. They chose the title for their brotherhood, as I have already mentioned, after looking over a book of engravings of Gozzoli's frescoes in the Campo Santo in Pisa. Here, says Hunt, they found 'that freedom from corruption, pride and disease for which we sought'. As original romantic artists the English Pre-Raphaelites set out honestly to enlarge their experience and to avoid the 'corruption, pride and disease' in degenerate contemporary derivative-popular and other forms of popular art. They based, that is to say, their idea of art on what they believed to have been the idea of art which had served as basis for Benozzo Gozzoli. But they could not possibly have been influenced by Gozzoli's technique because they had never seen it, and when pictures by Gozzoli arrived in the National Gallery, the Brotherhood existed no longer, and all the truly 'Pre-Raphaelite' pictures which these artists ever produced were already painted.[1]

[1] The first Italian Pre-Raphaelite works in the National Gallery were the panels of Saints by Lorenzo Monaco (Nos. 215 and 216). These were presented by G. W. Cunningham in 1848, but whether they were exhibited in that year or not I do not know. It is, of course, possible that the young men saw these pictures (which are painted in tempera on wood), that the pictures made a profound impression on them, and that they studied Lorenzo Monaco's technique and attempted to combine it with their attempt to achieve an 'all-in' naturalistic vision. But there is no evidence, I believe, that they had seen these pictures, and their own account of the selection of their group title is that which I have given in the text.

The two pictures by Gozzoli in the National Gallery were bought respectively in 1855 and 1857. The Pre-Raphaelite brotherhood only held together as a group till 1853.

The English Pre-Raphaelites' technique shows little or no influence from the formal Italian art which was based on mosaics. The technical basis of these English artists was, as I have said, a desire to rival the camera's all-in vision which they mistook for a power to record completely the generic character of physical objects and concrete things; and to this basis they added a prejudice for bright tints, derived probably from some Gothic manuscripts with which Rossetti had made them acquainted.[1]

Of the pseudo-romantic confusion of ideas so evident in the work of the degenerate followers of the Pre-Raphaelites I have written in an earlier section. Here I would merely remind the reader (a) that Rossetti himself shook off the confusion and became in his later years an original romantic artist, using romantic technical distortions to stress unusually emotive fragments in pictures which are generally considered his worst work, but which I hold to be original, truly romantic and therefore admirable;[2] (b) that Burne-Jones, in his ragoût of pseudo-romantic subjects and emotive fragments copied discreetly from Botticelli and Rossetti, used degenerate Pre-Raphaelite technique; (c) that Burne-Jones' followers were still more addled in mind and used a still more degenerate version of Pre-Raphaelite technique.[3]

(v) The Daguerreotype and Ingres

In France at first we find the same misconception in regard to the camera's vision that we find in England. For if we compare Ingres' *Odalisque* which was painted in 1814 with *La Source* which was painted in 1856, we feel that the differences cannot wholly be explained by the reflection that Ingres was thirty-four when he painted the first picture and was suffering a little from senile

---

[1] There was also the technical influence of the Flemish primitives. Rossetti and Hunt went to Paris and Belgium in 1849–50. They already knew Van Eyck's *Jan Arnolfini and his Wife*, which had been bought by the National Gallery in 1842. They were impressed by Van Eyck and Memlinc in Ghent and Bruges. In the Louvre, Hunt records, they looked at Fra Angelico's *Coronation of the Virgin*. This, with the possible addition of the Lorenzo Monaco pictures, already referred to, seems to have been the extent of their acquaintance with Italian Pre-Raphaelite technique.

[2] As I have already mentioned, I believe the sketch for Rossetti's *Annunciation*, 1849, if it exists, to be his best work and perhaps the most original religious picture painted in England in the nineteenth century. It should also be noted that in his illustrations to Tennyson's poems drawn in the 'fifties, Rossetti showed the influence of photographs by making the edge of the frame cut into figures in an arbitrary way as they are accidentally cut into by the frame in photographs. This trick was imitated later by Byam Shaw in his illustrations to Browning.

[3] Cf. my 'English Painting'. [1935 note.]

concupiscence when he painted the second. In the *Odalisque*, in fact, we have colour and modelling in the Italian Renaissance tradition of artists like Bronzino, whereas in *La Source* we have modelling curiously like the illusion of modelling in daguerreotypes and also a reflection of the metallic monochrome colour which permeates the daguerreotype image from the plate.[1]

Ingres, there is no doubt, was much influenced technically by daguerreotypes in later years, and this happened because he was a person who absorbed every influence that came his way. Ingres was a kind of Haydon.[2] He was at heart a romantic. When in Italy he imitated early Italian Renaissance pictures. When he returned to Paris after his Italian studies the accident that his pictures looked to the superficial observer more like the pictures of David than like those of Delacroix led the critics to regard him as the upholder of the classical tradition, and to hail him as the descendant of Raphael and Poussin. That position Ingres accepted, and he tried repeatedly to achieve classical architectural compositions. But like Haydon he never really grasped the architectural principle of classical art. He imagined that purity of line was the beginning and end of that conception. He was only happy when he could paint or draw a portrait and stress emotive fragments as the original romantic artist that he truly was. The real Ingres is seen in the finger nails of his portrait of *M. Bertin*, in the series of emotive fragments that go to the making of his portrait of *Madame Rivière*, in the emotive attitudes of the nudes in his *Bain turque*. His romantic work was never popular in kind—though sometimes it comes perilously near it. Ingres, in a word, was never at heart an architectural artist, the reinforcements whereby he turned his vision to perception were not essentially those called up by an artist preoccupied with formal relations, and such architectural reinforcements as he summoned were always mingled with and often dominated by the reinforcements that create romantic art.[3]

These comments are frankly a digression. My real point about Ingres at this stage of our inquiry is simply that we see the influence of the daguerreotype in the technique of his last period, and that thereby a twist was given to the naturalistic technique used by French derivative artists in the venal descriptive popular art which they evolved to meet the demands of the new French bourgeois created by the Revolution, and that it was the same twist as that which, as we have seen, led the English Pre-Raphaelites to the mistaken notion that the camera could completely and perfectly record forms, and that it was the artist's duty to rival the camera in purely mechanical non-selective vision.

[1] All the pictures by Ingres referred to in this section are in the Louvre.
[2] Cf. 'The Honest incompetent artist spectator' in Part IV.
[3] Cf. my 'French Painting' (Medici). [1935 note.]

(vi) Technique of Corot and the Impressionists

Ingres was one of the French artists who fell into this particular misconception of the camera's vision. Other French artists soon discovered that the camera's lens recorded not the generic character of physical objects and concrete things as perceived by representational descriptive artists, but that it recorded only effects of light; and by 1850 these French artists had started on attempts to contract their perception to the camera's true vision—attempts which were destined to debase pictorial technique in ways quite different from the way it was debased by artists who failed to understand the camera's eye.

Corot was the first French artist whose technique was undermined by an attempt to rival the camera's true vision. He was born in 1796, and from 1826 to 1850 he composed classical landscapes like *Le Colisée*,[1] *La Cathédrale de Chartres*,[1] *Saint André du Morvan*,[1] *Homère et les Bergers*[2] and *Honfleur— maisons sur les quais*.[3] The perception in these pictures is architectural. The physical objects and concrete things are here perceived in their formal relations one to another and this architectural enlargement of the artist's experience is synthetized in new formal relations which are the subject of each picture. But about 1850, when Corot evidently had seen some photographs, he adopted new manner in which formal order ceased to be the subject of his pictures and the suggestion of effects of light became the subject instead. Corot, in fact, after seeing photographs had discovered a short cut to make an effective picture and that short cut was to shut off perception and record the mechanical impression on his eyes. Fascinated by the meritorious results of his first experiments in this technique he began more and more to make pictures in which trees were registered as muzzy silhouettes and foliage registered as formless flecks of light (Pls. 35 and 37). Sometimes he painted an architectural or descriptive nude and surrounded it with formless degrees of light as a foliage background; at other times he painted both figures and landscapes in this photographic light-registering technique. From 1850 to 1870 he turned out hundreds of these paintings in which the much-vaunted silvery colour was only part of a general imitation of photographic greys. This photographic technique Corot used to express a romantic popular attitude which obtained contact with the public's familiar sentimental experience of landscape in misty weather. This new

[1] Louvre.
[2] Saint-Lô.
[3] Reproduced in my 'French Painting' (Medici). [1935 note.]

manner was accordingly at once successful; and is, I understand, admired by many people to this day.[1]

For twenty years Corot continued to supply the dealers with fluffy silvery landscapes in this photographic technique. But in 1870, when the war came, he was driven to Paris and the shelter of a studio. Here confronted with the problem of painting the living model in a studio—a problem scarcely attempted since his earliest days—he made in his seventy-fourth year a fresh effort to give play to more architectural perceptions; and in *L'Atelier*,[2] *La Femme à la Perle*[2] and *La Dame en Bleu*[2] we have once more architectural perception and relatively speaking architectural technique.

This studio period was exceedingly helpful to Corot; and when in 1871 he returned to landscape and painted *Le Beffroi de Douai*[2] he produced a picture nearer to *Honfleur—maisons sur les quais* painted in 1830 than any he had painted since 1850; for the camera's influence here has been excluded from the actual painting, though the picture provides evidence, in the way the buildings on each side in the foreground are cut off by the frame, that Corot had observed the possibility of exploiting in pictures the striking accidental compositions which the camera's records so frequently produce.[3]

Corot died in 1875. He thus lived long enough to see the first Impressionist Exhibition of 1874, to see, that is, his own coquetting with the camera's vision developed to a conscious system.

The Impressionists set out to evolve a species of painting in which specific forms would be suggested purely as the camera suggests them, by records of their effects in light. Many volumes have been written on French Impressionist technique which is now familiar to everyone. Here it is only necessary to point out (*a*) that the celebrated spectrum palette of the Impressionists and their method of juxtaposing colours and allowing them to fuse at a certain distance to the desired tint, was in fact merely an attempt to evolve a system of colouring which it was thought would be that seen in photographs if the camera could record its vision of colour, and (*b*) that this artificial palette became in the hands of the leading French Impressionists the means for effecting an architectural synthesis of an aspect of formal order, and that this aspect of formal order (which was to be systematized by Seurat) was the real subject of many of their pictures.

[1] Also as I have noted earlier the 'artistic' photographers now repay to Corot the compliment he paid the camera and fake their photographs to make them look like reproductions of these photographic pictures.

[2] Louvre.

[3] This as I have noted earlier had already been done by Rossetti; and, as I shall note a little later, it was destined to be done regularly by Degas and his followers.

The Impressionists' technique is tied at one end to the photographic art of Corot's middle period; it is tied at the other both to the modern movement and to the degenerate painting by the tone values which I shall discuss in the next section.

Monet, as is well known, painted a dozen or more pictures of the same haystack at different times of the day. He set out to prove that his perception of the haystack was the same as that of a camera which sees, from the limitations of its vision, a dozen different haystacks at different hours of the day. Monet failed to prove that he had only sight and not perception because his use of the arbitrary spectrum palette was an architectural synthesis in itself. But later on when English artists painted haystacks in the same spirit without the architectural synthesis of colour, they convinced us perfectly that they had succeeded in degrading their perception to purely mechanical vision of momentary effects of light.

Degas exploited the camera's fortuitous compositions which, as he was the first to observe, bore a singular resemblance to the original compositions found in Japanese prints.

Manet, when he was not imitating the Spaniards, was an original descriptive artist who exploited in his technique effects of light fusion in over-exposed photographs. In his most characteristic painting, he mixed up his colours on his palette and painted in the 'direct' photographic tone values technique which I am about to discuss. He painted with gusto and used the free emotive handling of the romantic tradition.[1]

The Impressionist movement ties onto the modern movement in the person of the aged Renoir who in his last years concentrated on the architectural relations of forms—which is why most artists of the modern movement prefer the classical pictures he painted when he was paralysed to the Impressionist pictures he painted in his youth.

The chorus of abuse that greeted the first Impressionist exhibitions in the 'seventies would have been comprehensible if it had taken the form of a protest against the photographic basis of Impressionist technique. The Philistine critics must be blamed for this and also for their failure to distinguish between the limited architectural achievements of Monet, the romantic-descriptive achievements of Degas, the architectural-romantic achievements of the youthful Renoir and the descriptive achievements of Manet. But they are not to be blamed for failing to appreciate the major architectural achievements of Renoir

[1] Manet's technical procedures are more fully discoursed in my 'Modern French Painters'. [1956 note.[

because these did not appear till the modern movement had been already launched, and at a time when, the Impressionists' battle being won, the Philistines had begun to use their work as a rod wherewith to chastise the newer movement.

The photographic vision took a terrible hold on the less intelligent artists in France. Fantin Latour's *Atelier de Manet*,[1] painted in 1879, is technically quite photographic. Eugène Carrière abandoned colour altogether and painted pictures which are essentially emotive fragments drawn by shadows in oil paint; and the full measure of the disastrous results of the French artists' determination to see like the camera appeared in the mechanically descriptive popular portraits by Bonnat on the one hand, and in Henner's romantic popular muzzy nudes on the other.

Thirty years after the French discovery of the camera's true vision the discovery crossed the Channel and began to drive from the field the English pictorial technique that resulted from the misconception of the camera's vision by the Pre-Raphaelites and Ruskin. From 1890 onwards relatively few degenerate imitations of the daguerreotype-Pre-Raphaelite-naturalistic technical tradition were produced in England. Since 1890 the exhibitions of the Royal Academy, the R.B.A., the R.O.I., etc., have been full instead of pictures where people sitting in sunlight and shadow under trees are painted in a technique that makes the pictures look like Kodak snapshots coloured on an easy system of yellowish splodges for the light parts and bluish splodges for the shadows—a technique which is, of course, a coarse derivative parody of the French Impressionists' spectrum palette of 1875.

This second twist given to naturalistic technique in the nineteenth century by the camera, the twist which we see in the pictures of Corot's middle period and in various types of degenerate Impressionism, is so important for our inquiry that I must now discuss it in further detail.

(vii) Naturalism and representation (ii)

Readers who recall my earlier section on the difference between naturalistic and representational technique in Part I, and have followed the rough sketch I have given in this part of the degeneration of nineteenth-century technique, will realize that the vast mass of work produced to-day, outside the modern movement, is executed in the debased photographic-naturalistic technique that appeared for the first time in the pictures of Corot in his middle period.

[1] Louvre.

122

That technique, as I have there mentioned, has been widely taught in the art schools since the 'eighties. It is based on the system of 'drawing by the shadows' and painting 'by the tone values', a vicious system that we must now examine.

The popular Dutch artists, who used the naturalistic technique, copied the appearances of phenomena in the particular light before them at the moment. But they did not do this consciously and as a system. The camera had not yet come to create the notion that to paint in this technique was the beginning and the end of art; and the photograph had not yet arrived to destroy the artists' perception of individual local colours.

In the section in which I discussed human perception I have submitted that the mechanical action of the human eye registers relations of colours in so far as they are relations of light and shade, and that our eye reacts to individual colours in a way that is different from the camera's present vision of individual colours. The difference between the Dutch painters' naturalistic technique and the debased photographic naturalism that arose from the camera's influence in the nineteenth century was simply this:

The Dutch painters, being descriptive artists, used their mechanical vision of individual local colours as a factor in their description. They gave us deliberate statements that the cook's skirt was red and her bodice black and they super-imposed this statement of their mechanical vision of individual local colours on to their statements of their mechanical vision of relations of light and shade. They did this also physically in their technique. That is to say they painted their pictures in monochrome and then applied the colours separately in transparent glazes; they thought of red and black and blue as red and black and blue when they applied them, not as parts of light and shade. Most of the Dutch artists did not reinforce their mechanical vision of *relations* of colours to conscious perception of those relations: it was only an architectural artist like Vermeer who could do this.[1]

Now the photographic naturalists of the nineteenth century were so delighted with the short cut to illusionist painting which Corot had evolved in imitation of the camera's records, that they suppressed even their mechanical vision of individual colours. They threw overboard the popular descriptive aim of the Dutch painters and made the imitation of the camera's records their sole pre-occupation. They drew by copying the lights and shadows, and they painted by copying the same thing in tinted lights and shadows in oil paint.

The method of drawing taught in the later part of the nineteenth century in the art schools was thus a method unknown and undreamed of by the old

[1] Cf. 'Architectural colour', Part III.

123

masters. Before 1850 no artist drew by copying the lights and shadows. All the old masters drew by making lines and tones symbolizing their perception of form. Their drawings were either symbolic statements of such perception or else imagined arrangements of light and shade serving as a note for the architectural or romantic disposition of light and shade in the picture or engraving for which the drawing was a study. It was not till after 1850 that artists began to make elaborate smears on paper which would remind the spectator of the appearance of a man, a tree or a bird as recorded by photographs. The final degradation was reached in 'stump' drawing where the student was given a dish of black powder and a paper stump and by this means in a few months he could produce a smear-copy of the lights and shadows before him which looked exactly like a photograph and did not contain a single line.

This twist given by the camera to nineteenth-century drawing was a debasement of the art of drawing because light-and-shade drawings of this kind, as I have stated earlier, are produced by a mechanical trick whereby the artist's hand copies mechanically the mechanical vision of his eye. For the execution of this technique the artist or art student need not reinforce his mechanical vision to perception. After some months of practice, if he has facility, or some years, if he has none, he can become so adept at this simple trick that he can think and talk of other things while he is doing it.[1]

Nineteenth-century photographic painting was simply this debased drawing executed in oil paint. The student was taught to paint with half-closed eyes, to contract his perception that is to the camera's vision. He was taught to suppress even his mechanical vision of individual local colours and to see colour relations as relations of tones. This system was called painting 'by the tone values'.

In practice this meant painting in greys (the photograph's range of colours), and if the model had a red skirt or a black bodice the student mixed some red or black with his grey paste. If, greatly daring, he chanced to put in a touch of bright red or strong black corresponding to his mechanical vision or his perception of individual colours, he was told that he had thrown his study 'out of tone'. As a result of this imitation of photographs in oil paints, colours completely vanished from late nineteenth-century naturalistic technique. At best

---

[1] Portrait draughtsmen who use this trick can chatter brightly to their sitters while at work. This from the standpoint of material success is a great advantage to the artist; because sitting to a silent artist is a boring business, while sitting to an artist who happens to be able to talk, though he has not learned to draw, but only acquired a drawing-trick, can be most agreeable; and more people will sit if sitting is agreeable than if sitting is an affair of silence and boredom. The same thing applies in a lesser degree in the case of photographically naturalistic portrait painters and their sitters. No artist using symbolic representational technique which requires mental synthesis can think or talk of other things while he is painting without damage to his work.

we got pictures in tinted greys, and at worst we got the works of Carrière and others who made photographic naturalistic imitations of light effects in monochrome.

It must further be observed that, as opposed to the Dutch naturalists, the nineteenth-century photographic naturalists did not paint their pictures by two processes but by one. They did not underpaint in monochrome and subsequently glaze colours on this preparation; they mixed up the final tint on the palette and applied it to canvas. This was known as the 'direct method' of painting and was considered a merit in itself. The notion that there was something admirable in this direct method was of course a debased version of the original romantic idea of emotive technique. It was more dashing to mix up a lilac tint of flake-white, rose-madder, blue and black, than to paint a monochromatic version in blue-grey and glaze the rose-madder later in the manner of the old masters; and because it was more dashing it was more 'artistic' to the pseudo-romantic mind.

This system of mixing up coloured tones on the palette, or 'direct' painting, was never employed by the old masters in their pictures for two reasons.

The first reason was that they knew that such painting could not physically last because the mixed-up tinted grey pastes all eventually return to uniform greyness. Such painting, as the old masters knew, could only last if the colours composing the paste were very loosely mixed together, and if they were applied to the canvas in one touch which was never afterwards manipulated by the brush, a form of dexterity which did not appeal to the old masters and, indeed, never occurred to any artists until the nineteenth-century romantics evolved the notion that it was a fine thing to see spots and dashes evidencing the fine fury of the artist at his work. The old masters only used the method for rough sketches where rapidity of execution was their principal aim, and very few old masters used it even in sketches.

The nineteenth-century painters who painted 'by the tone values' in the direct technique habitually pointed to Hals and Velasquez as their historical precedents. But they did not look carefully at the pictures by one artist or the other. Hals in fact glazed all the important pictures of his early and middle periods. He used the direct method only in his sketches and in certain late works. Indeed the only picture by Hals certainly painted in the direct manner, which I know, is the group *Men Guardians of the Old Men's Almshouses* in Haarlem, which was painted when he was over eighty. Velasquez also only used this method in his sketches. As everyone who has examined his pictures in the Prado knows, the only 'direct' Velasquez painting in that gallery is *Las Meninas*—an unfinished sketch that has lost a great deal of its brilliance in later years. But the technique of this picture has no relation to the finished pictures by Velasquez where the artist, like all artists, in their finished pictures, till the nineteenth century, always applied colours in successive layers and never mixed up finally tinted pastes.[1]

The second reason why the old masters never used the direct method of painting by the tone values was that the tradition of perception, whereby the artist separates in his mind the colours in phenomena before him from other aspects of those phenomena, obtained throughout Europe till it was destroyed by the camera. The architectural old masters perceived colours for architectural ends, the romantic old masters perceived them for romantic ends, the descriptive old masters, even the Dutch popular naturalistic painters, as I have already observed, perceived them for descriptive ends. The old masters did not atrophy their perception of colours and restrict it to mechanical vision of colour relations as part of relations of light and shade, because there were no photographs to tempt them to such a course and no art masters to tell them that to do so was the beginning and the end of art.

We commonly assume that the pictures by the old masters are richer and more varied in colour than those of the nineteenth-century painters because their actual colours were superior. This is nonsense. Nineteenth-century colour-men supplied excellent colours. The pictures painted in them are now grey and colourless partly because 'direct' painting loses in course of time whatever brilliance it may have had, and partly because pictures painted 'by the tone values' are not painted in colours but in tinted greys.

In 'Human perception' I suggested that our mechanical vision of individual local colours is more intense when we are near to an object than when the object is far away. The nineteenth-century painters who used the photographic naturalistic painting-by-the-tone-values technique always had the greatest difficulty with the foreground. For here their mechanical vision was in conflict with the photographic vision. They saw mechanically strong local colours; but they dared not put them in for fear of 'throwing their pictures out of tone'. So they usually looked over the foreground altogether, 'suggested' it with smears, and took a point of vision in the middle distance where everything, to their relief, could be photographically seen.

---

[1] Whether Velasquez ever intended to paint a picture from *Las Meninas* we shall never know. Obviously he was confronted with a situation that might never recur. Here was this little Infanta with her dogs, her dwarfs and her attendants in a group that he desired to paint. If the thing was to be done at all it had to be done quickly. Hence *Las Meninas* the central part of which was obviously painted at 'one go'.

That the pictures painted by their students in debased photographic naturalistic technique were colourless and would not physically last did not trouble the art masters of the late nineteenth century. For their business was to persuade the maximum number of students that since they were achieving proficiency in the easy tricks of drawing by the shadows and painting by the tone values, they were also achieving proficiency in art. What happened afterwards was not the art masters' concern.

What in point of fact happened was, of course, that the student left the art school, took a studio, called himself an artist and continued to do the only thing he could do—that is to say he went on making studies of models by the photographic naturalistic trick; the only difference being that whereas before he had brought them home as his art school 'studies' he now sent them to exhibitions in gold frames called *By the window*, *Portrait of an English girl*, or *Eve*. As everyone knows thousands of such productions were exhibited every year in every exhibition in the last quarter of the nineteenth century; and thousands are exhibited in all our exhibitions to this day. They are the work of men who can do one thing and one thing only; and that is the copying of lights and shadows on physical objects and concrete things before them; and they can only do this while the light is constant and while the objects, or the things, keep still.

The symbolic representational artist can always represent motion. The naturalistic artist can never do so. The camera also can never do this. The photograph of racehorses which I reproduce as Pl. 1, shows what the camera can do in this field. It far surpasses anything that a descriptive draughtsman using naturalistic technique could accomplish. But it does not begin to represent horses galloping as perceived by any human mind. The old artists' formula of the horses with four outstretched legs is one such perception. In the photograph reproduced the horses look as though they were about to fall and break their legs. We have to *correct* this impression when we look at the photograph by our knowledge that the horses will adjust their legs before touching the ground. Thus in looking at photographs we sometimes reinforce the camera's records with associated ideas, as I have noted in 'The camera's vision', and we sometimes correct them by the same means; and we are apt to forget that what the cinema provides is only a succession of still photographs.

In a picture by Jan Steen called *The Drawing Lesson* a plaster Cupid is shown suspended in a flying attitude from the studio ceiling. Naturalistic technique in Holland in the seventeenth century was saved from the complete degradation of the nineteenth-century procedure by the artist's use of individual colours;

but it was clearly as dependent on the immobility of objects before it. Henry Holiday in the nineteenth century, when he set out to paint a pseudo-romantic picture of the Rhine Maidens, posed wax models in a glass tank of water constructed in his studio for the purpose. Burne-Jones borrowed this tank when he embarked later on an 'imaginative' picture of a similar subject.

It must moreover be noted that the derivative painters who use photographically naturalistic technique combined with the yellow-for-the-light-and-purple-for-the-shadows formula (which as I have observed earlier is a popular parody of the French Impressionist's spectrum palette) are equally mechanical in their procedure and equally dependent on the immobility of objects and things and light.

Now, the technical procedure of the representational artist has obviously no relation to the degraded photographically naturalistic trick. Michelangelo and Raphael did not proceed in this manner. Nor did the great romantic artists. The immobility of the object or thing contemplated is not required by the representational artist. No bisons stood motionless before the artists in the caves of Altamira; Michelangelo did not hang a model from the ceiling when he painted God creating Adam; Raphael did not group his fifty figures in a temple and keep them motionless for a month or two while he painted the *School of Athens*. For representational artists see not only with their eyes but also with reinforcements converting their vision to perception; and their technical procedure is the creation of symbols for that actual or imagined perception.

The descriptive artist using a representational technique looks at an eye, and says to himself: 'This is an eye'; he then makes a symbol for its generic structure as an eye. The romantic artist making a representational technique looks at an eye, says to himself, 'This is an exciting eye', and then makes a symbol for the exciting aspect of the eye. The architectural artist using a representational technique looks at an eye, says to himself: 'This is an oval with a dark circle in the middle', or 'This is a convex oval of extremely subtle form', and then makes a symbol for the form to fit in with other symbols of adjacent forms perceived in the same way. The photographically naturalistic painter looks at an eye, says to himself nothing at all and mechanically copies the light and shadow that happen to be passing over the eye at the moment (Pls. 30, 32).

These contrasts become of course still more marked when the representational artists use imagined and not actual perception. When they do this the photographic naturalist is seen to be still more obviously a poor creature whose equipment as an artist consists in nothing but one degenerate trick.

We can now, I think, look with advantage at the technique of Sargent.

128

(viii) *Technique of Sargent*[1]

Roger Fry said repeatedly that Sargent was not an artist. If by this he meant that he was not an original classical architectural artist, I quite agree with him. For Sargent was a romantic popular artist who, except when he was imitating some old master, used in his portraits the photographic naturalistic technique, and in his landscapes the yellow-for-the-lights-and-purple-for-the-shadows pseudo-Impressionist formula.

Anyone who studied the pictures in the Sargent Memorial Exhibition and who has discovered from earlier parts of this inquiry exactly what I mean by a romantic popular artist will know what I mean when I describe Sargent as an artist of this kind. For he reacted habitually to emotive fragments within his familiar experience. Many of these fragments were of the fashionable-emotive variety. He made a fortune by painting portraits, but he was a disinterested, not, I fancy, a venal popular artist.[2] He did not paint to achieve contact with the familiar romantic experience of other people, he simply made records of familiar romantic experience of his own. He was not an original romantic artist; there is no reason to suppose from any of his pictures that he enlarged his romantic experience by his work; also he lacked the original romantic's courage to stress the emotive fragments in some original way; and his architectural perception was obviously rudimentary.

Both his portraits and his pictures were at first abused by Philistines as though they were works of original art because the pseudo-romantic and pseudo-Impressionist photographic naturalistic techniques in which they were painted were still unknown to the visitors to the Royal Academy at the time when they were first exhibited. But as soon as the Academy visitors got used to these techniques (a process made easier for them by the swarm of derivative painters who immediately copied them) they realized that what they had before them was not original romantic art, asking them to enlarge their romantic experience, but popular romantic art representing the familiar romantic experience of a man whose experience of that kind was very much their own; and the day came

[1] To young people to-day the comments which follow may seem flogging a dead horse. But when this book was written Sargent was generally more highly rated in England and America than say Matisse; and £167,000 (equivalent to perhaps £400,000 in present money) had just been paid at an auction for miscellaneous paintings and watercolours left in his studio when he died. The acquired value of his work has now greatly fallen in both places (cf. footnote at the end of this section); but as my comments on his technique are still quite actual I have left the section as I wrote it. [1956 note.]

[2] But cf. 'Value of romantic popular art', Part IV.

when they responded with enthusiasm to Sargent's paintings—which then said to each man among them: (*a*) 'You are a fine romantic fellow. You have often reacted yourself to the kind of emotive fragments here set forth'; and (*b*) 'You are a fine artistic fellow. This kind of photographic painting of lights and shades, and this yellow and purple colour formula have no longer any terrors for you. They are both already within your own familiar experience of art.'

Occasionally Sargent left his naturalistic techniques in his wardrobe and made a successful imitation of a portrait by Van Dyck. The picture *Lady Sassoon* is an example; though even here certain details like the rings and bracelets are seen as formless obstructions to and reflections of light with purely mechanical vision.

Occasionally moreover Sargent, by vigorous contracting of his perception to mechanical vision of light effects and by setting down degrees of light, obstructions to light and reflections of light with great accuracy, produced photographic naturalistic painting that has never been surpassed. But most of his photographic portraits show little more skill in this degraded technique than can be seen in the paintings by hundreds of other camera-rivalling European painters between 1850 and the 1914–1918 war.

Sargent's interiors were fundamentally photographic, being nothing more nor less than imitations of effects of light; and his landscapes were all parodies of the original architectural landscapes by Monet and Sisley, made hybrid by his romantic popular bias and carried out in the debased yellow and purple parody of their spectrum palette.

Sargent has been called a descriptive artist. But his attitude, motives and procedure were not those of descriptive artists who depict the generic character of physical objects and concrete things. Sargent never attempted to do this. He depicted physical objects and concrete things before him as obstructions to and reflections of light. His vision was not reinforced to perception of generic character. Such reinforcements as his vision had were of the kind that produce romantic-fashionable perception, or of the kind that produce derivative popular art. 'I chronicle' Sargent used to say; 'I do not comment.' This was not quite accurate. There was romantic popular comment in most of Sargent's work. Had he said 'I chronicle momentary effects of light and shade; I do not describe; when I am painting I allow my familiar experience of emotive fragments to affect me but apart from this I never think', he would have told us what happened when he worked (Pls. 34, 36).

The character of Sargent's technique will be recognized by all readers who have (*a*) examined carefully the technique in his portraits; (*b*) appreciated the distinctions I have drawn earlier between naturalistic and representational painting; and (c) followed the account I have given of the twist given to nine-teenth-century naturalistic technique in France when the artists began to imitate photographs and rival the camera's vision.

Sargent's technique is sometimes credited with the quality called style. This, too, is an error. What passed for style in Sargent's pictures was merely a vulgar interpretation of the romantic movement's doctrine that technique itself should be emotive and expressive of the artist's temperament. Sargent suffered from the romantic heresy which tried to persuade us that virile spontaneous 'direct' brushwork was a merit in itself. His showy handling was a debased equivalent of the '*heureuse saleté*' of Delacroix's '*brosse ivre*'. It lacked the quality of style in the representational techniques of architectural, romantic or even descriptive art because at bottom it was naturalistic. The difference between Sargent's most brilliant portraits and the portraits painted by an artist whose technique has style can be seen if we compare the eyes in his portrait *Henry James* with the eyes in a head by Rubens. Sargent did not perceive an eye as a generic eye, or as an unusual eye, or as an architectural form. He merely copied the lights and shadows that happened to be on the eye before him at the moment. Rubens was fundamentally an original descriptive artist whose representational technique had style. An eye in a Rubens portrait is a symbol for the artist's perception of generic form, and the accidental light and shade of the moment play little or no part in the creation of the symbol (Pls. 30, 32).[1]

An important aspect of Sargent's attitude is the popular character of his romantic reaction to emotive fragments. His portraits of women often have romantic points of focus in the eyes and mouth which are of course exactly the points of focus which the romantic popular illustrators give us on the covers of magazines. Another point of focus in Sargent's portraits is frequently the hands which were always painted as fashionable-emotive fragments, the artist having reacted to the familiar fashionable-emotive elegance of long fingers, manicured nails and so forth.

Around the emotive fragments we find in Sargent's pictures the habitual slush of degenerate romantic technique which always fails to co-ordinate the points of focus. There is, perhaps, no passage in any other picture in the National Gallery as degraded, technically, as the juncture of 'Ena's' skirt and the large jar in the famous group *Ena and Betty Wertheimer* (Pls. 31, 33). It has no archi-tectural, romantic, or descriptive justification. The artist simply did not know what to do with this juncture. Not being an architectural artist the juncture as form did not interest him; not being a descriptive artist he took no interest in the

[1] For the use of the word 'style' in this passage see footnote on p. 70. [1956 note.]

131

generic forms of skirts and pots; and the fragments were not emotive to him in any familiar way; so he just 'slushed' and hoped nobody would look at the passage as it was some distance from the bright eyes, the smiling lips, the alabaster bosoms and the fashionable-emotive hands that are the points of focus in the picture.

What I submit then is (1) that Sargent's technique in his most personal and accomplished portraits was, at its best, degraded photographic naturalism (i.e. direct painting by the tone values) exceedingly well done; (2) that in his less accomplished portraits and in the countless portraits where as dishonest artist-spectator he passed them out as 'right' when he knew they were wrong, his technique was this trick less well or extremely badly done;[1] (3) that in his landscapes his technique was the photographic naturalistic yellow-and-purple parody of the French Impressionist's spectrum palette; (4) that in his derivative portraits his technique being derivative was pseudo-technique with no character of its own; (5) that what passes for style in his pictures is the old romantic heresy that an artist's technique should talk about the artist; (6) that what passes for characterization in his pictures is a popular record of familiar emotive fragments; (7) that compared with any original romantic artist he was unable to discover unusual emotive fragments and too timid to stress them in any original way; and (8) that his romantic settings to his points of focus rarely co-ordinate those points of focus but are often dismally degraded slush.[2]

C. RECONSTRUCTION IN FRANCE AND ENGLAND

In the foregoing sections and the earlier parts of this inquiry I have tried to indicate the general character of nineteenth-century art and nineteenth-century technique as they appeared to the pioneer artists of the modern movement when they decided to return to the idea of classical architectural formal art as a basis and to evolve new classical architectural formal techniques of their own.[3]

I have said that the movement started in Paris about 1884; and Cézanne and

[1] Cf. 'The dishonest artist-spectator', Part IV.

[2] For the value of Sargent's portraits deriving from the appreciation of many English and American spectators at the present time and the value that may be conferred on them at some future time by spectators regarding them as historical documents which are both varieties of *acquired* value, cf. Part IV *passim*.

[3] As I stated in the Preface, I do not pretend to have given a complete account of nineteenth-century art. I have merely tried to give a bird's-eye view from the angle of the artists of the modern movement who saw it as a mass of confused ideas and degenerate technique and reacted violently against it.

Seurat are now recognized as its most significant pioneers. I have instanced the work of Sargent and the yellow-and-purple parodies of the Impressionists' technique as among the types of painting against which the pioneers protested—though Sargent's work and that of his imitators was mainly produced in the 'nineties and in the first decades of the present century.

To explain this I must remind the reader that I have not yet insisted on the distinction between the commencement of the movement in Paris and the first comprehension of its character and the first contributions towards it here in England.

For the last hundred years Paris has seen the birth of all the attempts to find a *raison d'être* for plastic art and a criterion of its value to replace the basis and criterion formerly provided by religion.[1] Or in other words all the artistic movements of the last hundred years have originated in Paris. In each case it has taken thirty years for the particular attempt to be understood in England. At any moment between 1826 and 1926 we have therefore, in France, a new movement surrounded by derivative parodies of the last movement and by other forms of popular art; and, in England, a movement which was called new, but which was always really a tardy contribution to a movement that was the last but one, or two, in France; the English tardy pioneers being of course likewise surrounded by derivative parodies of earlier movements and by other forms of popular art.

It must be clearly recognized that what has been happening since 1826 has again and again been this. A group of artists in Paris have thought out a basis for their art and made experiments on that basis. Ten years later a swarm of derivative popular artists arose in Paris and reaped the fruits of the pioneers' experiments. Ten years later still, another group of French artists thought out another basis as a development of the last one or as a reaction against it; and ten years later than that they in their turn were imitated by derivative artists. Somewhere in the middle of the third decade artists in England began to understand what the first French group had been after and those of them who were original tried to enlarge their experience on that basis, while those who were incapable of enlarging their experience either abused the French movement or joined the French imitators of its productions. Except in the case of the Pre-Raphaelites in the early 'fifties and Whistler in the 'sixties and 'seventies it is true to say that in the last hundred years the advanced art in England has always been an art which was advanced in Paris thirty years before and which as an experimental basis had already been superseded in that city.

[1] Cf. 'Religious and non-religious art', Part I.

The New English Art Club, for example, which was considered most revolutionary at its inception, was founded in 1886 at a time when, in France, the Impressionist basis of the late 'sixties and 'seventies had just been abandoned for the revival of the classical idea by Seurat and Cézanne. Most of the early New English artists had been to Paris and had had a chance to take part if not in the Seurat-Cézanne movement—that perhaps would have been asking too much— at any rate to take part somewhat tardily in the Impressionist adventure. But in 1886 very few of the New English artists had seen the point of the Impressionist movement, still less of the really advanced movement of the time. Clausen was in Paris in the 'seventies. He must have seen pictures by Manet, Renoir, and Monet. He came back to England and painted *The Girl at the Gate* in the Tate Gallery. It was not till 1904 that Clausen realized the point of the French Impressionist experiments which he had presumably seen in Paris in the 'seventies, and then, keeping clear of the spectrum palette, he sat down and copied the momentary light and shade on haystacks, in barns, and so forth, in a photographic monochrome technique that out-Coroted Corot's imitations of the camera's vision. Somewhere about 1916 Clausen saw the point of the classical architectural basis on which Seurat and Cézanne were working in 1886; and since then he has produced some figure studies solving formal problems of an architectural kind.[1]

Some new English artists saw the point of Impressionism in the 'nineties. When Harland printed Impressionist sketches in the 'Yellow Book' in 1894, and lashed English Philistines to fury, both the Impressionist and Post-Impressionist battles had already been won in France, Seurat had been dead three years, Van Gogh four, Gauguin was already back from Tahiti, and Cézanne had painted most of his most important works.[2]

The first Post-Impressionist Exhibition in London, representing the experiments made on the new classical basis chosen by Seurat and Cézanne in 1884, was in 1910; and though many people abused the paintings and some praised them *nobody* treated them as what they were—examples of the art produced

[1] This passage must not be interpreted as a *criticism* of Clausen's work as an artist. I am engaged here solely with the relation of Clausen's technique to the modern movement. I do not pretend to have given even a complete historical statement of Clausen's position which would have indicated that though always thirty years behind the advanced original art of his time he has always been thirty years ahead of most of his colleagues in the Academy. I stress this because Clausen's disinterested courage in repeatedly burning his boats is acknowledged and respected by critics of all schools. My point is simply that there has been no justification for considering him 'advanced' at any stage of his career. Cf. 'The value of technique', Part IV.

[2] For Sickert's contacts with French painting cf. 'Sickert' by Lillian Browse and R. H. Wilenski (Faber). [1945 note.] Cf. also the additional chapter in my 'English Painting' 1954 edition. [1956 note.]

in Paris a quarter of a century before. The pictures were both praised and howled at as the very latest thing, though in Paris by 1910 the Cubist movement, which was a development of Post-Impressionism, and the result of a new determination to force it back to its logical foundations, was already launched. There was only one artist in England between 1910 and the 1914–1918 war who saw the point of the contemporary Cubist experiments. That artist was Wyndham Lewis. All other artists in England at that time were either tardy converts to Post-Impressionism or had still completely failed to understand it.[1]

Throughout the nineteenth century, as I have noted earlier, the only genuinely 'advanced' artists in England were the Pre-Raphaelites in the first few years of their movement, and later Whistler who saw the point of Impressionism at the very beginning, who saw its weak spot, and used its methods only in his watercolours and other sketches, and who saw that the path of salvation would be found in a deliberate return to purely architectural formal art which he himself achieved in *Miss Alexander*, *M. Duret* and several other works, contributing thereby almost as much to the modern movement as his contemporaries, the official pioneers in France.[2]

When, therefore, I referred to Sargent's works of the 'nineties as works upon which the first artists of the modern movement turned their backs, I was thinking of the English recruits who joined the movement after 1910. To the French artists who had returned to the modern architectural basis in the 'eighties the techniques of Sargent and all the other pseudo-Impressionists between 1890 and 1920 appeared the backwash of the French Impressionist technique of the 'seventies—which, of course, is exactly what they were. The negative lesson which such works taught had been already learned by the most intelligent artists in France at the beginning of the 'eighties. But in England in 1910, when artists began to take an interest in the technique of the modern movement, Sargent's pictures and those of the yellow and purple snapshot makers who followed him had still a salutary negative technical lesson to teach.

[1] Art historians of the future will find it intriguing to trace the relation of the plates in the Vorticist publications by Lewis (1914) to the work of some English painters of the nineteen fifties, and of his drawings in 'The Enemy' (1927) to that of Graham Sutherland. [1956 note.]

[2] Whistler was not, however, able to escape the influence of the camera. Both the portrait of his mother and the portrait of Carlyle are painted in the photograph's monochromatic range; and there was a good deal of grey-tinting in his use of colour in many other pictures. In his best work, technically speaking, he escaped this pitfall. In the *Girls in White on a Sofa*, for example, and in his blue Nocturnes he escaped it. When he did not escape it his pictures have all turned or are turning to grey blackness. Whistler would have advanced further along the line to architectural composition had he been able to escape more completely from the romantic tradition of a point of focus. In certain of his pictures, notably the two mentioned in the text, he achieved this escape; but in many others he adopted a point of focus, and he always adopted this romantic technique in his etchings. Cf. 'Architectural form', Part III.

I have referred to them for this reason and to stress the point that what the pioneer artists of the modern movement saw around them in France in the 'seventies and 'eighties was in fact much the same kind of thing which the English artists saw around them in 1910, and which I am afraid it must be admitted they still see around them here in England at the present day.

Roughly, then, the art which both groups have abandoned is (*a*) original romantic art, romantic popular art and pseudo-romantic art; (*b*) original descriptive art and descriptive popular art; and (*c*) derivative art of all kinds. They have abandoned all these forms of art in favour of an art based on the classical idea that architecture is the mother of the arts.

Technically speaking, they have abandoned the emotive technique of the original romantics and the various degenerate forms of 'free' emotive handling that derive from it; they have abandoned the daguerreotype 'all-in' naturalism of the Pre-Raphaelites and their imitators which was based on a misconception of the camera's vision; the photographic naturalism of Corot in his middle period and all the other imitations of the camera's true vision, particularly the degraded procedures known as 'drawing by the shadows' and painting 'by the tone values' in tinted greys; and all forms of derivative techniques imitating the particular way of painting of some artists living or dead.

This being, I hope, clear, we can now look at their own attempts to construct a new classical architectural technique.

Part III

TECHNIQUE
OF THE MOVEMENT

A. ARCHITECTURAL FORM

POST-IMPRESSIONISM AND CUBISM

Every original modern artist has, by the fact of his originality, a separate technique. But there are certain general principles which govern such artists' technique and distinguish it from the technique governed by the principles of original romantic or original descriptive art. I have already outlined these general principles in various connections. I must now try to examine them a little further.

I begin with the principles which govern the modern artist's attitude to architectural forms and the relations of such forms, and his creation of architectural pictorial form. Architectural colour, architectural distortion, and the use of perspective are all parts of architectural pictorial form. But for the sake of clarity I have split the inquiry into those separate sections; and I begin with the forms.

A basic idea of the modern movement is, as we have seen, that the business of the architectural artist is fundamentally the same as that of the architect. It is held as a first principle that the artist must be free, as the architect is free, to introduce representational details in his work or not; that representational details are no more a necessary part of a picture or a piece of sculpture than they are a necessary part of a cathedral. It is also held that if the painter or the sculptor decides to introduce such details he must do so by the architect's procedure; that he cannot achieve an architectural construction by degrading his perception to mechanical vision and imitating the momentary appearance of some fragment at some point of time and space. It is held, in other words, that he must not copy fragments in photographically naturalistic technique but must (*a*) reinforce his vision to actual or imagined perception; (*b*) perceive not fragments but formal relations; and (*c*) force his perception to the point of creating a definite organized and complete formal symbol compounded of smaller symbols homogeneous and consistent one with another and with the symbol as a whole. This general principle I have already referred to in 'Naturalism and representation', Parts I and II.

Now what does the modern architectural artist actually do? What is his procedure (*a*) when the enlargement of his formal experience is the result of actual perception; and (*b*) when that enlargement is the result of imagined perception? How does he set to work to make a picture?

Let us take the first case first. Confronted with an arrangement of physical objects and concrete things he separates in his mind firstly his perception of individual forms from his perception of the architectural relations of those forms one to another; he separates, that is, forms from architectural form. Then he separates in his mind his mechanical vision of individual forms in the momentary effect of light before him from his knowledge of the generic character and function of those forms; then he separates that knowledge of the forms from his knowledge of their generic formal relations one to another; then he separates his knowledge of those generic formal relations from his mechanical vision of the effect of these relations in the light and shade of the moment; and then he separates his consciousness of any reactions in himself to emotive fragments from his consciousness of reaction in himself to the architectural relations of forms before him one to another; and so on and so forth.

Confronted, for example, with a cottage, an oak tree, and a sky behind, the artist of this calibre separates in his mind his perception of the individual forms from his perception of the architectural relations of those forms one to another—he separates, that is, the forms from the form. Then he separates in his mind the image mechanically seen by his eye of the lights and shadows on the cottage, the tree, and the sky, from his knowledge that the cottage is a cottage with a bad roof which lets the rain in, that the tree is an oak tree which at a certain season carries acorns, that the sky is one which means that it will probably be fine for at least ten minutes, and so on; then he separates that type of knowledge from the knowledge that the tree is so close to the cottage that it constitutes a danger, and his knowledge that the sky which appears so close to the tree is thousands of miles away; then he separates his knowledge of that kind from his knowledge that one half of the cottage is darker than the other because the sun is behind the tree and the tree is therefore casting a shadow on the cottage and creating a fantastic pattern on the garden path; and then he separates that knowledge from his consciousness of any emotional effect the cottage or tree may have on him because the cottage happens to be his home or because it has an 'old-world' character; and he separates that consciousness from his consciousness that the formal relations he perceives with the appropriate reinforcements to this vision are such as please him and make him want to paint a picture which shall be a symbol of those relations. This general process is repeated in respect of each detail perceived until the artist has arrived by the process at separated perception of the relation of the verticals of the cottage to the roof, of the column of the tree trunk to the dome of the foliage that crowns it, and so on; eventually he has in his mind a series of symbolic fragments which he fits together like a jigsaw puzzle[1] to create a single symbol for his general perception of formal relations which is the subject of his picture.

The process is much simpler in the second case when the artist's perception of formal relations is not actual but imagined, when the artist, that is to say, is not impelled to paint a picture by the perception of formal relations before him in nature but is impelled to paint a picture by formal relations imagined in his mind. The process is simpler because the separations I have indicated are not involved. This difference apart, the procedure in the one case or in the other is the same. The imaginative architectural artist is in fact simply a man who can imagine formal relations to the point of symbolic concrete form, just as the imaginative romantic artist is a man who can imagine unusually emotive fragments to the same point, and the imaginative descriptive artist is a man who can imagine descriptive experience to the same point also.

When a spectator says: 'I do not believe the artist saw it (or perceived it) in that way', he is generally making one of two errors. He is either assuming that the formal relations symbolized are untrue because he has never observed them in nature himself, or he is assuming that the artist was symbolizing some particular formal relations observed in nature when, in fact, his picture symbolizes some formal relations imagined.[2]

As I have indicated in Part I, in the section discussing the architect's procedure, the materials with which the architect or the architectural artist works are proportion, balance, line, recessions and so on—words which stand for perceived or imagined architectural relations of form in space. Having extracted these relations from the scene which he has actually perceived, or perceived in imagination, he sets to work to make a concrete symbol the subject of which is these formal relations (which if he be a painter include of course colour); and since his attitude is architectural his symbol must have a definite architectural character and be composed of parts definitely architectural in themselves, of parts, that is, which have each a definitely architectural character and shape.

This principle was not pressed back to its logical basis by the first artists of the movement who are known as Post-Impressionists. Seurat was the first nineteenth-century artist to attempt a consciously architectural technique to symbolize forms and form.[3] Cézanne only arrived at it after forty years' search for

---

[1] Cézanne, when he was pleased with a piece of work, used to slip the fingers of one hand between the fingers of the other and say: 'I've got it.'

[2] It is, of course, outside my purpose to speculate here on the parts played by memories and other experience in the artist's imagination, as such speculations are the province of the psychologist.

[3] I have discussed Seurat's technique in my Faber Gallery 'Seurat,' 1949. [1950 note.]

the architectural secret. Both Seurat and Cézanne attempted and achieved what might then have been thought the impossible; they contrived to retain representational elements in pictures the subjects of which are as formal as the Parthenon; and it may be that the years which have passed since they died have produced no more perfect solutions of this particular problem. Cézanne arrived at his discovery by studying classical architectural art in the museums and by turning his back on the romantic heresy. He set out to achieve architectural symbols not only for relations of light but also for relations of colours and forms. That is what he meant by his famous declaration that he was trying to make Impressionism a classical art like the art of the old masters.

Van Gogh, who was fundamentally a romantic artist, is a transitional figure in the modern movement. His art was not based on the classical art of Raphael— it was based on the romantic art of the Northern artists, particularly on the art of Rembrandt; and the technique of his art was based on the nineteenth-century romantic tradition of spontaneous emotive handling. In his last years when he painted the chair, his bedroom, and the corner of the street with the bright blue sky, he was beginning to realize the meaning of architectural art. But his main output was romantic.[1]

Gauguin was also a romantic and a transitional figure. He never completely understood the classical principle of architectural representational symbols creating together a single symbol for formal relations. He perceived forms rather than form and perceived them fundamentally in the romantic way. The pattern of his pictures moreover was often to some extent derivative—a superficial imitation of classical compositions, as anyone can realize who thinks away his coloured maidens and tropical foliage and imagines pseudo-classical figures and western foliage to replace them.[2]

Both Van Gogh and Gauguin used sometimes romantic and sometimes architectural technique. But they did nevertheless contribute to the modern movement's attempt to regenerate painting and pictorial technique on the classical architectural basis. Unfortunately their pictures, admirable though they are, have also greatly confused the issue, and impeded progress, since they did not help the world to realize that the art of the twentieth century had been created by Seurat and Cézanne as, first and foremost, a reaction against the romantic heresy of the nineteenth century.

Renoir was another transitional artist. In his later years he began to study

---

[1] The use of colours by Van Gogh and Gauguin is discussed in the next section.
[2] But cf. Addendum to the 1938 edition; also 'The influence of Gauguin' in the 'Preface to the 1956 edition'. [1956 note.]

formal relations; and the monumental grandeur of his latest nudes marked him a convert to the new movement. But here again we have an artist who was really a romantic. In his late work he abandoned the stressing of his nymph's eyes and of the whiteness of their bosoms which characterized his early work. But the charming pictures that made his reputation are fundamentally romantic in kind.

While Van Gogh, Gauguin and Renoir, all artists of great distinction, were at one and the same time subscribing to the new movement and confusing the issue, more and more intelligent young men began to look back again to the pioneer work of Seurat and Cézanne, and to feel the need to press back the architectural concept to its foundations. 'flat-pattern' Cubism and 'mountain-of-bricks' Cubism were the result of this return to the root idea.

The development of flat-pattern Cubism must be considered first. Here we had artists who said to themselves: 'I must approach my problem like an architect. The architect achieves formal harmony without representing physical objects and concrete things, I must do the same. I must make pictures which shall be frankly symbols on a flat surface for formal proportions, harmonies, recessions and so on which I have perceived in nature or which I may be able to perceive in my mind's eye, and I must give my symbols definite architectural shapes.'[1]

That was the idea behind those diagrammatic organizations of superimposed planes which I have called flat-pattern Cubism. If we examine the experiments made on this basis by the most intelligent artists we find extreme ingenuity in symbolizing on a flat surface the 'abstract' material with which the architect works. Recession, for example, was symbolized without the aid of perspective by devices which I shall describe later; for these artists, in their technical reactions against illusionist photographic naturalism, made it a point of honour to refrain from any procedure which conveyed the illusion that any part of the picture was farther from the spectator than the actual canvas. The canvas itself, they argued, must appear to be what it actually is, i.e. the most distant part of the physical contents of the surrounding frame. The picture, therefore, had to be composed of surfaces obviously imposed one over the other; and the architectural relations between those surfaces had to lead the eye back to the canvas but no farther. The artists admitted, as it were, the creation of symbols for recession *forwards* from the canvas but refused to countenance the creation of an illusion of recession from the canvas *backwards* into space.[2]

---

[1] 'The picture is finished as soon as the purely abstract surfaces dividing it are organized.' Lhôte.

[2] Cf. 'Architectural perspective' in this part.

Hence those curious pictures where pieces of coloured paper, buttons and so forth were applied to the surface of the canvas as units in the creation of formal design—pictures which it is indisputable broke entirely fresh ground in pictorial technique.

This stage was followed by an experiment made by certain Cubists who composed their pictures with symbols for formal relations perceived from several points of view. They said to themselves: 'The architect does not stand in one place and make his architectural composition a symbol for a single perception of formal relations; he makes his composition a symbol for a formal order discovered by different perceptions of formal relations experienced at different times and in different places. We are architectural painters; we will do the same.' Hence those architectural compositions where one part of a violin, perceived from the side, is placed in a formal relation to another part of a violin perceived from the front, where half a full-face forms an angle with a profile hat and so on (Pl. 15). The argument in justification was this: 'In the creation of a symbol for formal order on the classical principle the architectural artist's perception of formal relations, i.e. of what we call "form", is more important than his perception of individual forms; he is, therefore, justified in developing his perceptions of formal relations which are essential to his art at the expense of his perception of individual forms which are not essential or not so essential for his purpose.'

Italian Futurism was a perversion of this quite justifiable experiment. For the Italian Futurists were romantic popular, not architectural artists. They composed their pictures with symbols of fragments observed from different points of view. But the subject of their pictures was not the formal relations of such fragments; the subject was the emotive character of the fragments. A Futurist picture was the world as a romantic popular artist saw it while going round and round on a merry-go-round, or travelling in a car.[1] That was obviously an entirely different kind of picture from an architectural composition composed of symbols for formal relations which had been perceived from several points of view *as formal relations* without romantic interest in the fragments which revealed those relations. The public found Futurism easier to understand than the form of Cubism which it perverted, but the more intelligent Cubist artists recognized at the outset that Futurist pictures were romantic popular, and not original architectural art.

The various forms of flat-pattern Cubism were a contribution as a reaction

[1] The world, in fact, as presented to us by the restless cinema and television cameras of to-day (cf. Preface to the 1956 edition). [1956 note.]

144

against illusionist technique resulting from vision unreinforced to perception; they were a contribution also as a means of forcing the architectural idea of art to a root foundation upon which a new classical technique could be constructed; and it is true to say that as a result of those experiments no intelligent artist to-day is wholly uninfluenced by the classical architectural idea of art or wholly blind to the degenerate character of photographic naturalistic illusionist technique.

Cubist technique in the flat-pattern pictures was geometrical in aesthetic. The architectural symbols used were variations of the square, the circle, the triangle, and so forth. From this the artists soon advanced to a technique using the cube, the sphere, the cone, the cylinder and so forth. From pictures composed of ordered formal flatnesses symbolizing actual or imagined perception of formal relations the Cubists proceeded to organize order by means of symbols for three-dimensional forms; they started to build up their pictures with pictorial signs for cubes, spheres, cones and so on, and sections and segments of such three-dimensional forms. The argument here was: 'We seek to perceive formal relations in nature. For the purpose of our architectural task we find ourselves perceiving a tree as a column and the boughs and foliage above it as a segment of a sphere; we find ourselves perceiving a human arm as two cylinders, one beneath the other, and a third cylinder divided into five cylinders (called fingers). It should be possible to create architectural symbols for the relations of forms thus architecturally perceived. Let us try to do it and see what happens.'

Hence, as a first stage, those mountain-of-bricks Cubist pictures where pictorial signs for cubes, spheres, cylinders and cones were combined together into one symbol for some actual or imagined perception of formal relations.[1]

These pictures also served useful purposes; they served to help artists to an architectural perception of a head as a conglomeration of forms all equally important to replace the romantic artist's perception of a head as a setting for emotive eyes or an emotive mouth, or the same kind of artist's perception of an old man's head as essentially a snow-white beard or emotive wrinkles; and they served to help artists to achieve architectural composition rather than romantic composition with a point of focus.

From this first stage of mountain-of-bricks non-representational Cubism the artists turned back once again to Seurat and Cézanne. I have said above that Cézanne contrived to retain representational elements in pictures the subjects of which are as formal as the Parthenon. This is how Cézanne's pictures strike us to-day when we look at them after our experience of flat-pattern and

[1] For the part played in this by Cézanne's famous *dicta* cf. my 'Modern French Painters'. [1945 note.]

mountain-of-bricks Cubist pictures. But to spectators at the time, Cézanne's pictures seemed to be just representational pictures very badly done. For it was assumed that Cézanne was a descriptive artist who had set out to describe the generic character of mountains and trees or of oranges and apples. When the Cubists looked back to Cézanne, after their own experiments, the extent to which he had introduced symbolic representation into the symbol for formal relations which was the subject of his picture, struck them as simply miraculous. With great efforts they had themselves succeeded in creating architectural pictures where such representation was almost or entirely eliminated. Here was a man who had achieved the same thing without sacrificing representation to anything like the same extent.

They set out accordingly to train their own perception to rival Cézanne's achievement which they looked on as more varied and subtle not only than their own non-representational architectural productions but as also more varied and subtle than the productions of Seurat who had forced the architectural concept nearer to its foundation with a better trained intellect but less sensibility than Cézanne.

On this task the artists of the modern movement bent all their efforts; and it is this task upon which many are still engaged to-day.[1]

These artists do not set out to describe, and make, incidentally, a decoration recalling some architectural composition familiar to those familiar with works of art. They do not set out to stress emotive fragments and make settings for their points of focus. They set out to perceive or imagine formal relations and force their perception or imagination to symbolic architectural concrete form; they set out also to perceive or imagine the formal relations one to another of the parts of individual forms and to force that perception or imagination also to the point of symbolic form, all such forms being homogeneous and consistent with one another and with the symbolic architectural structure as a whole; they set out to avoid the austerity of flat Cubism and of mountain-of-bricks Cubism, on the one hand, and romantic and descriptive characters on the other; they are architects, who, incidentally and on occasion, see fit to represent.

B. ARCHITECTURAL COLOUR

In the section discussing 'Human perception' in Part II, I have submitted that our mechanical vision registers relations of colours in so far as they are part

[1] i.e. December 1926. [1956 note.]

of relations of light, and that our mechanical vision also registers individual colours.

The Dutch seventeenth-century painters, as I have also indicated, produced their naturalistic descriptive popular pictures by the use of this mechanical vision of individual colours; while the photographic naturalistic painters of the second half of the nineteenth century, rivalling the camera's vision, atrophied their mechanical vision of individual colours and crushed all colours to tinted greys.

The architectural artists of the modern movement set out to revive and reconstruct the use of colours and relations of colour (which artists call colour) on the classical basis. They are not content to use colours in the Dutch way, still less to atrophy their vision of colour to the 'tone values' level. They are also not concerned with using colours and colour in the way in which they are used by romantic and descriptive artists.

I have already pointed out that original romantic artists use individual colours and colour to stress emotive fragments; and I must now point out that romantic artists sometimes use individual colours as emotive agents producing emotive associated ideas; they use them, that is to say, as part of their emotive technique.[1]

In descriptive art individual colours are either used as emotive individual colours or else purely and simply as agents in description. The Dutch painters gave full rein to their mechanical vision of individual colours. They made the cook's skirt red and her bodice black because they saw red and black as such. The nineteenth-century photographic naturalists atrophied their mechanical vision of individual colours; they tinted the grey paste they used for the cook's skirt with red, and the grey paste they used for her bodice with black as agents in their description of the light and shade effects on the skirt and bodice before them.

Now the architectural artist's perception of individual colours is exactly the same in character as his perception of architectural forms. That is to say, he separates in his mind his perception of colours from his perception of forms; and he then proceeds to perceive relations of the separated colours.

The architectural artist's perception of individual colours is thus a separate process but one which is of necessity a preliminary to a study of their mutual relations; and it is such mutual relations which form the colour-subject of his picture, which is part of its architectural form-subject.

---

[1] In early Christian religious art colours were also frequently used with deliberate reference to their emotive associated ideas.

147

In contrast to this architectural procedure, involving as a necessary condition the study of the mutual relations of separately perceived colours, we have, on the one hand, the romantic artists' procedure where the use of colour-relations is optional and serves only as a setting for stressing an emotive point of focus, and, on the other, the procedure of the descriptive artist, where the use of such relations is again optional and serves only as an agent in the description.

Let us suppose artists of the romantic, descriptive, and architectural characters looking at a young girl's face. The first perceives her lips as an emotive fragment and paints them red to stress that perception; the second perceives her rosy cheeks as a generic character of a healthy face and paints them red as an agent in such description (or if he uses the photographic naturalistic technique he paints them a pinkish grey in his description of colour as part of the accidental light and shade before him); the third perceives the red of the lips as one red and the red of the cheeks as another, and makes in his picture a symbolic equivalent of the relation of the two reds.

We must also remember (a) that in the case of architectural artists the perceived colour-relations are not imitated but symbolized, and they may be, and frequently are, transformed to meet the requirements of the general formal organization of the picture; and (b) that the artist's colour-perception may be actual or imagined.

The spectator who says 'I do not believe that the artist saw (or perceived) the colour in that way' is therefore generally making one of two errors of the same kind as the spectator who makes a similar remark in respect of the forms or form in a picture. He is either assuming that the colour relations set down are untrue because he has never himself observed those relations in nature, or else he is assuming that the artist was symbolizing an actual perception when, in fact, the colour is a symbol for relations which the artist imagined.

The history of the use of colours and colour by the artists of the modern movement is rather curious. Cézanne and Seurat proceeded in the way I have described. But when we get to the transitional artists Van Gogh and Gauguin we find confusion in their use of colour comparable to the other confusions in their work.

Van Gogh I have described as a romantic artist; and he generally used individual colours to achieve romantic stress. But to do this he often used individual colours as agents producing emotive associated ideas. It is clear not only from his work but from his letters that in the mind of Van Gogh light blue was emotive as the colour of the sky, and that yellow was emotive as the colour of the sun; and I believe it is possible that he regularly perceived individual colours as agents producing emotive associated ideas and had the greatest difficulty in achieving architectural perception of relations of colour and creating symbols of such relations in his pictures. Van Gogh's use of colours must be regarded as the extremity of reaction from the photographically naturalistic vision of the 'tone values' painters; as such it was a contribution to the modern movement. But to-day we can recognize that his frequently romantic use of colours and colour obscured the true character of the modern movement at an early and critical stage of its existence.[1]

Gauguin sometimes used individual colours for romantic stress of a point of focus. But he varied this procedure with perception and creation of architectural colour-form relations; sometimes we get the one thing and the other side by side in the same picture.

The use of colours and colour by Renoir was different. In his youth and middle period he disciplined his natural inclination to romantic stress by the use of the architectural spectrum palette. Later, when he threw in his lot with the modern movement he abandoned both procedures. He then concentrated on the creation of monumental architectural form of which his colour subject was a part.

When the keener intellects at the end of the century decided that the Post-Impressionists had confused the issue and began to press back the architectural idea to its root foundation, they subjected the use of colour to the same intransigent process.

The flat-pattern Cubists sometimes made relations of colours the dominant subject of their experiments; and they thus produced some pictures which competed with Western experience of Oriental carpets or with what I presume to be Oriental experience of Scotch plaids.

The mountain-of-bricks Cubists worked mainly in monochrome.

The Cubist experiments made it possible for modern artists to return to Seurat and Cézanne with the typical architectural use of colours, and colour, clearly in their minds. To-day they are in possession of this secret; and avoiding the Scotch plaid on the one hand and romantic and descriptive uses of colours on the other, they use relations of colours as part of their form-subject which, as in all classical architectural art, is always the real subject of their picture.

---

[1] I am speaking, of course, of the work of 1888 and later. He worked through several derivative stages, imitating J. F. Millet and the Impressionists and others, before he became the original artist that we mean when we say 'Van Gogh'.

C. ARCHITECTURAL
AND OTHER DISTORTIONS

There have been five main kinds of distortion in all periods of art: (1) accidental distortion; (2) religious distortion; (3) romantic distortion; (4) descriptive distortion and (5) architectural distortion.

Of these the first, as its name implies, is accidental, and the other four are, and always have been, deliberate and for a definite purpose.

Accidental distortions arise when a descriptive artist is trying to record the generic character of some physical object or concrete thing and describes it inaccurately (*a*) through defective mechanical vision or (*b*) through lack of skill of hand or (*c*) through some subconscious abnormality which he is unable to overcome. The first case can generally be remedied by glasses, and the second by another six months' or another six years' practice; neither is of any consequence to students of art history because the results produced, being accidental, do not enter the domain of art. The third case is more interesting. What I have in mind here is the artist who has an abnormally small head who always draws figures with abnormally small heads, or the artist with abnormally short legs who always draws figures with the same peculiarity. Anyone who has worked at an art school will remember such cases and will also have noticed that there is sometimes a tendency to produce an opposite distortion. Here presumably the distortion is the result of a complex in the artist. Psychologists may be able to explain it, and psycho-analysts may be able to remove it, I am only concerned with the results of the complex which again, being accidental, do not enter the domain of art.

Among deliberate distortions the religious distortions are perhaps the most interesting—as they are certainly the most numerous. Such distortions occur in magic images, in divine images, and even in narrative religious art; and the governing principle, I fancy, is always exaggeration.[1]

In the magic image the artist took some aspect of man, or beast, and exaggerated it. The aspect or part which was to work magically was distorted by exaggeration—it was made, that is to say, as the image-maker perceived it, only

[1] In the Preface and the first chapter of this inquiry I have explained that I have not judged it necessary for my purpose to discuss religious art. But I have found it necessary at one or two points to refer to certain of its characteristics, which I submit tentatively and as suppositions. This is one such point (*cf.* Preface to the 1956 Edition, p. 31 [1956 note]).

more so, in the hope that this exaggeration would make assurance doubly sure. When images were made to scare the devil the distortions were doubtless fundamentally of the same character. All theriomorphic and anthropomorphic magic images, and combinations of the two (as in Egyptian magic art), are distorted on this principle. The artists made the image like certain aspects of beasts or men but *more so*—the 'more so', expressed by deliberate exaggerated distortion, being resorted to in order to make the desired effect more likely to occur.

The same principle obtained in Egyptian funeral carvings which had magic functions connected with the protection of the dead. The full-face eye in profile heads in Egyptian art was possibly given that form because, while man's profile was perceived as most characteristically man, his full-face eye was perceived as most characteristically an eye, and when the full-face eye was distorted in size and shape to a prominent symbol it was felt that evil spirits would recognize the sculpture as *eternally watching* and so a formidable foe. It was the magic function of Egyptian art which accounts for its extreme formality. The little clay figures placed within the tombs had no magic function; they were intended for the convenience of the departed who was supposed to continue his earthly occupations in another world and might have need of servants to help him hunt, fish and so on; as these figures were not expected to do anything but obey the dead man's orders, no distortion for a magic purpose was necessary; and these figures were accordingly without distortions and are realistically modelled.

It is frequently assumed that the Egyptians who drew full-face eyes in profile faces for thousands of years never discovered how to draw an eye in profile. But it is, of course, absurd to suppose that the artists who created the magnificent religious and dynastic arts of Egypt were not intelligent enough to discover the tricks of naturalistic drawing which thousands now learn easily every year in our art schools. All peoples everywhere must soon have attained to a certain power in 'realistically' descriptive drawing and modelling. But they never used it in their magic art. In early religious art, which was always magic, the most original artists available must have been called upon to invent exaggerated distortions which might reasonably be expected to 'work'. When these distortions had apparently worked, they were retained and repeated by magic-religious derivative artists because they had worked and would presumably work again. This is doubtless why the technique of Egyptian magic-religious sculpture remained stationary for so long, though there must have been lots of artists who could draw as 'realistically' as a Dutch painter and model as 'realistically' as a nineteenth-century French sculptor, and who did so when engaged on portraits, caricatures, and illustrations of everyday life.

It may also be observed that in Egyptian *dynastic* art exaggerated distortions were invented as a form of flattery. The majesty, power and pomp of the Pharaohs was symbolized in sculpture which exaggerated and so distorted the figure to suggest superlative majesty, power and pomp. Hence the enormous scale of Egyptian dynastic sculpture and hence also the Great Sphinx, which is a huge head of Pharaoh typifying his great wisdom on the body of a lioness typifying his great courage. The great Pyramids are presumably survivals of a time when a pile of stones was put over a grave to protect the body from jackals. The tombs of the Pharaohs retained the shape of the mound of stones, but the shape was exaggerated and distorted to formalism in order to achieve the magic purpose of greater and more durable protection for a great king's grave. In the celebrated Assyrian Lion Hunt in the British Museum the lions, as everyone knows, are 'realistically' perceived and drawn; but the king is drawn with deliberate formal distortion exaggerating his royal and unruffled calm.

In Greek art we come to divine images, that is to say, to images where the artist has tried to perceive a divine aspect in man and to give that aspect form. The Greek religious artists making symbols for such perception seized on certain aspects of the human form which seemed to them appropriate and exaggerated them. Hence perhaps the familiar Greek distortion of the human nose and brow in the facial type which we habitually speak of as the type of the Greek god.

The Greeks used a modification of their god-distortions for demi-gods; when they were representing mortals in their popular art on vases and so on, they perceived and drew 'realistically' and sometimes they perceived and drew in a romantic way. When they wanted to represent beings who were the opposite of gods, they used distortions which were the exact opposite of their god-distortions; thus satyrs were always given a broken snub nose and a wrinkled brow; and the agitation against Socrates was doubtless made easier by the fact that he looked like the public's familiar experience of the appearance of typically ungodlike men as portrayed in art. In Greek religious art we have, in fact, what we have everywhere, the employment of original artists to invent distortions for a religious end (in this case the creation of the divine image) and the employment of derivative popular artists to copy these distortions when their special character had been passed as satisfactory from the religious point of view; and in Greece at all periods there were also romantic and descriptive popular artists using various forms of 'realistic' techniques—witness the well-known story of the Greek painter whose cherries were so naturalistically copied that they are said to have been pecked at by the birds.

When we get to early Christian divine images the distortions are of a different character; and the ascetic spiritual nature of early Christianity is very evident. The distortions in this religious art, which Watts-Dunton attributed to a crippling of the artist's strength by 'slavery to monkish traditions of asceticism',[1] were the expression of that passionate separation of the flesh from the spirit which was the essence of mediæval religious thought. The early Christian artists seeking to perceive an aspect of man suitable for a divine image thought away the flesh and distorted the human body to make it as uncorporeal as possible.

The early paintings of Christ and the Virgin do not look like men and women because they were not intended to look like men and women; the figures were intended to be spirits, they were not intended to be flesh. Hence those flatnesses and angularities that seemed to Watts-Dunton such pitiful examples of artistic weakness. Russian religious art used such distortions till very recent times. We find them also to this day in those Spanish Madonna images where the Virgin's velvet robe is a flat triangular shape within which no body is enclosed or intended to be thought of as enclosed.[2]

After the invention of divine images original Christian religious artists began to be employed in narrative religious art where distortions in most cases were not called for to the same extent. But even here the sacred figures are often deliberately dehumanized, and later we get El Greco's hysterically saintly saints where the human figure is distorted to make it seem more saintly and divine.[3]

In earlier parts of this inquiry I have indicated the nature of deliberate distortions in original romantic art. Here it is only necessary to add that, when the romantic artist distorts in stressing the emotive aspect of his chosen fragments, this procedure is also habitually a stress by exaggeration.[4]

I have not made references to deliberate distortion in original descriptive art because in that form of art such distortions are relatively rare. But the original descriptive artist seeking to enlarge his experience of the generic character of

---

[1] Cf. pp. 103 and 104.

[2] I am not called upon in this inquiry to discuss the *effects on the spectator* of distortions in various forms of religious art. But I venture to remark in passing that the very formalized distorted flat Madonnas are often regarded as peculiarly sacred by the populace, and often selected for processions. To the reader who is interested in religious art I commend *Religion and Art* by A. Della Seta.

[3] El Greco's religious distortion is worth a study in itself. He had undoubtedly in his mind the notion of the human spirit as a *flame*. He watched autos-da-fé at Toledo. The idea of purification by flame was a madness in the air; and the writhing of the flames round heretics at the stake may have influenced the characteristic writhing line that he used in the distortions of his later work (cf. note on p. 59).

[4] Caricaturists, who are generally original romantic or romantic popular artists, as already noted, always use exaggeration as the basis of their distortions. Cf. my 'English Painting'. [1935 note.]

physical objects and concrete things or his experience of a social-historical or moral kind does sometimes give form to such enlargements by exaggerated distortions in the normal way. Signorelli, for example, gave us not men but flayed anatomical figures in his *Last Judgment* in Orvieto Cathedral; he distorted by removing the top layer and made his anatomically constructed figures 'more so' by this means.

Architectural distortions, the kind used by the original artists of the modern movement, are also sometimes based on the 'more so' principle. The artist here perceives forms and form architecturally. In his architectural perception of a tree-trunk and the boughs and foliage above it he perceives the trunk as a cylinder surmounted by a segment of a sphere, or in some other architectural way; in his architectural perception of a nude man's body he perceives that also as a related series of architectural forms. In creating on the classical principle synoptic symbols for such perceptions in his pictures, he frequently exaggerates such architectural perceptions in architectural distortions which are quite deliberate and serve as elements in the creation of new architectural form. This was the character of the distortions used by the mountain-of-bricks Cubists.

On the other hand, in the reactionary aspect of Post-Cubism (by which I mean the development of the modern movement since the present return to the representational Cubism of Cézanne and Seurat), the character of the distortions, though the same, is much less obvious, because the architectural character of the artist's form-subject is generally very much less pronounced and the artist's perceptions of individual forms are also less evidently architectural in character.

All these types of exaggerated distortions by original artists are thus deliberately evolved for their separate purposes. The non-representational Cubists went still further. They claimed, as we have seen, the architect's right to assemble in one work architectural experience gained by a *series* of architectural perceptions. The distortions of the violins, newspapers, and so forth, shown from several angles, and in separated parts, in flat-pattern Cubism, are thus not exaggerated distortions but distortions which pay little or no regard to the formal structure of individual forms as such. There are those who hold that such drastic transformation of several perceptions into an ordered architectural unity goes beyond any legitimate uses of distortion. Frankly this objection seems to me quite arbitrary. Unless we rule out perception in favour of mechanical vision we must accept human perception as at least as 'true' as mechanical vision. If we once accept perception in this way—and if we do not we rule out all art except art executed in the easy mechanical naturalistic technique—I do not see how we are logically to determine the point beyond which we must forbid the artist to go in reinforcing his vision to perception. The distortions of flat-pattern Cubism are, I admit, without precedent in religious, romantic, descriptive or architectural pictures and sculpture. But they are not without precedent in architecture, as the Cubist artists of this type pointed out; and there can be no doubt that they opened up an unexplored avenue in pictorial design.

In any case it is important to remember (a) that this use of distortion by the flat-pattern Cubists is the only step taken by any artists of the modern movement which is without precedent in architectural painting and sculpture; and that the architectural distortions by the mountain-of-bricks Cubists and by the original modern artists who have since returned to base their art on the pictures by Cézanne and Seurat, are normal exaggerated distortions parallel to the exaggerated distortions by original religious, descriptive and romantic artists of all times and places;[1] and (b) that it is much harder to evolve an exaggerated distortion for the special purposes of any form of art than it is to sit down and copy lights and shadows in the naturalistic technique.[2]

Unless the spectator understands the religious, romantic, descriptive or architectural purpose of such distortions he inevitably finds them disquieting at first glance; and he fails to capture contact with the work's essential character till he has overcome this disquiet. But we must also note here a sixth form of distortion—*distortion intended to record disquiet*, such as we encounter in the works of Hieronymus Bosch. In such cases, of course, the spectator can only gain contact with the work's essential nature if he feels that disquiet at once and retains the feeling on longer contemplation.[3]

D. ARCHITECTURAL PERSPECTIVE

The Cubist artists who pressed back the architectural idea of art to its logical foundation made it a point of honour to avoid illusionist naturalistic painting,

[1] The question of distortions by popular artists has been touched on in 'Romantic popular art', Part I, and 'Degeneration of technique', Part II. There I called attention to the well-known romantic popular distortions on magazine covers and fashionable emotive illustrations cf. Plate 38. In 'Popular Cubism' I shall refer again to derivative popular distortions.

[2] I know this from personal experience, as I have mentioned in the Preface.

[3] I have added this paragraph in this edition because such distortions to record disquiet appear in some works by Neo-Surrealist painters and Romantic-Expressionist sculptors—Giacometti for example (Pl. 28). They also occur in Picasso's Surrealist pictures referred to in the 'Epilogue to the 1935 edition', in his *Frightened women by the sea* (reproduced in my 'Modern French Painters'), in his *Guernica* and the terribly distressing series of *Weeping women* that went with it, in the protests against Hitler's war referred to in the 'Preface to the 1956 Edition' and in *Boy and Birds* (Pl. 47). For my views on the work of Hieronymus Bosch cf. my 'Bosch' in the Faber Gallery series. [1956 note.]

and when they reached rock bottom they refused, as we have seen, to admit any suggestion of recession behind the physical flatness of the canvas. In other words they refused to use illusionist perspective. The 'correct' use of perspective was held in the nineteenth century to be a merit in itself, though it was only one element in a particular technique. By the eighteenth century, or earlier, an optical instrument had been invented by means of which the artist saw the scene before him reflected in perspective on his paper. Canaletto is said to have used it; and an instrument doing the same thing is sold by artists' colourmen to this day. 'Correct' perspective can therefore be quite mechanically used. Moreover the elementary perspective used by artists is very easy to learn, and 'correct' perspective can therefore be quite easily used without an instrument. The laws of perspective, after all, are only the systematization of human mechanical vision. The artist needs no reinforcements to his vision to see his grandmother as a pigmy at the bottom of the garden and as apparently a quarter the size of a child of four by the window; but he has to call up reinforcements to counteract this mechanical vision by his knowledge of the real relative sizes of the figures.

On this foundation the Cubists started to experiment with methods of suggesting recession without the aid of this science which had first been used as an architectural element in Italian renaissance architectural art and had eventually become a mere agent in naturalistic illusionist technique.

The first experiments were made by the flat-pattern Cubists, who were responsible for the ingenious idea of suggesting recession by arbitrary variation of the colour and tone of a flat plane in order to suggest different distances between that plane and various planes before it. Thus a flat-pattern Cubist would put a space of red and across that a space of black; across the two he would write 'Le Journal' or some other letters. The colour and tone of the different letters would be devised in order to suggest that the red space was much farther away than the black space. The letters LEJOU against the black might be dark grey and the last letters RNAL against the red might be black or white; as the contrast between the grey letters LEJOU and the black space behind was less violent than the contrast between the black or white letters RNAL and the red space behind them, the distance between the letters LEJOU and the plane behind appeared to be less than the distance between the letters RNAL and the planes behind them.

The violin bow in the picture by Gris which I reproduce (Pl. 15) is used in this way to suggest varying recession in the various forms behind it, and the page of music in its turn does the same thing. Gris, moreover, it should be noted, in his picture has made use of cast shadows in some places to suggest recession—a procedure regarded as unclassical by pure Cubist doctrine. But in his use of cast shadows in this picture the artist has avoided naturalism since his violin seen from two angles also casts shadows caused by different angles of light.

A less radical use of this system can be found in paintings by Cézanne who deliberately avoided stereoscopic realism in his landscapes and suggested recession by varying the colour and tone of each object to stress its relation to the objects on every hand. Thus a white wall of a cottage by Cézanne is made dark at the edge against lighter forms beyond and becomes lighter and lighter till it reaches the roof the edge of which is dark; and against the ground Cézanne's white wall is again dark. These variations in the several parts of the flat wall were not seen by the artist in the particular effect of light and shade before him at the moment. The wall was probably mechanically seen as a blaze of uniformly white colour. But the artist made the variations in order that his painting of the wall at every point should state clearly his perception of the wall's formal relation to each and all the surrounding forms, and not merely state his mechanical vision of the wall's momentary effect in some particular light.

The flat-pattern Cubists in their system of perspective, where the variations of the upper or nearer forms created the recessions in the forms which were below or farther back, were thus merely pressing back Cézanne's methods to their architectural foundation; and they also imposed upon themselves the arbitrary limitation which forbade the suggestion of a recession farther from the spectator than the physical plane of the canvas itself; by which limitation they went further on Cézanne's path than Cézanne himself had presumably thought wise or possible.

This experiment, which was of great assistance to the new architectural artists in their study of formal relations, was followed by others.

'Our art', it was now argued, 'is an organization of our perception. It is not a record of our mechanical vision. Why should we use this science of perspective which is merely a formulation of our mechanical vision into rules? Why should an artist say in a picture that one of his figures is six feet high and another only two when he *knows* that all men are approximately the same height? Why should we say in a picture that railway lines join together half a mile away when we *know* that if they did no train could move a yard? Why should we continue to tell these stupid lies? Let us look instead at the pictures by artists of the Orient, at Byzantine mosaics, at the works of Duccio and Lorenzo Monaco and the other primitives who were not led by perspective to these perversions of the truth.

157

Uccello sat up all night working out problems of perspective and Donatello told him that he was deserting the substance for the shadow. Donatello was obviously right from the classical standpoint to which we have now returned. We will not desert the substance for the shadow. We will not paint railway lines converging as they appear to our mechanical vision. We will paint them parallel as our perception, reinforced by knowledge, tells us that they really are.'

This argument, for what it is worth, is of course unanswerable; and the Cubist pictures produced on this principle were also of great assistance in the modern reconstruction of classical art.

The mountain-of-bricks Cubists went yet a step further. Reacting against illusionist perspective they made apparently converging lines run outwards if the organization of the lines and forms in the plan of their picture was assisted by lines running outwards in some particular place; and they then proceeded to unite this experiment with the flat-pattern Cubist notion of the artist's right to create form from a series of formal perceptions; and those pictures where table-tops perceived from above are set on legs perceived from some other angle were the result of this particular architectural experiment.[1]

Finally we get to Giorgio Chirico, who recognized that the lines used in 'correct' perspective have both architectural and psychological significance. From the middle of the Renaissance to the end of the nineteenth century the possibility of anything but a purely illusionist use of perspective had been forgotten. The modern artists for that reason first turned their backs on perspective altogether; they then invented new ways of suggesting recession, and finally, led by Chirico, they have tried to force perspective back to its proper rôle of a technical expedient which the artist is free to use in an emotive or any other manner or to ignore as he may please.[2]

E. THE POSITION TO-DAY[3]

The technical history of the modern movement can therefore be summarized as follows: The movement was founded by two artists, Cézanne and Seurat, who rescued painting from the technical degeneration of the nineteenth century

---

[1] I am not suggesting that there was a precise chronological sequence in these experiments; in point of fact, of course, they overlapped. But it is convenient for exposition to describe them in this way.

[2] Cf. Epilogue to the 1935 Edition p. 47.   [3] December 1926.

by concentrating on the creation of architectural symbols for formal relations actually or imaginatively perceived. Then came the period of the Cubist investigation of the foundation of the architectural idea of art and of the architectural conception of technique. It was then recognized that both Van Gogh and Gauguin had failed to find the main path and had obscured the issue by reason of their romantic bias and their neurotic maladies; but that Cézanne and Seurat had themselves advanced a long distance along that path which later experiments had proved to be so fruitful and still, relatively speaking, so unexplored.

Matisse and Picasso have explored this path further. The technique of Matisse is calligraphic. His representational style is composed of calligraphic symbols resembling in character the calligraphic symbols of Oriental painting. This type of handling is always as conspicuous in a picture as the emotive handling of the romantics. The romantic's emotive handling talks about the artist—his verve, his energy, his nevrosity, and so on, as I have indicated earlier. The calligraphic artist's technique talks about the symbolic nature of the presentation. Matisse's calligraphy (which includes a stylistic handling of spaces of pigments and spots of pigment as well as of lines) is obviously a symbolic language just as Michelangelo's calligraphy was a symbolic language; but the imitators of Matisse mistake his calligraphy for emotive romantic handling, which it is not.

Incidentally, it may be noted that Matisse, as an architectural artist, relies mainly on an extremely nice adjustment of relative scale. The size of every symbol in a characteristic picture by this artist is determined by its architectural relations to the other symbols in the picture. If Matisse enlarges eyes he does not enlarge them as a romantic painter enlarges them, in order to make them an emotive point of focus, he enlarges them because two ovals of this particular size are the formal requirements in this particular part of this particular picture. Rousseau le Douanier made this same adjustment of relative scale his main architectural preoccupation. The little front dog in his *Old Juniet's Cart* (Pl. 39) determines the scale for all the physical objects and concrete things perceived as material for this picture; if the dog is covered over, the cart and pony, the people, the trees and the sky shrink to half their size at once, the stretch of ground back to the distant trees on the right is much restricted, and the whole sense of infinity, the sense that is, of everything being a part of a universe that continues beyond the four sides of the picture, immediately disappears. In the same way, if Matisse paints a girl in a plaid overcoat the size of the squares will not be determined by the squares on the actual coat before him but will be

159

determined by the relation of the squares to the oval of the face, to the form of the hat, and to the other architectural symbols in the picture.[1]

Picasso after an early romantic period and his period of austere 'abstract' architectural experiment, set himself the problem of building a new monumental classical art. The technique in these works is neither romantic-emotive nor calligraphic. Picasso tries here to be supremely impersonal (Pl. 22). In a self-conscious age this artist has been able to forget himself in architectural tasks. His influence has been enormous; and imitations of his achievements are legion.[2]

The three great original artists so far produced by the movement are thus Cézanne, Seurat and Picasso. The other outstanding painters are on a different plane. Derain is temperamentally a romantic. Segonzac strikes me as temperamentally an eighteenth-century artist led to a rather brutal handling of pigment in his architecturally constructed pictures by a desire to overcome a natural perception of grace and prettiness.

Maillol in sculpture has made a contribution. Technical flourishes and emotive handling are excluded from his architectural art. Like Picasso he has captured the true secret of classical architectural art. This secret has also been captured in sculpture by Brancusi, who, metaphysically speaking, is a realist while Maillol is an idealist. Brancusi believes that the formal order with which he seeks to attain contact is inseparable from the physical stone or metal upon which he is working; and this deep-seated respect for his material determines throughout the character of his supremely classical and architectural art.

Both France and England have produced original romantic and descriptive artists in recent years as well as the original architectural artists of the modern movement. For the purposes of this inquiry there is, however, no need to refer to such artists in France except to remind the reader that Rouault and Rouveyre are original romantics, as exceptional among the vast host of derivative popular and other popular French artists as the original architectural French artists are exceptional in another way.

In England, John and Epstein (Pl. 25), as I have indicated earlier, are original romantic artists, both of whom have tried their hand at architectural art. John made his effort in his large *Galway* decoration in the Tate Gallery, which has romantic details but is a magnificent beginning for an architectural picture;

---

[1] Cf. 'Epilogue to the 1935 edition', 'Addendum to the 1938 edition' and my 'Modern French Painters' (Index, 'Matisse'). [1945 note.]

[2] Cf. 'Epilogue to the 1935 edition', 'Addendum to the 1938 edition' and my 'Modern French Painters' (Index, 'Picasso'). [1945 note.]

39. Rousseau le Douanier: *Old Juniet's Cart*

40. Matisse: *Interior*

41. Gauguin: *The White Horse*

42. Matisse: *Etretat: Women on the Shore*

43. Ivon Hitchens: *Blue Shadows*

45. Chirico: *Horses by the Sea*

44. Cecil Collins: *Evening*

46. Paul Nash: *November Moon*

47. Picasso: *Boy and Birds*

48. Patrick Heron: *The Round Table*   49. Patrick Heron: *Balcony Window
with Black Fish*

50. Patrick Heron: *Night Still Life*

51. Frederick McWilliam: *Kneeling Figure*

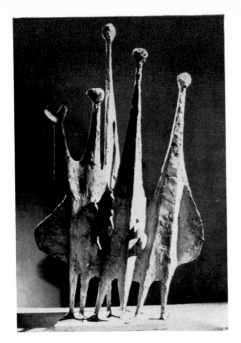

52. Kenneth Armitage: *People
in a Wind*   53. Kenneth Armitage: *People
in a Wind*

54. Alan Reynolds: *Seeding in Winter*

55. Frederick McWilliam: *Father and Daughter*

56. Victor Pasmore: *Spiral motif in Black and White (Snowstorm)*

57. Ben Nicholson: *March*

58. Pierre Soulages: *Peinture: 23 Mai* 1953

59. W. Barns Graham: *Green Moon and Lilac*

60. William Gear: *Duet*

61. Henry Moore: *Family Group*

62. Merlyn Evans: *Recumbent forms in an Interior*

63. Bernard Meadows: *Black Crab*   64. Bernard Meadows: *Crab*

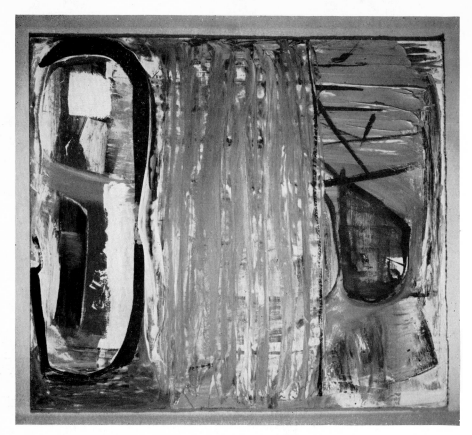

66. Peter Lanyon: *Tide Race*

65. Douglas Hamilton Fraser: *Beach*

Epstein made his architectural effort in his carvings: the *Wilde Memorial*, the *Doves*, *Rima* and so forth.[1]

Round these two original romantic artists in England there are others of less eminence; and the usual horde of romantic popular performers.

It must also be noted that in England the war produced a number of original descriptive pictures. I have referred earlier to the extraordinary difficulty of original descriptive art since specialists and machines have usurped so much of the material with which the descriptive artists work. In the case of the young artists, who went through the ordeal, the war provided a great enlargement of moral experience. Paul Nash, William Roberts, Nevinson, Stanley Spencer and Eric Kennington all produced works of original descriptive art symbolic of their enlarged moral experience in the war. These artists, or some of them, evolved for their works a representational technique based on their own earlier experiments in the architectural art of the modern movement which they had been studying before they went into the trenches. Their earlier experiments thus helped them to give form to the enlargement of their experience. But the character of their technique was merely incidental—as always in original descriptive art. The works in character were not basically architectural; they were original and descriptive, and perhaps the only original descriptive art of modern times. I refer particularly to Paul Nash's war landscapes (Pl. 12), Roberts' *Gas Attack*, Nevinson's hospital picture, Spencer's *Unveiling a War Memorial at Cookham* (Pl. 13) and other works, and Kennington's *Kensingtons at Laventie* (Pl. 11), his Canadian War Memorial painting and his Twenty-fourth Division memorial in Battersea Park. Wyndham Lewis, whom I have already instanced as the first artist to understand Cubism in England, even immediately after the experience of war-service remained a classical artist concerned fundamentally with architectural form; though before that his art had had romantic moments.

Since the war Stanley Spencer has consistently developed his splendid original powers; Kennington has turned to the carving of large symbolic sculpture; and Paul Nash has resumed his study of architectural form (Pl. 6) and is now, in my view, the leading, because the most subtle, artist of the modern movement in this country. Among the other architectural painters here in England are Mark Gertler (Pl. 8), Edward Wadsworth (Pl. 4), and Keith Baynes (Pl. 10).[2]

---

[1] Cf. my 'The Meaning of Modern Sculpture' (Index, 'Epstein'). [1935 note.]

[2] Duncan Grant, Roger Fry, and their followers paint with architectural purpose. Grant sometimes uses romantic-emotive technique, and in some of his recent works seems to me to have failed in separating perception of formal relations from vision of momentary light and shade. But whether this mixed quality must be ascribed to the power of the genius to 'get away' with inconsistencies, or to some confusion, I am not required to say.

The most original architectural sculptor so far produced by the modern movement in England was Gaudier Brzeska who was killed in the war. Leon Underwood is a creative and imaginative personality. Frank Dobson (Pl. 33) is working at present in the path opened up by Maillol.[1]

To-day in England we have thus a few original architectural artists, a few working with original architectural purpose but handicapped by confusions, and a few original descriptive artists; and we have thousands of romantic popular, descriptive popular, and derivative popular artists of all kinds, using various derivative techniques, including all the degenerate romantic and degenerate descriptive techniques of the nineteenth century.

This, as I have said earlier, is inevitable, because it is easier to remain within one's architectural, romantic, or descriptive experience than to enlarge it, and because it is easier to work in naturalistic or derivative technique than to invent a technique to symbolize any kind of enlargement of experience.[2]

F. POPULAR CUBISM

Commenting on derivative art in various earlier sections of this inquiry I have pointed out that after a certain period the public becomes familiar with original art, and that then derivative popular artists always appear and reap a harvest by imitating the original art which has become familiar.

This has already happened to the original artists of the modern movement. Imitations of their work are to be seen on every hand. These rank, of course, with derivative popular art of other kinds because the men who produce them set out either to imitate like apes as a pastime or to achieve contact with the public's familiar experience of this kind of art.

Imitations of original Post-Impressionist, Cubist, and Post-Cubist art are not confined to actual works of painting and sculpture; they are seen in contemporary interior decoration, in posters, clothes, theatrical designs, in advertisements in newspapers and, of course, in architecture itself.

Derivative popular artists in these fields have mostly remained at a stage when they imitate Van Gogh's romantic use of individual colours, but a few

[1] Henry Moore is not mentioned because his first exhibition was not till February 1928, a year after this book was first published. My illustrated article on his work in *Apollo*, December 1930, aroused a long controversy in the *Morning Post*, 13 December 1930–16 January 1931. Cf. also my 'The Meaning of Modern Sculpture', 1932, *passim*. [1945 note.]

[2] The 'Preface to the 1956 Edition' (pp. 15–43) is designed as a brief conspectus of developments since this section was written in 1926. [1956 note.]

have advanced to imitations of the original modern artists' architectural use of colour-relations. The 'jazz' curtains and sunshades, the vermilion shoes and jade hats, and the prevalence of bright tints in the theatre and on the hoardings are all the work of derivative popular artists imitating original art produced by painters who were reacting against the colourless 'tone-values' pictures by the nineteenth-century photographic naturalists.

It is worth noting incidentally that whereas the most 'artistic' London shop twenty years ago (1906) was a place which specialized in olive-green and grey velvets which 'artistic' young ladies made up into dresses with square-cut yokes, the most 'artistic' emporium of to-day, actuated by the same kind of derivative pseudo-artistic notions, specializes in vermilion chairs and emerald green beds.

In all this Diaghileff's Russian Ballet played a part. But the Russian Ballet was the work not of derivative popular but of original artists. It was part and parcel of the modern movement. The pictorial aspect of the ballets it has produced (which is the only aspect within the scope of this inquiry) shows a progression from the romantic-emotive use of individual colours by Bakst to classical architectural colour creations by Picasso.

The pseudo-Cubist use of colour by derivative popular artists to-day is paralleled by their pseudo-Cubist methods in respect to form. The work of the original Cubist is imitated on all sides in decorative objects; and we are all familiar with war memorials imitated from the original mountain-of-bricks Cubist pictures.

The treatment of forms in original Cubist pictures is also imitated by derivative popular painters and designers of advertisements. What such artists do is this: they make a photographic naturalistic drawing 'by the shadows' (or get the same result by an enlarged photograph); they then make the *shadows* into triangles and other geometrical forms. This procedure, of course, is simply a degenerate parody of the difficult procedures of architectural perception and imagination; and the artist who resorts to it is always either muddle-headed or frankly venal and out to make money by disguising photographic naturalism as original architectural art.[1]

Between the photographic naturalistic posters of the nineteenth century and the pseudo-architectural brightly-coloured posters of our own day we have had (and still have) derivative popular posters in the yellow-for-the-lights-and-purple-for-the-shadows technique of the derivative popular pseudo-impres-

[1] McKnight Kauffer must not be confused with such performers. He is an original artist of the modern movement who happens to design posters.

sionist painters. Such posters are generally produced as follows: The artist photographs his subject in sunlight; he gets the print enlarged and bleached; he then puts yellow on the light parts and purple on the dark parts of the bleached print; he then adds a little pseudo-spontaneous splodging imitating the derivative romantic popular painter's imitation of original romantic emotive handling—and the thing is done.

Part IV

RELATIVE VALUES

A. CRITERIONS OF VALUE

In the first part of this inquiry I have considered the *character* of certain categories of art. In this part I shall try to examine their respective *values*.

In the preceding sections I have tried throughout to keep separated in my mind the notion of a value in works of art arising from the artist's attitude, motives and procedure and the notion of a value arising from the work's contact with a spectator arriving on the scene when it is finished.[1]

But to keep these notions of value distinct is extremely difficult. Few æstheticians or art critics have ever succeeded in doing it. To-day there are even some critics who deliberately refuse to make the attempt, and regard their own reactions to works of art as so important that no other criterion of value for a picture appears to them justifiable or even necessary.

Mr. Clive Bell's writings constitute a contemporary example of this egotistical method of approaching works of art. Mr. Bell postulates in himself, and people like himself, a special capacity for reacting to plastic art. Such people, he tells us, when confronted with a work of plastic art, experience an emotion of an exceptional kind. This emotion he calls the æsthetic emotion, and he describes it as a 'passionate emotion', an 'intense rapture', a 'superhuman ecstasy', which transports the spectator to 'superb peaks of æsthetic exaltation'.

This reaction Mr. Bell sets up as the criterion of value of the works contemplated. If this thrilling emotion arises, then the work contemplated can be classed as 'art'; if it does not, the work contemplated is not 'art' but something else.[2]

Most people, I fancy, analysing their own reactions to plastic art, will be disposed to accuse Mr. Bell of hyperbolic statement. But it may, of course, be true that Mr. Bell reacts in this hysterical way to pictures and sculpture. In that case, as I shall try to show, his reactions give an acquired value to the works he contemplates; but they cannot be accepted as a criterion of any original work's *intrinsic* worth.

[1] I have, so far, avoided references to the *effects* oi any kind of work of art on myself or any other spectator. I have made references, in two notes, to the effects of photographs, where I pointed out that we have to reinforce and correct the camera's records by associated ideas. I have also made references to the effects of Sargent's pictures. But I have tried as far as possible up to this point to leave the spectator's reactions entirely on one side. This part of my inquiry is, however, partly devoted to their consideration.

[2] 'I have no right to consider anything a work of art to which I cannot react emotionally; and I have no right to look for the essential quality in anything that I have not felt to be a work of art' (Clive Bell, *Art*).

For if we accept the aesthete's emotional reaction as the criterion of value of original art, we are led to the absurd conclusion that a great work of art is valueless if it happens to be produced in a society so poor in aesthetes that nobody reacts to it; and to the equally absurd conclusion that a work of art has a high value if aesthetic spectators chance to see it on a day when they are capable of a high degree of ecstasy, and a low value if they see it on a day when their receptivity happens to be below the mark. For it can, I think, be taken for granted that the degree of the aesthete's receptivity, like that of all other spectators, is a variable quantity affected by temporary and accidental factors of physiological and other kinds. It must also be observed that the aesthetic spectator who assumes that his own reactions are the criterion of a work of art's intrinsic value is generally led to assume also that the activity which produces the works to which he reacts must be an activity similar in character to his own reactions. Thus Mr. Clive Bell, who tells us that he experiences 'superhuman ecstasy' when he contemplates formal architectural art, tells us also that the artist's business is 'the translation into material form of something that he felt in a spasm of ecstasy', a description which might be accepted (with allowances made for Mr. Bell's hyperbolical vocabulary) if he were speaking of the original romantic artist's activity, but which as a description of the way architecture, architectural painting and architectural sculpture come into being is exceedingly misleading. This description has been responsible, I fancy, for a degree of confusion between the romantic and architectural standpoints in the minds of certain artists on whom, for good or evil, Mr. Bell's writings have had an influence; it has also been responsible for a great deal of confusion in the mind of the public which is led by Mr. Bell's description of the modern artist's activity to assume that the movement is a species of hysterical romantic art which, as I have tried throughout this inquiry to demonstrate, is just what it is not.

But it is not only the *aesthetic* spectator's reactions to works of art which cannot be taken as the criterion of their intrinsic value. *In my view no reactions on the part of any spectator can be held to be the criterion of such value.* For the character of the spectator's reactions varies with each individual, and each spectator's degree of receptivity also varies at different times. It must also be remembered that a work of plastic art (the only kind of art with which we are here concerned) is a concrete object. Its own physical appearance is subject to variation. In the case of architecture and sculpture that physical appearance varies obviously in different effects of light; it also varies as the spectator moves about. In the case of pictures both types of variation also occur, though not to quite the same extent. To assess a work of art's intrinsic value by the incidence or non-incidence of some particular reaction on the part of the spectator is thus to assess it in fact by a gauge that varies continually in a number of different ways, both when the spectator is the ordinary plain man and when he makes a claim to some special aesthetic capacity for reacting emotionally to works of art.

The theory of values which I am about to submit postulates:

(*a*) that a work of original art of the architectural, romantic or descriptive kind has intrinsic value implicit in the attitude, motives and procedure of the man who made it and in that man's perfect fulfilment of his initial purpose of enlarging his experience in the work;

(*b*) that the original artist produces his work without reference to its effects on spectators (other than himself);

(*c*) that spectators (other than the artist) who arrive on the scene when an original work of art is finished, cannot affect the work's intrinsic value by their reactions towards it though they can give it another kind of value which can be described as an 'acquired' value.

This theory, which may sound paradoxical to the average egotistical spectator, is a truism for the original artist.[1]

No original artist will admit that the criterion of value of his work is the incidence or non-incidence of any special reaction on the part of spectators other than himself, and in this I am convinced the original artist is quite right.

The original artist admits that the *acquired* value of his work must be assessed by its effects upon spectators. But he refuses and rightly refuses to confuse such acquired value with the intrinsic value of his work which he knows to be established for all time the moment the work is finished. From the point of view of the original artist nothing happening after such a work is finished, like the arrival of a spectator at an exhibition, can possibly detract from its intrinsic value, alter it or contribute to it further value *of that kind*. If the spectator ignores the work or dislikes it, nothing has happened. If he likes it he contributes the value of his interest or appreciation or the value of his aesthetic thrills; but that is an *acquired* value, and no quantity of acquired value can affect the intrinsic value of an original work of art.

---

[1] But it is not a truism for the popular artist. This is the real basis of the inveterate hostility between original and popular artists, which breaks out into open warfare when an episode like the *Rima* controversy provides the occasion. Original artists regard popular artists as traitors and popular artists regard original artists as 'too impossibly highbrow for this world'. Artists who have been original in their youth and have crossed the Rubicon to the popular side in middle age are generally peculiarly bitter opponents of new adherents in the younger generation to the faith which they themselves have abandoned.

The criterion of the intrinsic value of original art which I submit in place of the spectator's variable reactions is simply *the comprehension of the artist's purpose and the extent of its fulfilment*. The intrinsic value, as I have said, I believe to be implicit in the artist's attitude, motives and procedure and equally in the original artist's perfect fulfilment of his initial purpose of enlarging his experience in his work. To assess that value we must be able to comprehend it. We can achieve this by intuition or by knowledge. We may fail to achieve it; in the case of a great work of original art we are indeed almost bound so to fail until we have seen it many times, and to fail even then without the aid provided by knowledge of the artist's life, historical position and artistic creed. But we must not argue from such failure that there is no intrinsic value to be discovered in original art; or that, because the task of discovering it is difficult, we must therefore abandon it and assume that the work's value consists only in the other kind of value which it acquires from contact with our own reactions towards it.

B. THE ARTIST AS SPECTATOR

It follows from the foregoing that theoretically the man most competent to assess the intrinsic value of an original work of art is the artist who made it.[1]

Writers on aesthetic and art critics seem habitually to forget that the artist is necessarily a spectator of his own work; that he is the only spectator whose judgment can cause alterations in his work's character; and that if he is an original artist he is an essential spectator and the only spectator who can, and in fact does, change his work's intrinsic value by his activities as spectator.

This applies equally to original architectural, romantic and descriptive artists. Every original artist as spectator has to discover (*a*) whether the initial impulse of his work was, in fact, an enlargement of his architectural, romantic or descriptive experience; (*b*) whether the work is, in fact, a perfect concrete symbol of that enlargement.

---

[1] Original artists frequently look with indifference on work done a year or two ago. But this habit does not invalidate the theory I submit in these sections. The crucial moment when the intrinsic value of the work is decided by the honest-competent artist-spectator is the moment when he passes it as 'right' and therefore 'finished'. When he progresses to fresh experience in a year's time naturally the achieved symbol of his earlier experience interests him less than the yet-to-be-achieved symbol of his new experience. When the artist says that the work he did last year is 'no good' he does not mean that it was once good, and has now ceased to be so, but that it has ceased to interest him.

The greatness of great original artists consists to a large extent in their capacity to play the honest and competent spectator to their own work. Many original artists fail because they are incompetent or dishonest as artist-spectators of their own work. There are, in fact, three types of artist-spectator: (1) the honest and competent; (2) the dishonest; and (3) the honest but incompetent.

Let us look attentively at the original artist as spectator of his own work and begin by an examination of the original architectural artist confronted with this task.

C. THE ORIGINAL ARCHITECTURAL ARTIST-SPECTATOR

I. THE HONEST COMPETENT ARTIST-SPECTATOR

The original architectural artist—be he architect, sculptor, potter or painter producing work analogous to architecture—is, as we have seen, a man engaged in enlarging his experience of formal relations and in crystallizing that enlargement in the concrete form of a building, picture, carving or pot. In other words, the task of such an artist is to communicate his enlarged architectural experience in finite form to himself. The artist *qua* architectural-experiencing man communicates the new experience to himself *qua* spectator-man.

As I have indicated earlier, his activity is a triple enlargement of experience because the execution of every original work, as every original artist knows, is of necessity an enlargement of his technical experience, and between that technical enlargement and the initial enlargement of architectural experience there is a mental synthesis inventing a symbolic language of communication which is also an enlargement, because precision of experience is a form of enlargement in itself.

Such an artist will not begin a piece of work unless this triple enlargement of experience is its real subject and motive. Once he has started, his task is to play the spectator to his work's progress stage by stage. This can be achieved because the artist is a human being. As such he habitually goes to bed. When he comes down next morning he is a human spectator of the work he did the day before.

If, as honest artist-spectator, he perceives that the work he did the day before is, in fact, a concrete symbolic equivalent of his initial enlargement of architectural experience, it is his obvious duty to call it 'right' and to add nothing to it. If he perceives that it does not communicate to him what he intended it to communicate, it is his task to discover where the work fails and to make the necessary additions, subtractions, adjustments, or possibly to proceed to a necessary destruction or to begin again. If he is unable to decide whether the work is right or wrong it is his duty to leave the thing till the next day or the next year or for whatever time may be necessary to enable him to judge it.

If the work fails to satisfy his scrutiny it is, of course, a most delicate and difficult business for the artist-spectator to discover the cause of the trouble; for the leak in the vessel may be in any of the three constituent processes.

It may be, for example, that the initial perception, actual or imagined, which first prompted the work was not really an enlargement of experience or was not really of an architectural character. Or it may be that the initial perception has been forgotten in the later processes, for, as we all know, there are artists—mentally incapable of retaining enlargement of experience—who make valuable sketches but fail in all attempts at elaborate completed work. Or it may be that the synthetic language of communication used is inadequate or unsuitable or that the artist has not invented this but taken it over from some other artist and thus crushed his original experience in a popular mould. Or it may be that the manual execution, is inadequate, unsuitable or derived.

The original architectural artist who is honest and competent as spectator of his own work is (*a*) a man who knows when he is enlarging his experience and when he is merely jaunting comfortably within it; (*b*) a man who knows exactly the difference between architectural experience and experience of other kinds and can pull himself up if through some momentary confusion he has embarked on a work in one way and continued it in another; (*c*) a man who can retain initial architectural experience in his mind for any period that may be necessary for the perfect completion of the work; (*d*) a man who—if he discovers that his initial experience was not in fact an enlargement or was non-architectural in character or that he has forgotten it, has the courage to destroy his work as valueless the moment he has made the discovery; (*e*) a man who can analyse the synthetic language he has invented as a symbolic precision of his initial experience and discover if it is appropriate or not; (*f*) a man who—if he discovers that his language is inappropriate because it is a formula taken from some other artist living or dead or that it is inappropriate from some other cause—has the courage to invent another for his purpose, or destroy the work; (*g*) a man who can discover when and where and why his hand has failed him and has the courage to do the whole or part of the work again or destroy it for that reason.

Such an artist-spectator's task is indeed difficult. But it is essential. For it is only when such an artist has analysed what it was he set out to communicate to himself and the extent to which his concrete work communicates it, and when he has had the moral courage to call his work obstinately 'wrong' and 'unfinished' until he knows it to be really 'right' and so 'finished' that he has produced a perfect work of original architectural art.

In the case of art of this calibre the artist's honest and correct judgment as spectator constitutes, I submit, not only theoretically but in fact the fundamental criterion of the work's intrinsic value. If the work fails to satisfy that judgment it is a horse which has failed at the first fence. If the artist judges his work right, and rightly judges it right, then it has an intrinsic value that can neither be destroyed nor altered by any reaction towards it on the part of any other spectator at any time or place.

II. THE DISHONEST ARTIST-SPECTATOR

Every original architectural artist knows the temptations to shirk his duty as spectator of his own work. For example:

(a) When, surveying his work, he recognizes that his initial motive was not in fact an enlargement of his experience but merely an excursion within experience already won, stolen or received as a gift, such an artist is frequently tempted to throw bad labour after bad and to go on with his work because it contains some fragments that are individually well done or because he has been persuaded by some foolish friends that the work is too good to be thrown away. In such cases, knowing in his mind that the work, from the character of the initial impulse, is not original but popular in kind, he often endeavours to give it 'originality' by some novelty in handling or technique. All such devices are dishonest and of no avail. For if the artist's initial attitude was popular, if, in truth, he set out either for a jaunt within his own experience or remained for venal motives at the outset within what he knew to be the familiar experience of other people, then no parade of a novel or personal handling, no invention of a new way of painting in spots or dashes or what not, can make his work original or give it the particular character of original architectural art where the synthetic language is really the symbol of the enlarged architectural experience.

(b) Much the same temptations arise when the artist-spectator discovers that his initial impulse, though a genuine enlargement of experience, was an enlargement of an experience of a non-architectural kind. In such cases he is frequently tempted to continue his work in the architectural manner. This

173

procedure is also both dishonest and a waste of time, and the result is inevitably a hybrid work which is neither truly architectural nor truly romantic or descriptive in kind.[1] The honest original architectural artist confronted with this dilemma, if true to his principles, relentlessly destroys the work; or he may without dishonesty yield to the temptation to recommence it on the basis of the true initial impulse and make it a frankly romantic or descriptive work. The dishonest artist-spectator is the man who lacks the courage to destroy or recommence and continues his work to a hybrid 'finish' of no intrinsic worth.

(c) When the artist-spectator discovers that, in the course of his work, he has forgotten his initial enlargement of architectural experience, he often imagines that he can remedy the loss by extraneous additions or by haphazard deletions.

In the first case he may put noses and toes on figures which he had perceived or imagined as silhouettes that he has since forgotten; or he may put folds into draperies originally perceived or imagined as a flat shape of colour; or put tree-trunks or pillars into what was originally experienced architecturally as a recession without details; and so on and so forth. When the artist does this, his work ceases with the first nose or fold or pillar to be integral; it is no longer honest; it is no longer right. Morally it is little better than venal descriptive popular art where such redundancies are inserted from the venal motive of remaining within the average spectator's familiar experience of generic forms.[2]

In the second case the artist frequently resorts to what is called 'simplification' in the hope that the elimination of details will remedy what he recognizes to be defects. The artist who simplifies in a haphazard fashion is also dishonest, and morally little better than the artist who simplifies in the manner of the venal derivative popular artist who simplifies because 'simplification' rather than elaboration may chance to be at the moment within the familiar experience of 'artistic' folk.

Artist-spectators who find that their initial enlargement of architectural experience has been forgotten in the course of their work are also tempted to other devices. They may try to remedy the defects they recognize by making naturalistic studies of particular details and grafting these studies on to an original architectural sketch; or they may take details from prints or photo-

---

[1] But cf. 'Genius and the critic', Part I, and 'The value of genius' in this part.

[2] For the difference between Constable's honest sketches and his relatively dishonest pictures elaborated from them, cf. my 'English Painting.' [1935 note.]

graphs, and graft them on in the same way. These procedures are likewise dishonest and futile.

(*d*) The artist-spectator who finds that his work fails to symbolize the initial enlargement of experience through his use of inadequate, unsuitable, or derived symbolic language, is tempted either to leave the trouble unremedied or to invent or borrow another language equally inadequate or unsuitable; or to have recourse to facile naturalism in place of representational symbols; and (*e*) the artist-spectator who recognizes that his work fails in execution is tempted to fake the failure by some device to draw the spectator's eye from the points of weakness; he is tempted to paint dark slush over a background which looks 'worried' because he has failed to handle it in any appropriate way; or to strengthen the colour in the sky to attract attention from the clumsy handling of the trees, or to intensify the high lights that the coarse touch in the half-tones may be less evident; and so on and so forth. Whenever the artist leaves inadequate technique unremedied or attempts to fake it instead of recommencing or destroying the work he is dishonest and the work is without intrinsic worth.

(*f*) Many dishonesties arise from sheer impatience. The artist-spectator is frequently tempted to proceed with his work before he has discovered the source of the defects which he knows to be there. He may fail to give the necessary time for reflection and consideration through yielding to a childish desire to see his work 'finished', or through yielding to a venal desire to get the work done in time for the Academy, or in time to show to a rich man who is coming to tea and may possibly buy it. In such cases the impatient artist either continues his work in a haphazard fashion hoping that the defects will be remedied by accident, or else continues it with the deliberately venal intention of concealing the defects by camouflage and fake. All such yielding to impatience is dishonest, and the artist who botches and fiddles hoping for accident, or botches and fiddles evolving fakes, knows in his mind that his work is wrong and that he has shirked the problem of how to set it right.

Many more examples of dishonesty in the artist-spectator could, as all artists know, be given. All soi-disant architectural works dishonestly passed as 'right' by an artist-spectator who knows in his mind that they are 'wrong' are without the intrinsic value of original architectural art whatever the artist's intention may have been when he began them. However great the appreciation of such works by other spectators, and however numerous those appreciative spectators may be, or in other words whatever *acquired* value such works may eventually secure, they must remain fakes and failures till the crack of doom; for they are aspects of humbug, not aspects of truth.

III. THE HONEST INCOMPETENT ARTIST-
SPECTATOR (THE CASE OF HAYDON)

Between the honest competent artist-spectator and the dishonest artist-spectator there is the figure of the honest incompetent artist-spectator, the man, that is, who is morally relentless in judging his own work but incapable of analysing his own perception, motives and procedure and is therefore incapable of judging the extent to which his work has fulfilled its purpose.

There are many more honest-incompetent than honest-competent artist-spectators. But there are many more dishonest artist-spectators than honest-incompetents.[1]

Benjamin Haydon who lived and worked a hundred years ago was a good example of an honest incompetent artist-spectator. His attitude, motives and procedure are known to us with certainty, because though most of his pictures are not now accessible, we have his autobiography and journals to inform us of his mind.

Haydon, it is clear from his memoirs, was a man of scrupulous honesty of purpose in judging his own work. In the affairs of the world he was casual. He borrowed sums amounting to hundreds of pounds from all kinds of people and trusted to luck, or, as he would have put it, to the justice of God, to enable him to repay the debts. But he was not casual about principle when he surveyed his pictures.

Haydon believed himself an original architectural artist. He imagined that he was engaged in the same category of task as Raphael was engaged in when he painted the *School of Athens* or as the artists of the modern movement are engaged in to-day. But in this he was mistaken. As artist-spectator of his own work he was incompetent. He did not realize that the initial motive behind his *Dentatus*, his *Judgment of Solomon* and his *Christ entering Jerusalem* was not in any of the three cases an enlargement of his own architectural experience but in each and all firstly the proving to the world that he, Haydon, was a great artist, and secondly the enlarging of his own romantic and not his own architectural experience.

---

[1] When the honest artist-spectator fails in judging his own work the cause is always, I believe, muddle-headedness. I have selected Haydon as a typical example (*a*) because the work in question in his case was soi-disant architectural in character (i.e. the kind of work I am still discussing) and (*b*) because he is frequently instanced by those who deny the artist's competence to assess his own productions. Haydon failed as artist-spectator. I have tried to show why and to indicate by that means the difference between Haydon and the genuine original architectural artist who can and does succeed.

176

Haydon imagined that he worked like the true original architectural artist without reference to the effect of his work on spectators other than himself. In fact, it is clear from his memoirs, the effect of his work on eventual spectators was always present in his mind. As artist-spectator of his own work he failed to discover that he was for this reason not an original but a popular artist, that he had embarked on the achievement of contact with eventual spectators, that he had set out, not exclusively to solve the original architectural artist's specific problem, but to persuade the world that he was the kind of person who could solve it. He was unable to discover if his work had or had not solved the original architectural artist's problem because he was never able to discover what that problem was.

Haydon was temperamentally not an architectural but a romantic artist. The reinforcements by which he converted his mechanical vision to perception were the kind of reinforcements that lead a man to perceive the emotive character of fragments, not the kind of reinforcements that enable a man to perceive relations of form—it was as emotive fragments that he admired the Elgin marbles. As a Romantic he was excited by expressive eyes. He set out to rival Raphael's *School of Athens* though his idea of art was that of the third-rate actor who imagines art to be the grimacing records of emotions. When he started his *Raising of Lazarus* he scrawled about with his brush, he tells us, and in so doing, 'gave an expression' to the eye of Lazarus. 'I instantly got interested' he continues 'and before two I had hit it.' This might have been written by a follower of Delacroix; and a follower of Delacroix also would have sympathized with Haydon's interest in Napoleon musing at St. Helena.

It was of course partly the romantic strain in Haydon that endeared him to Keats and Wordsworth; it was also his romantic dramatization of his own position that imposed upon so many kinds of people when they came in contact with him; and it was his failure to discover his romantic bent that made all his pseudo-architectural pictures hybrid productions of low intrinsic worth.

Had Haydon been born at the same date in France he would have been swept automatically into the romantic movement; he would not have wasted his life trying to combine the romantic and the classical ideals without truly comprehending either. Had he been able to ignore the public he might have discovered his romantic bias and discovered at the same time the true nature of architectural art; if instead of trying to impress eventual spectators he had been content, like his friend Wilkie, to attempt to make money by pleasing them, he might have been a successful popular artist. But fate permitted none of these things. Fate decreed that he should be an artist whose work is without intrinsic

M

or acquired value because he was never able to discover what in fact he had set out to do, and failed by the same token, as artist-spectator, to discover whether he had achieved his aim or not.[1]

Since the world regards an honest muddle-headed man as a more sympathetic figure than a clear-headed knave, the spectacle of the honest incompetent artist-spectator is less offensive to us than that of the artist-spectator who is deliberately dishonest. But the fact that such a man excites our friendly pity rather than our dislike cannot give his work intrinsic value. For any soi-disant original architectural artist who hands us a work which for any cause is not the perfect epitome of his enlarged architectural perception is handing us what is commonly called a 'pup'. When such an artist says: 'It is not what I wanted', it is often assumed that he is being modest. He is not. He is confessing failure or dishonesty.

Unfortunately artists of all kinds habitually send their failures and dishonest productions to exhibitions and contribute thereby to prevailing confusions in respect to values.

D. THE ORIGINAL ARTIST AS SALESMAN[2]

When a work of original art (of any kind) is finished and exhibited, the original artist does not expect the spectator to be able to appreciate or understand it; nor does he grant him the right to criticize or assess it; but he expects him to *buy* it, because to the original artist the spectator is not a man but a purse.

The original artist thinks his intrinsically right pictures above all price because their intrinsic value, as records of his vital experience, cannot be translated into terms of money. He never really wants to part with such works; but, unless he is financially quite independent, he frequently needs money and so he sells these right works and hates the world for parsimony however large the sum he gets for them.

On the other hand he knows that his failures, his wrong pictures, are without intrinsic value; he dislikes the sight of them in his house or studio because he knows he ought to destroy them; so, unless he destroys them, he sells them as

---

[1] Haydon's genre pictures in the Tate Gallery—*Punch or May Day* and *Chairing the Member* —though hybrid have some measure of intrinsic value as original descriptive art. But there is surely no intrinsic value in his huge *Raising of Lazarus* (14 feet by 20 feet) which the National Gallery transferred as a white elephant to the Tate Gallery in 1929. [1956 note.]

[2] This section is added in this edition. [1956 note.]

soon as possible, persuading himself that the money does no more than pay him for the unproductive time he spent on them, and despising the world for its idiocy in paying money for anything so worthless.

If the original artist's intrinsically right pictures come back to him unsold from the market, he hoards them for ever—though he may never feel the need to look at them because his interest has moved on; but unless he sells his failures quickly he will always inevitably sooner or later destroy them.[1]

What I have submitted then, in the foregoing sections, is this:

(*a*) The first test of value of a work of original architectural art is whether it has been honestly and correctly passed as right by the artist himself in his capacity of spectator.

(*b*) When a work of this kind has been honestly and correctly passed as right by the artist-spectator it has intrinsic value which cannot be affected by the addition or non-addition of acquired value given to it by other spectators.

(*c*) But the artist through dishonesty or incompetence often passes his work as right when in fact it is wrong.

(*d*) Works which have been passed as right by the incompetent or dishonest artist-spectator when in fact they are wrong, have no intrinsic value. They have failed at the first fence. No amount of acquired value subsequently given from other spectators can make them less intrinsically worthless.

(*e*) The original artist as salesman regards the spectator as nothing but a purse.

E. VALUE OF
ORIGINAL ARCHITECTURAL ART

We must now look more closely at the intrinsic value of the original work of architectural art which has been passed as right by the honest and competent artist-spectator; and consider the relation of that value to other spectators when the work stands before them.

In Part I of this inquiry I have stressed the normality of modern original architectural art. I have tried to show that the modern movement is a phase of the search for a fundament to the artistic activity to replace the fundament of service to a religion, a search in which countless intelligent artists of Western

---

[1] For the application of the above to Turner, and Ruskin's bewilderment in that connection cf. my 'Ruskin', pp. 267–9 (Faber).

Europe have been engaged since the middle of the Italian Renaissance. I have stressed in other words the normality of the original architectural artist in basing his art on a consciously-held idea of art. I have now to consider the human value of the architectural attitude and its value to the normal man.

All reasonable people contemplating the great original architectural buildings, sculpture and pictures in the world must recognize, I think, that the artists who made them were men of fundamental normality, great energy, great intelligence and great organizing power. No reasonable being can suppose Raphael's *School of Athens* (Pl. 3) or Seurat's *The Bathers* (Pl. 7) to be works by men whose intellect is in any way out of touch with the intellect of normal men. All architectural art is in fact the result of a normal human attitude to the universe and a normal human energy; every man is to an extent an original architectural artist; the difference between Raphael or Seurat and the man at present passing in the street is not a difference of kind but a difference of degree; original architectural art is an activity characteristic not only of original architectural artists but in some measure of every normal man.

What then, humanly speaking, is this activity? What is the essential character of the attitude and energy that produce it?

The answer I believe is to be found in Einstein's reference to the '*positive motive which impels men to seek a simplified synoptic view of the world conformable to their own nature, overcoming the world by replacing it with this picture*'.

There is unquestionably in every man an urge, an impulse, an energy—call it what you will—which compels him to desire to arrive at ever greater comprehension and appreciation of the universe. This urge or instinct is seen in the men who attempt to supply an explanation of the universe by a religious system, in the men who seek to discover scientific laws, in the men who struggle to arrive at greater comprehension and appreciation by philosophy or metaphysic; it is the instinct that has driven certain men to want desperately to make the whole of mankind conform to some religion or system of government; and in its most obvious form it is the instinct that drives the housewife to arrange bibelots symmetrically on the parlour shelf or dispose a bunch of varied flowers in considered proportions in a pot.[1]

Man displays a thousand different aspects of this desire to convert vaguely realized formal experience to precise, concrete and ordered form. The original architectural artist displays the desire and his satisfaction of it when he achieves

---

[1] It may be objected that even architectural artists are frequently untidy people. But, of course, the objection is a confusion. The artist is not a housewife. He is not concerned with the elementary aspects of order. His business is the enlargement of experience in that field. He must not be expected to refuse to perceive the wood and spend his time examining the trees.

contact with formal order and creates a synoptic symbol of that order by his work.

The work of men who set out to enlarge their perception of order by science, philosophy or metaphysic has been credited through the ages with a high intrinsic value; and I submit that a work which symbolizes an artist's enlarged perception of formal order can also be credited with an intrinsic value that is high.

Now what happens to the spectator who apprehends the character and value of such a work? My submission is that the spectator is of the same clay as the artist and has within him, developed in more or less degree, the same architectural aspirations, the same impulse towards order; that he secures therefore a satisfaction, analogous to the artist's satisfaction, from the spectacle of a work of art which is in fact a finite ordering of architectural experience in a form comprehensible to the human mind.

When we appreciate an original work of architectural art we recognize that the artist has made clear to us something that, as human beings like himself, we desired to perceive clearly but were not able to perceive without his aid; we realize that he has *tidied-up* for us an aspect or a corner of the universe which, as human beings like the artist, we would have liked to have 'tidied-up' ourselves; we realize that he has helped us one step farther to a goal towards which as human beings we are all instinctively impelled; and that he has done this as the result of an impulse, an intellectual energy and an organizing ability not different in kind from our own impulses, intellectual energies and organizing abilities, but merely greater and more powerful in degree.

Confronted with a work of art of this calibre we thus recognize 'a simplified synoptic view of the world conformable to our own nature'; we experience an intellectual satisfaction of the kind experienced by the contemplation of any other intellectual problem solved in what seems to us a conclusive and final way. Pater, writing of Raphael's *Ansidei Madonna* said that it gave him something of the pleasure one has in a proposition of Euclid. That appreciation will be comprehensible to the reader if he has followed my argument to this point. Pater's pleasure, I submit, was a normal human pleasure at the contemplation of a high normal human activity.

This pleasure can be experienced by anyone before any work of original architectural art, once the spectator has recognized the problem which the artist in each case has set out to solve and once he has acquired the means of following the solution. With such pleasure the spectator adds to his own familiar experience; he is one step farther towards a desired comprehension and appreciation of order; and he is prepared for a further step to-morrow.

The man, therefore, who can truly understand the formal problems solved by the original architectural artists of the past is prepared for the understanding of the art of the modern movement; the man who can truly understand the formal problems solved by the original artists of the modern movement is prepared to appreciate the architectural art of to-morrow. True appreciation of this kind of art marks an enlargement of the spectator's experience of architecture in the universe.

Original architectural art can thus contribute value to spectators who board the waiting train in the station and are carried with each work a little farther in a direction which, as men, they desire to go. Spectators who arrive too late at the station, or who revile the uncommon shape of the carriage doors instead of opening the doors and getting in, are just left standing on the platform.

It may be objected that the spectator, though willing to secure enlargement of experience by the appreciation of such art and though able to apprehend the nature of the artist's architectural problem, may still be unable to follow the solution because of the unintelligibility of the artist's symbolic language. This, I submit, is like saying that a French professor's lecture on Rembrandt is unintelligible because one happens to be ignorant of French. If we are not familiar with that language we must learn it or miss the benefits which work expressed in that language may provide. Every original architectural artist invents, to some extent, his own language for every work. There is no such thing as a universal language of art.[1]

Any man who will take the necessary trouble can understand the language of any true original architectural work of art, if that language has been honestly and competently accepted by the artist as a perfect means of communication between himself, the artist-experiencing-man, and himself, the artist-spectator-man. What has been honestly and competently passed as intelligible communication to one normal man—the artist—must be intelligible communication to other normal men.[2]

If I am right in submitting that the nature of our reaction to such art is a species of satisfaction at the contemplation of a synoptic symbol for formal order it follows that our reaction to the *colour-subject* of an architectural work, which is part of this form-subject, must be the same in character.

[1] The assumption that the naturalistic technique was a universal language of art, which all artists have always used or tried to use, was common in the nineteenth century, and was the cause of much confusion in respect to values. (Cf. Parts II and III *passim* and 'The value of technique' in this part.)

[2] Some people are quick at learning artists' languages; others are slow. I happen to be slow myself. But I have always found the labour involved worth while and I never assume that I can assess a work of art on any solid basis till I have discovered the particular symbolic principle on which the artist has based his language, or else discovered that he has confused a number of principles or worked without a principle at all. The wise critic does not say: 'This is unintelligible' but 'This, so far, I cannot read'.

182

This I believe to be the case. The colour-subject in a work of this kind is always, as I have indicated, a relation of colours. Our reaction when we contemplate a relation of colours in a work of art is, I believe, the same kind of satisfaction that we get when we contemplate a work of art's relation of forms. It is a kind of gratitude to the artist for having symbolized a relation which we had ourselves desired to perceive to the point of concrete form but which we ourselves were unable to perceive to such a point of precision.

There are those who tell us that we react purely sensationally to individual colours and also to relations of colours. There are others who believe that our reactions in both cases are the result of associations of ideas. Both points are worth examination.

In regard to our reactions to individual colours I have submitted earlier that there is a mechanical reaction in our eye to individual colours, and that this reaction is different from the reaction of the camera's eye as at present constructed. How far our mechanical vision communicates to sensation without associated ideas from the brain is an open question. In the case of the normal man the communication between the eye and sensation is probably much less direct than is commonly supposed. I believe that nine times out of ten our sensational reactions are the result of associated ideas; that lake reds elate us if we associate them with roses and the bloom of youth on healthy cheeks, while the same range of reds depress us if we associate them with heavy pomp and pools of blood; I believe that cadmium yellow cheers us if we associate it with daffodils and sunlight; and that black depresses us if we associate it with darkness and with death. It is easy to confuse pure sensational reaction with sensational reaction caused by association of ideas; and though I do not venture to suggest that pure sensational reactions never happen from contemplation of individual colours I believe that great caution must be exercised before assuming that our reactions to individual colours are anything approaching purely direct effects of those individual colours on our sensations.

This (a point I have touched on earlier in 'Human perception') is one of the reasons why comparisons between our reactions to music and our reactions to pictures are so dangerous. For, to begin with, music assaults us through the ear, an organ which is much less intimately and elaborately connected with the brain than the eye, and music for this physiological reason can make a more direct communication to our senses; and then we must remember that I am speaking at this point not of colour (i.e. relations of colour) but of *individual colours*. Most comparisons between painting and music compare our reaction to a splash of red or yellow to our reaction to a *series* of sounds. The only comparisons that are possible at all are first a comparison between our reactions to a splash of red or yellow and our reactions to a *single note* of an instrument or voice; second a comparison between our reactions to a relation of colours in a work of plastic art and our reactions to a chord; and third a comparison between our reactions to a series of relations of colours in a work of plastic art and our reactions to a series of notes and chords. But for the reason I have given, and also because music is a progression whereas a work of plastic art is relatively static, I believe all such comparisons to be more entertaining than helpful in the study of the individual arts.[1]

Romantic artists use individual colours as emotive agents. Original artists of this class have in mind the colour's effect on their own sensation as determined by romantic associated ideas. Popular artists of this class use individual colours in the same way to achieve contact with the spectator's familiar ideas romantically associated with such colours. When we react to the one use or the other we are only too apt to imagine that our reaction is a pure sensation when it is in fact due to new or familiar romantic associated ideas.

In discussing our mechanical vision as opposed to perception I have suggested that we mechanically see *relations of colours* in so far as they are relations of light and shade in much the same way as the camera sees them. We must now observe that to *perceive* such relations we have to call up reinforcements to our mechanical vision to convert it to perception. For this reason it seems to me dangerous to suggest that we react purely sensationally to relations of colours; and it is equally dangerous to suggest that we react to such relations purely on the stimulus of associated ideas. We do not, I believe, react to a combination of red and yellow in a picture in a mechanically sensational manner as we react to the movement of a cross-Channel steamer, nor do we react to it purely because we associate a similar combination of colours with the Spanish flag or with oranges and tomatoes on the quay at Venice; we react to it, I believe, as to a combination, we like it if it appears to be evidence of deliberate well-devised symbolic order and we dislike it if it appears to be a combination that is accidental and so without symbolic sense;[2] we react to it, that is to say, in exactly the same way that we react to any other component part of architectural form.

Now it may be suggested that the spectator's appreciation of original architectural art, his satisfaction at the contemplation of a problem admirably solved, must contribute to the work's intrinsic value even if it be admitted that the

---

[1] As stated in the 'Preface to the 1956 edition', Calder's mobiles are the nearest equivalent to music in the plastic arts. [1956 note.]

[2] It is for this reason, for example, that I personally dislike Van Gogh's colour in many of his pictures. [1956 note.]

work also has intrinsic value of the kind I have submitted at the beginning of this section. This as I have tried to indicate throughout this inquiry I believe to be a fallacy. The acquired value taken on by such a work from the spectator's satisfaction is a value of quite a different character from its intrinsic value. The intrinsic value of an original work of art is constant. The acquired value is always an unknown and a variable quantity which has relation only to itself. It can be a criterion of the spectator's value from certain points of view; but it can never be the criterion of an original work's intrinsic value or mingle with that value or detract from it. If I pour oil upon water I do not increase the amount of water or detract from it. The water remains where it was before I arrived on the scene.

It may further be objected that, if the truly valuable effect of such art is the enlargement of the spectator's experience of a certain kind—then, when the enlargement has been effected the work, on the one hand, will cease to have intrinsic value and the spectator, on the other, will cease to derive satisfaction from it. This, I submit, is a confusion between the intrinsic value of a work and the work's effects. If I discover a terrific explosive the discovery may enable an engineer to build a tunnel which would benefit a great number of people; it may also enable a general to blow a vast number of boys and men to tiny pieces. The intrinsic value of a scientific discovery resides in the apprehension of the general laws which the discovery represents; it resides in the new knowledge that $a+b+c$ will blow a mountain or a thousand men to blazes. That value cannot be altered by the accident that one man is pleased with it because it can add to man's convenience while another is pleased with it because it can destroy a thousand people in two minutes. In the same way the intrinsic value of a work of original architectural art is independent of its effects on subsequent spectators.

Such a work moreover has its store of intrinsic value which it can contribute over and over again. To a fresh spectator it can always obviously contribute full value. To a spectator to whom it is already known it can contribute ever fresh value until the total enlargement which it represents has become part and parcel of the spectator's familiar formal experience; then for that spectator its work is done; and the spectator is in the position of the original artist who looks back on the work he did last year as no longer of interest. The spectator may return to it and give it the acquired value of his patronage; but unless he has reached a stage when he is no longer capable of enlarging his formal experience by art he will leave it with a greeting and pass on to a picture which can give him value that he has not yet acquired.

Nevertheless there are, I believe, few actual works of art which can contribute value to a spectator for *very long* unless that spectator has ceased to be able to react to enlargements of his experience in the work's particular field. The greater the work the longer it has intrinsic value to give the receptive spectator. There may be works that would satisfy a receptive spectator throughout his whole lifetime, though he saw them continually every day. But when a man says that he never tires of Raphael's *School of Athens* the truth is generally that he has seen the work a dozen times (or less) at intervals of years, that he has never on any of those occasions received its full value, and that between the visits he has forgotten a good deal of the value he had absorbed before; or else the truth is that he has reached a stage when his receptivity has diminished, and that, in once again appreciating the work, he is really remaining within his acquired experience and giving the work the acquired value of that re-appreciation, instead of deriving value from the work by appreciating the order it symbolizes more completely than he had ever appreciated it before.

If a great work like Raphael's *School of Athens* would fail to contribute value daily for fifty years to a receptive spectator—as I believe it would—simple or minor works would obviously fail under a much less stringent test.

My answer to the last objection is therefore this: (*a*) the intrinsic value of a work of original architectural art does not depend on the amount of value it contributes to you and me, because that value does not depend on its effects; (*b*) there may be works which can continue to give value for fifty years to a continuously receptive spectator but such works are certainly most rare; and to the question, 'Why do we not tire of great original works of art?' I answer, 'We do tire of them if we ever reach the stage of having absorbed the value they can give.'[1]

F. VALUE OF ORIGINAL ROMANTIC ART

In the sections of Part I headed 'The romantic heresy' and 'Original romantic art' I have briefly described the character of the original romantic artist's activity. We have now to consider the intrinsic and acquired value of such art.

The task of such an artist as spectator of his own work is to decide whether or not his work is a perfect symbol of that enlargement of his experience which he

[1] To say 'I should never tire of Chartres Cathedral' is not a valid objection at this point. Because Chartres is the work not of one original artist but a hundred. It has therefore a hundred times as much value to confer. I am speaking in this inquiry of single works produced by individual artists.

186

set out to achieve. This obviously is the same kind of task as that of the original architectural artist-spectator, and it is as frequently done badly through incompetence or dishonesty in the various ways I have described and also in certain other ways peculiar to itself which it is unnecessary for our purpose to examine.

When the original romantic artist-spectator has failed in his task, then his work has, of course, no intrinsic value; it is again the horse that has failed at the first fence. When the artist has succeeded and has honestly and correctly passed his work as right, can it be said to have an intrinsic value equivalent to that of original architectural art honestly and correctly passed in the same way?

This is a difficult question. I submit that the intrinsic value of such works—which are, of course, as rare as original architectural works—is a high value but not so high as that of original architectural art.

There is, I think, a difference in value, because the original romantic artist sets out to achieve contact, not with any universal order, but with fragments; and by such contact he strives to achieve an enlargement, not of his formal, but of his emotional experience, and, as we have seen, to effect his purpose he usually concentrates on a point of focus and invents for that point an appropriate setting.

Now the impulse towards enlarged perception of unusually emotive fragments is no less normal in man than the impulse towards enlarged perception of formal order. But the activity of the original romantic artist is from first to last empirical—and so a kind of activity that is always ranked lower than the deliberate search for universal laws.

To take the very obvious example of an original architectural artist and an original romantic both painting a woman's head. The former is concerned with the formal relations of the parts of the head one to another, and the formal relation of his representational symbols for those parts (and for the whole head) to that symbol of universal order which he has set out to create by his architectural picture. He is concerned from first to last with a search for a creation of a formal order. The original romantic artist is concerned only with such details of this particular woman's head as have enlarged his emotional experience. He may be concerned with the expression of her eye, or the shape of her mouth, or the movement of her neck. The emotive details may be formal. That does not matter. The difference between the two men is that the first is concerned with formal relations, that is to say, with an order, while the second is concerned with formal or other fragments perceived as unusually emotive. When the original romantic artist has forced his romantic perception of the woman's eyes or the shape of her mouth or whatever it may be to the point of symbolic

187

romantic expression, his work is done; and in our own day, when artists are much freer than they have ever been before, original romantics habitually stop that point. But I cannot help feeling that the intrinsic value of this achievement is lower than the intrinsic value of a picture which, like a work of architecture, is from first to last a symbol of the artist's actual or imagined perception of a formal order.

Now how does original romantic art affect the spectator? Obviously it helps him to perform a task which, as a normal human being with a normal desire to enlarge his comprehension and appreciation of unusually emotive fragments, he would like to do himself but cannot. We all know that as we move about the world we continually recognize with pleasurable emotion some emotive frag-ments which, we say, remind us of some romantic artist's pictures. When we say this we *should* say that we have perceived these fragments as emotive because some artist has pointed out their emotive qualities, or in other words, that the artist's work has made this type of fragment part of our familiar experience of emotive fragments. Bosanquet said that all our familiar ideas of 'beauty' derive from art; and it is probably true that all our *familiar* experience of formal order derives from architectural art and all our familiar experience of emotive fragments derives from our experience of romantic art. The original romantic work of art can thus enlarge both our experience of art and our experience of the fragments of life which it has stressed as emotive; and it can prepare us for further enlargements of both kinds to-morrow.

Whether the type of experience enlarged in the spectator by architectural art is more or less valuable than the type of experience enlarged by romantic art, it is not necessary for our purpose to inquire. But I am tempted to suggest that at certain times one kind of enlargement is more valuable while at others the higher value must be conceded to the other. This applies, I think, both to individuals and to communities. There are times in every normal man's life when, to obtain the satisfactions he most desires at the moment, he is disposed to enlarge his romantic experience; there are other times, in the same process, when he is more disposed to further experience of order; possibly, in each case the more valuable art for him at each time is not the kind he welcomes but the other—but that again is a question I can leave aside. In the same way com-munities in certain circumstances are disposed to the one form of enlargement while in other circumstances they are disposed to the other; this swing of the pendulum corresponds to the analogous swing in general thought; in times and places where individualism holds the field a community asks for enlargement of its romantic experience—when an enlargement of formal experience might be better for its health; in times when uniform order and collectivism hold sway in thought, a community tends to desire to perceive formal order when, it may be, increased appreciation and comprehension of unusually emotive fragments might do it little harm.

We have still to consider the acquired value given to original romantic art by the appreciation of the spectator. That 'acquired' value is of course of the same kind as the acquired value given to original architectural art; it is equally an unknown quantity, equally variable, equally different from the work's intrinsic value and equally useless as a criterion of that value. But it is often an index to the psychological condition both of individual spectators and communities at the time.

G. VALUE OF
ORIGINAL DESCRIPTIVE ART

Now what is the intrinsic value and the acquired value of original descriptive art?

The task of such an artist as spectator of his own work is to decide whether or not his work is a perfect symbol of the initial enlargement of his own experience which prompted it. This again is obviously the same kind of task as the tasks of the original architectural and romantic artists which we have been considering. Again, obviously, the task is frequently done badly through incompetence or dishonesty in the ways I have described earlier and in other ways peculiarly its own. Again, also, such work has no intrinsic value if dishonestly or incompetently passed as 'right' by the artist-spectator when, in fact, it is not a perfect expression of his original initial purpose. Again in such a case it is a horse which has failed at the first fence.

But when such an artist has honestly and competently passed his work as right then his work, I submit, has intrinsic value because the artist has obeyed an impulse towards increased comprehension of everyday life, an impulse which is as normal as the formal and romantic impulses.

This intrinsic value I set lower than the intrinsic value of original architectural art; and indeed the enlarged perception of everyday life is habitually lower than enlarged perception of a formal order.

Whether there is or is not a justification for this difference in valuation is a more complicated question than is commonly supposed. It is undeniable that the activity of the original descriptive artist is held in particularly low esteem at the

189

moment because we have been told so often that such an artist is engaged in an activity more suited to the historian, the novelist, the parson or the photographer, that we have begun to believe it. A picture we have been told again and again should not 'tell a story'; but the reason given is really only a statement of a fact I have already indicated, the fact that specialists in other fields have now robbed the artist of his 'descriptive' task. In other words, the critics have said to the original descriptive artist: 'Mr. Jones the historian, Mr. Brown the scientist, Mr. White the psychologist, Mr. Green the journalist, Mr. Smith the parson and Mr. Robinson the photographer have now robbed you of all your lounge suits. Therefore, it is obvious, lounge suits do not suit your style of beauty. You must always appear in a morning coat or evening dress.'[1]

The prejudice against art of this character in the modern world is largely based on a confusion between the activity of the original descriptive artist and that of the popular descriptive artist, the value of whose work I shall examine later on. I am not tempted to suggest that the intrinsic value of original descriptive art is as high as that of original architectural art, but I believe it is possible to argue that it is as high as that of the original romantic artist's contribution, and that it may be higher, because the original descriptive artist is concerned with the acquisition and symbolizing of generic experience and is thus nearer to the original architectural artist who is concerned with the acquisition and symbolizing of universal experience than to the original romantic artist who is concerned with the perception of fragments.

But the artists of the modern movement are probably well advised to regard originality in this form of art as almost impossibly difficult of achievement in the modern world. The argument that painting is unsuited to such achievement is, as I have suggested above, palpably ridiculous. But the artist robbed by Messrs. Jones, Brown, White, Green, Smith and Robinson of all his lounge suits, though lounge suits may become him, is only showing reasonable adaptability to circumstances when he concentrates his attention on his morning coats and evening dress.

Actually, as we all know, there are scarcely any original descriptive artists in the modern world at all. With so few exceptions that it is difficult to name them, descriptive artists since the Renaissance have all been popular in kind. But such original descriptive art as exists to-day has, I submit, an intrinsic value somewhere between the intrinsic values of original architectural and original romantic art.

Now what is the effect on the spectator of original descriptive art? Clearly once again it helps him to perform a task which, as a normal human being with

[1] To this list we must, of course, now add Mr. Brick-Red the colour-cinema man and Mr. Grey the television operator. [1956 note.]

190

a normal impulse to greater comprehension and appreciation of scientific, social-historical and moral aspects of everyday life, he desires to perform himself but cannot. The value of the enlargement effected for us by original descriptive art must thus be assessed by standards of ethics and education.

Finally, we must observe that the acquired value given to original descriptive art by the spectator, like the acquired value in the case of other forms of original art, is a variable factor, different in kind from the work's intrinsic value and, here again, we must observe that such acquired value cannot be made the criterion of the intrinsic value of the work, though it may be an index to the educational and ethical standards of the spectator.

H. IMAGINATIVE ILLUSTRATION[1]

Narrative pictures and illustrations record the artist's imagined experience of physical objects and concrete things in particular conjunctions; they differ only from descriptive genre pictures in the degree of the story-telling suggested by the conjunctions; and it is possible therefore to regard them as aspects of descriptive art. But narrative art has its own problems and its own groups of associated ideas. For it ranges from illustrations to the Passion and the legends of the Saints to trivial anecdotes of everyday life. Book illustration, when not purely ornamental in purpose, covers the same wide field; and it is therefore arguable that narrative art, including illustration, should be thought of as an activity apart; and in that case its intrinsic value must be sought in the originality of the artist's action.

Religious art is outside the scope of this inquiry, but I must note in passing that, by the standards here submitted, the artists who personally imagine the scenes from the sacred stories must be accounted the original artists whose work has intrinsic value, whereas those who follow the instructions of theologians, or imitate existing pictures, must be ranked as popular practitioners; and that the amount of acquired value given by spectators to such pictures considered as religious illustrations depends on each spectator's religious experience, his education, and the degree of his active or passive acceptance of the dogmas of his church.

When illustrating episodes in secular stories or poems, the original narrative artist enlarges his experience by translating the words and ideas into visual

[1] This section is added in this edition. [1956 note.]

191

images of equal or higher quality and with parallel import; and his work in that way has intrinsic value. But if he can only image the episodes in terms of genre painting with appropriate period trappings, he remains within his own and other people's familiar experience and must rank as a popular descriptive artist.

It follows that it is less difficult to illustrate the writings of a popular or second rate author than those of a great one; it is easier for example to make original illustrations to FitzGerald's version of Omar Khayyam's 'Rubaiyat' than to the plays and poems of Shakespeare; and illustrations to Shakespeare tend, in fact, to remain on the popular level.

Some artists paint pictures, or make drawings, illustrating narratives or poems written by themselves; or write such texts after painting their pictures or making their drawings. But there are few examples of this by original artists, because the professional processes in the two arts are so different that the man who can perform both on the same level is extremely rare; and because if an artist has enlarged his experience to perfection in one way he has normally no urge to do anything further about it. The man who writes a book or poem and then sets out to illustrate it acknowledges thereby that he feels the verbal ideas and images to be incomplete; and if he works first as painter and draughtsman he acknowledges some failure also if he feels the need thereafter to exteriorize the same experience in words.[1]

There remains the case of the original artist illustrating narratives or poems vaguely in his mind but not written down. In such cases, which are more common, it is arguable, I think, that the unwritten narrative or poem is unwritten because the author could not completely realize it in verbal terms; and that, if he does in fact realize it in terms of a painting or drawing, the result, as the enlargement of that particular experience, has the intrinsic value of original art.[2]

I. THE PHILISTINE AND ORIGINAL ART

In the foregoing considerations of the value of various forms of original art and of their effects on the spectator I have assumed the normality of the spectator, because most abnormal spectators can be disregarded.

[1] When original artists write explanations of their personal attitudes, motives and procedures, and instance some particular pictures, they often produce most admirable prose and make most revealing comments; but that, of course, is a different thing from attempting a verbal illustration of a particular painting, i.e. an original equivalent in words.

[2] Thus Paul Nash's final pictures are referred to in the 'Preface to the 1956 edition' as illustrations to unwritten lyric poems by himself and assessed as original art; and the work of Cecil Collins (Pl. 44) must also, in my judgment, be considered in that category.

We have no need to speculate on the reactions of mad spectators or of eccentric spectators of most kinds. But there is one class of abnormal spectator which is so numerous that it must be separately considered. That class of spectator is the Philistine.

The Philistine is the man who is obstinately determined to remain within his familiar experience in every field, holding any further experience to be quite unnecessary; he is the man whose normal impulses towards further experience of any kind have become atrophied; he is the man who has reached a point in his development where he says to himself: 'This is enough. I am what I am. I know what I know. I like what I like. I do not desire to alter in any way.'

The Philistine always detests original art. When normal men tell him that he should make an effort to understand it, when they suggest, that is, that he should enlarge his experience by art, he flies into a passion. Confronted with original architectural art the Philistine says: 'This is not architectural art,' when he should say: 'I have never seen architectural art of this kind before.' Confronted with original romantic art he says: 'This is not romantic beauty,' when he should say: 'I have never regarded this particular fragment as romantically emotive in life or seen it stressed as romantically emotive in art before.' Confronted with original descriptive art he says: 'This is not true to nature,' when he should say: 'I have never noticed this in everyday life.' Also most frequently he confuses the issue, and abuses formal art because it does not fall within his familiar romantic experience, and romantic art because it does not correspond to his familiar experience of everyday life, and so on.

The Philistine is not only abnormal in this way. He is also abnormal because he is a person with a permanent grievance. He is a person with a permanent grievance against original artists *as such*, because he knows that their work is carried through from start to finish without reference to its effects upon himself. This standing grievance flames into active hostility when the Philistine is confronted with an actual work of original art. To save his face in that situation the Philistine says that he resents the attempt of the original artist to 'pull his leg'; what he would say if he had the courage is that he resents the original artist's complete lack of concern with his leg or any other part of him. If he does not suggest that the original artist is pulling his leg he suggests that he is mad; and such is the Philistine's conviction of his own importance that, in calling those who ignore him madmen, he is perfectly sincere.

The only type of art which is understood by the Philistine is venal popular art, the value of which we must now consider.

J. VALUE OF ROMANTIC POPULAR ART

In estimating the intrinsic value of any form of popular art we must not forget the distinction I have indicated in Part I between the activity of the disinterested popular artist working to please himself and that of the venal popular artist working to please other people and extract their money.

Let us consider first the value of the venal romantic popular artist. As artist-spectator such a man is clearly not faced with any problem comparable with that of any original artist. The initial impulse of his work, its form and character are all determined with a view to achieving contact with other people's familiar, snobbish, erotic, sensational or sentimental experience of emotive fragments. He is therefore quite unable to call his work 'right' or 'wrong' until he has discovered whether the spectators whom he had in mind react in the way desired or fail to do so.

The original architectural artist who paints a portrait of my wife can pronounce it right if it fulfils the enlargement of his experience of formal order which he set out to achieve. The original romantic artist can also judge his portrait of my wife by his own standard. But the venal romantic popular artist who paints a portrait of my wife to achieve contact with my familiar experience of my wife's head considered as an emotive fragment, cannot pronounce his work right until I have seen the portrait and reacted in the way desired. The work of the venal romantic popular artist can never have intrinsic value, deriving from the artist's honest competent judgment of it as the perfect fulfilment of his purpose before it is seen by other people, because his purpose is fulfilled not by himself but by the spectators whom he set out to attract and please.

In point of fact if the romantic popular artist knows his business the effect of such works on the average spectator is generally automatic. A romantic popular work says to the spectator: 'You have seen the fragments here portrayed before and you have felt them emotive. They fall within your familiar experience of romantic 'beauty'. The man who made me is an artist, a specialist in 'beauty', and he has the same experience of fragments that you have and feels them emotive in the same way. You are a fine romantic fellow whose familiar experience of emotive fragments is also the experience of an artist. There is therefore no need for you to enlarge your familiar experience in this field; your romantic sensibility is all that could be desired.' When a man buys a romantic picture because the central figure is like his little daughter or his mistress he is

194

responding to this type of flattery. When he buys a romantic landscape because it reminds him of the place where he spent his holiday or his honeymoon he is doing the same thing. When he buys a romantic landscape because it reminds him of the sunset he admired yesterday he is also responding in the same way.

The spectator responds to this flattery and gives the picture the acquired value of his appreciation. This is *the only sort of value* a work of venal romantic popular art can ever have; and it is high or low according as many or few people chance to have opportunities of seeing the picture and responding to its flattery.

Such works do not contribute value to the spectator but derive merely a variable value from his appreciation; and in admiring them the spectator is indulging in the pleasure of receiving flattery.

I refer in the next section to the relatively constant acquired value of romantic popular art when it is designed to achieve contact with very elementary and constantly familiar emotional experience in the spectator and I give the case of Sir Luke Fildes' *The Doctor* as an example. But unless the familiar emotional experience in question is very elementary, and so constant, the acquired value of such work is extremely variable. When the artist sets out for example to achieve contact with the spectator's familiar experience of fashionable-emotive fragments the acquired value of his work changes as the fashions change (Pl. 38). Romantic popular illustrators generally continue all their life to draw women the shape that they found emotive in their youth. That is why no popular illustrator over fifty can draw what the public at that time thinks an 'attractive' woman, and why there is always a call for young illustrators in Fleet Street. It must however be observed that a hundred years later the acquired value of the romantic popular illustrator's work again increases because the fashions become once more emotive as being 'quaint' and 'old world', i.e. remote in time. Much the same thing happens to the acquired value of romantic popular portraits.

It must be clearly understood that we are responding to flattery when we go to the Royal Academy or the National Gallery and admire romantic popular pictures as records of emotive fragments with which we are familiar in life. For such pictures merely tell us that our own familiar, snobbish, erotic, sensational or sentimental experience is a suitable content for a work of art.

Now let us consider the value of the work produced by the disinterested romantic popular artist who works not to please and attract other people but to please himself.

The reader, who remembers the description of this type of artist's activity, which I have already given, will realize that in my view such an artist is an average snob, sensualist or sentimentalist who has the eccentricity of thinking it worth while to spend all his time in the relatively harmless and completely safe amusement of painting pictures within his familiar romantic experience.[1]

The task of judging his own work as an artist-spectator is obviously quite a simple one for such an artist, because the difficult problem of achieving perfect form for an enlargement of his experience is not involved. Moreover, the experience recorded being familiar, it does not call for anything but familiar procedure to record it. Artists of this calibre when they are dishonest or incompetent as artist-spectators sometimes try to express their familiar romantic experience in original technique. But such cases are rare because popular romantic artists are usually men of low mental energy with no impulse towards invention of any kind; and always, of course, the result in such cases is without intrinsic value because an original language is not a suitable means of communicating the familiar experience which is the subject of the work.

If through incompetence or dishonesty such an artist passes his work as 'right' when it is 'wrong' it is of course without intrinsic value. But if the work has been honestly and competently passed by the romantic popular painter as the perfect expression of his romantic popular experience, can we then attribute to the work intrinsic value and if so is it high?

We must, I think, admit a low degree of intrinsic value. But we must not forget that the disinterested romantic popular artist's activity is as empirical at all stages as that of the original romantic; and, as the experience of emotive fragments which he records is familiar experience, the intrinsic value of his achievement cannot, I submit, be anything but lower than that of the achievement of his original romantic brother.

The effects of disinterested romantic popular art on the spectator are rather curious. Such art in practice is often produced by men who can afford to paint or sculpt without making money. The romantic popular artist of this class is thus as likely to ignore the average spectator's familiar experience as completely as it is ignored by the original romantic artist—though of course he is led to this position by an entirely different route. The work of such a man, like the work of an original artist, is produced without reference to its effects on spectators other than the artist (for if the artist works for praise instead of money he is none the less venal and is merely asking for payment of another kind). The work of such an artist has a measure of intrinsic value because the artist's purpose is achieved when he has honestly and competently passed his work as right. Its value is not solely the acquired value received from spectators as is the case with venal art

[1] 'Romantic popular art', Part I.

196

of this character. It has its intrinsic value, such as it is, without reference to any spectator other than the artist.

Evidence of this independence of the financially independent artist generally creeps into his work which for that reason is frequently mistaken by the spectator for original romantic art. The Philistine when confronted with such work often feels his characteristic grievance; he sees here and there a sign that his reactions have not preoccupied the artist; and he immediately abuses the work in the same way that he abuses original art. But the offending elements in such productions are not usually as thoroughgoing as the offending elements in original art because the artists are men of less vigorous attitudes of mind, and, living in comfort, they are prone to the notion that art, like everything else in leisured circles, should be sophisticated and urbane; and for this reason the Philistine is not usually impelled to abuse them with as much vehemence.

On the other hand those who admire original art often fall into this same error of confusing disinterested romantic popular art with original romantic art. They see evidence that the artist has not concerned himself with their reactions and attribute the independence to originality, when, in fact, it derives from money in the bank.[1]

I am not of course suggesting that all disinterested romantic popular artists are rich men; or that all artists with an independent income paint romantic popular art; or that there is any difference between the original romantic artist with no money and the same kind of artist with an independent income—except that the latter's work is more likely to be sophisticated and urbane. But it is, I think, a fact that most romantic popular artists who are disinterested are romantic popular artists who have no material temptation to be venal. The romantic popular artist is after all a man of low intellectual energy; if he had high intellectual energy he would feel the urge to enlarge his romantic experience and not be content to spend his days in producing art of the romantic popular kind. It must also be remembered that the disinterested romantic popular artist is frequently a man of middle age who has produced original romantic art in his youth which chanced to find appreciation and bring him money, and who has since yielded to the temptation to imitate his own work and thus degenerate from an original to a derivative popular artist.[2]

What I submit, then, is that disinterested romantic popular art can have an

[1] Sargent, to whom I have referred in Part II as a disinterested romantic popular artist, was disinterested on a sound financial basis. He became a rich man early in life. When he abandoned portraits for derivative impressionist landscapes he was already wealthy.

[2] The relation of the disinterested to the venal artist of this kind and the effects of his work on the spectator I shall discuss under 'Value of derivative popular art' in this part.

intrinsic value of the same kind as the intrinsic value of original romantic art, but much lower in degree; that it can also have acquired value from the spectator's appreciation; but that whereas in the case of venal romantic popular art the acquired value is the sole kind of value possible and the amount of that acquired value is the sole criterion of the work's value, in the case of disinterested work of the same kind the acquired value cannot be the sole criterion because there is a certain low degree of intrinsic value in the work.

K. VALUE OF DESCRIPTIVE POPULAR ART

Now let us consider the value of the work produced by the venal descriptive popular artist, and his disinterested brother who makes descriptive records in the spirit in which other men play golf.[1]

As artist-spectator the venal artist in this category is in the same position as the venal romantic popular artist. The initial impulse of his work, its form and character, have all been dictated with a view to achieving contact with other people's familiar experience of everyday life; he cannot for that reason pronounce his work right or finished or wrong or unfinished until he has discovered whether the spectators whom he had in mind do or do not react in the way desired. The work of the venal descriptive popular artist can never have intrinsic value deriving from the artist's honest competent judgment of it as the perfect fulfilment of his purpose before it is seen by other people.

Such works do not contribute value to the spectator. The only kind of value which they can ever have is acquired value from the spectator's appreciation. That appreciation is a response to flattery of a kind analogous to the spectator's response to venal romantic popular art. For such work says to the spectator: 'You have already frequently experienced the generic character of these physical objects and concrete things, or the social historical, or moral aspects of everyday life that are here portrayed. You are an intelligent observant fellow with no foolish romantic notions and no "highbrow" ideas of architectural art; your observation coincides with the observation of a descriptive artist who is a specialist in observation; there is no need for you to enlarge your familiar experience of everyday life; you know all that is necessary to know about it already.'

[1] Cf. 'Descriptive popular art', Part I.

The only criterion of the value of such art is the amount of the acquired value presented to the work by the spectator's appreciation, since such art being venal has no intrinsic worth of any kind.

The spectator with whom venal descriptive popular artists set out to achieve contact is the man in the street. This kind of art tends to have a high acquired value because it is generally admired by a great number of spectators. Also its value formerly was fairly constant because the average man's familiar experience of everyday life used to be much the same everywhere for generations. But, as a result of the advance of education, the labours of specialists and the productions of machines, venal popular art in the modern world tends to change its acquired value with each generation, and, since the criterion of value of such work is the sum total of the spectator's appreciation, the work must be said to have only a variable value which changes in general education and social conditions can considerably increase, diminish and even sometimes totally destroy.

The value of a descriptive popular work like Frith's *Paddington Station*, which is solely acquired value made up of the sum total of spectator's appreciation, is obviously less to-day than it was at the time when people, recognizing its topical generic descriptions, crowded round it in the Academy and bought hundreds of engravings of it for their homes. Eventually it will only be given historical value by the few spectators who take an interest in social-historical details of the past, and so, having very few admirers, its value will then be very small. On the other hand the acquired value of *romantic* popular art, which I examined in the last section, is much more constant if the work achieves the desired contact with constantly familiar emotions in mankind. Sir Luke Fildes' *The Doctor* is a picture of this character. It has lost much of its acquired value presented by the appreciation of 'artistic' spectators (as I remark in my next section discussing the value of derivative art), but the acquired value presented to the picture by people responding to its flattery of their familiar sentimental experience is probably as high to-day as it ever has been and it is likely to remain so.

Now what is the value of the work produced by the disinterested descriptive popular artist? Here again we have a parallel with disinterested romantic popular art. The work if incompetently or dishonestly passed by the artist-spectator has no intrinsic value being a horse that has failed at the first fence, and if honestly and competently passed it has the same kind of intrinsic value as original art of its class though that value is much lower in degree.

The effects of disinterested descriptive popular art on the spectator are again much the same in kind as the effects of disinterested romantic art: that is to say such work is often mistaken for original art by the Philistine and disliked by him for that reason, and it is as often mistaken for original art by the man who admires original art and is admired by him for that reason, the explanation being in both cases that the spectator is aware of a certain independence in the artist's attitude, a certain non-concern with the spectator's reactions, and that he mistakes this independence for the attitude of the original artist when frequently it is merely an independence deriving from a balance at the bank.

What I submit then on this point of the value of descriptive popular art is (a) that venal art of this calibre has no intrinsic value but only a variable acquired value deriving from the spectator's appreciation and that the amount of the variable acquired value is the sole criterion of its worth; and (b) that disinterested art of this character is the work of a man who paints his pictures in the same spirit that another man plays golf; that it may have the same kind of intrinsic value as original descriptive art though much lower in degree; and that it may have also acquired value from the spectator's appreciation; but that the amount of that acquired value cannot be the sole criterion of the work's value, because disinterested popular art like original art is produced without reference to its effects on the spectator and has a certain low degree of intrinsic value deriving from the artist's attitude.

L. VALUE OF DERIVATIVE POPULAR ART

I now come to the value of the work produced by venal and disinterested derivative popular artists. In the case of these artists there is no question of comparing the value of their productions with the value of original art of the same kind for there is, as I have observed before, no such thing as original derivative art since all derivative art is popular in kind.

I have defined the derivative popular artist as a man who works within his own familiar experience of art or within what he believes to be certain other people's familiar experience of art.

As artist-spectator the venal artist in this category is in the same position as venal romantic popular and venal descriptive popular artists. The initial impulse of his work, its form and character have all been determined with a view to achieving contact with 'artistic' people's familiar experience of art; he cannot for that reason pronounce his work right or finished or wrong or unfinished until he has discovered whether the spectators whom he had in mind do or do not react in the way desired.

The work of the venal derivative popular artist can never have intrinsic value arising from the artist's honest competent judgment of it as the perfect fulfilment of his purpose before it is seen by other people because his purpose has not been completed until 'artistic' people have approved it as familiar.

Works by this type of artist do not contribute value to the spectator. The only kind of value which they can ever have is acquired value from the spectator's appreciation.

When a man sets out to imitate a picture by Titian, Constable, Pissarro, Sargent, Cézanne, Matisse, Picasso or any other artist living or dead, in the spirit of a tradesman setting out to provide goods for an existing market, the customer whom he sets out to please is not the man in the street but the man who thinks he knows something about art. The patron whom he hopes to attract and please is the man who frequents the art museums, the Royal Academy, the New English Art Club, the London Group and so on, or the studios of artists. He attempts to achieve contact with that kind of spectator's familiar experience of the kind of pictures he has seen in places where in his opinion he has seen works of art displayed. The spectator's appreciation of such work is once again a response to flattery, for venal derivative popular art says to the spectator: 'You have frequently seen pictures or sculpture of my kind before. I am one of the kinds of picture or statue that you consider art. You are a cultivated fellow and recognize art when you see it. There is no need for you to enlarge your experience of art. You know all that is necessary to know about it already.'

The only criterion of the value of such art is the amount of the acquired value presented to the work by artistic spectators' appreciation, since such art being venal has not intrinsic worth of any kind; and, we may observe in passing, the attitude of the man who produces such work is singularly contemptible, because, in practice he often imitates superficial characteristics of original art produced by men who were despised and reviled, and thus obtains the material rewards for his labours which the original artists had to do without.

The amount of the total acquired value presented to such art by the spectator's appreciation is frequently at a given moment very high. But it is even more variable than the acquired value of either romantic or descriptive popular art because the taste of the 'artistic' public changes notoriously with each generation.

201

In the 'nineties of the last century most venal derivative popular artists established contact with the vague pseudo-romantic Keats-Tennyson-Rossetti-Morris-Wardour-Street-costume ideas of art that prevailed in the heads of the average visitors to the Royal Academy. To-day the average 'artistic' spectator reacts to derivative Impressionist or derivative Post-Impressionist pictures; and he regards the *Belle Dame sans Merci* type of Academy tableau as nonsense. As a result all the derivative pseudo-romantic costume pictures that exist have lost in value; and if a time comes when no 'artistic' spectator recognizes familiar experience of art in the nineteenth-century Knight-in-armour-Morte-d'Arthur-beauty-poetry-art formula then such pictures will have lost all their acquired value and be without value of any sort or kind.[1]

As I remarked in the last section the acquired value of a work of romantic popular art like Sir Luke Fildes' *The Doctor* is relatively constant among people who respond to its flattery of their familiar emotional experience; but at the time when it was painted acquired value was also given to this picture by people who regarded it as a familiar type of art. Large romantic popular 'subject pictures' of this kind now no longer achieve contact with 'artistic' spectators and *The Doctor* has therefore lost the acquired value given to it by such spectators, though it has retained its acquired value of the other kind.

It should also be observed that the acquired value of venal derivative popular art may *increase* as a result of changes in the 'artistic' public's taste. The derivative pictures by Mazo, the pupil, imitator and son-in-law of Velasquez, for example, were not given any acquired value by 'artistic' spectators at the end of the eighteenth century. A hundred years, later when the 'direct' painters had discovered Velasquez's *Las Meninas* and Whistler was handling paint very much like Mazo, there were numerous 'artistic' spectators who gave Mazo's pictures the acquired value of their appreciation. To-day when the technical reaction against 'direct' painting 'by the tone values' has been operating for half a century, 'artistic' spectators give the derivative popular works by Mazo the same passing glances that they received in the eighteenth century, and Mazo's pictures are now once more relatively low in acquired value. Or, again, the understanding of Cézanne's art has caused in our own time increased appreciation of the later works by El Greco; but writing in 1805 Fuseli described El Greco as a painter who began by successfully imitating Titian and 'afterwards attempted a new style and completely failed'; and Sir William Stirling Maxwell

[1] If the pseudo-romantic costume subject was not the real subject of the picture but merely incidental in a work expressing original formal or original romantic perception, then the work of course was original formal or original romantic and not derivative in kind, and it has and will always have its original intrinsic value.

202

writing in 1848 described the *Saint Maurice and the Theban Legion* as 'from an artistic point of view, little less extravagant and atrocious than the massacre it recorded'.

In the same way, of course, the imitations of original works by Manet, Renoir, Cézanne, Van Gogh, Picasso, Matisse, Maillol, Brancusi and Ozenfant have more acquired value given to them by 'artistic' spectators to-day than they had twenty, or even ten years ago, and more also than they will have given them by such spectators when the art of these original artists has ceased to be thought of as especially 'artistic' art and has become merely a recognized part of the art possessions of the world.

Now what is the value of the work produced by the disinterested derivative popular artist? Here the artist, in one set of circumstances, is in much the same position as romantic and descriptive popular artists of this kind. If as artist-spectator he incompetently or dishonestly passes his work as right, when it is wrong, then his work has no intrinsic value being once more a horse that has failed at the first fence; but if he has honestly and competently passed his work as right there can in this case be no comparison of its intrinsic value with the intrinsic value of original art of the same class, because there is no such thing as original derivative art. The attitude of the disinterested derivative popular artist as spectator is simply that of a man deciding whether or not he has successfully played the rôle of the sedulous ape. This activity seems to me so palpably contemptible that even though it be different from the venal spirit of the tradesman I cannot see any ground for attributing to it any kind of intrinsic worth; and the acquired value of such work is of course subject to the same inevitable fluctuations of artistic taste as is the work of the venal artist of this calibre.

It should also be noted that the work of the disinterested derivative popular artist is frequently mistaken for original art both by the Philistine and by those who admire original art, the explanation being the same as in the case of work produced by disinterested romantic and descriptive popular artists; and that many disinterested derivative popular artists are men who were original artists in their youth, and have made money by their original work, and use the independence thus secured to degenerate into derivative artists imitating their own earlier work.

Disinterested artists of the romantic popular and descriptive popular kinds tend, as I have observed, to show a certain independence in their work. But the disinterested derivative artist is generally so poor a creature that, even when placed in a position of security by the result of his own earlier labours, he rarely takes advantage of that security to work without reference to spectators other than himself. Nearly all derivative artists are venal; and very frequently they set out to achieve contact with 'artistic' spectators' familiar experience of their own earlier work and to attract such spectators' money by that means.

What I submit then on this point of the value of derivative popular art is:

(*a*) that venal art of this character has no intrinsic value, but only an especially variable acquired value derived from 'artistic' spectators' appreciation and that the amount of that exceedingly variable acquired value is the sole criterion of the work's worth;

(*b*) that disinterested art of this character is the work of a man who paints his pictures in the same spirit that another man imitates bird-calls, that it can never have any intrinsic value because this imitative activity is in itself contemptible; but that it may have acquired value from the spectators' appreciation, the amount of which in this case is the sole criterion of its worth.[1]

M. THE VALUE OF TECHNIQUE

Technique has no intrinsic value. At its highest it is the original artist's language of communication to himself which other people must learn if they wish to secure the value that his work can give them. At its lowest it is just a trick.

I have pointed out earlier that in the nineteenth century the degenerate naturalistic technique derived from the camera and from the easy 'drawing by the shadows' and 'painting by the tone values' taught in the art schools was mistaken by many people for a type of art and was indeed regarded by them as so basically a type of art that they imagined all types of art which employed other techniques to be 'untrue to nature'. The reader who has followed this inquiry is not likely, I hope, to fall into these errors. He is not likely, I hope, to assume that the mechanical vision of the human eye, the part, that is, of our perception which is like the camera's vision, is the only part of our perception capable of recording truth.

I have devoted a good deal of space, in various places, to the examination of these particular misconceptions because we live in an age where we are even more surrounded by photographs than were our ancestors in the nineteenth

---

[1] It must be understood that I mean these remarks to apply to those who imitate original architectural works by other artists (or by themselves) as well as to those who imitate original or derived works of other kinds.

century. We all see dozens of photographs every day; and those who go to cinemas see hundreds at every visit. Unless we sit down and think about it we are therefore ourselves liable to these nineteenth-century misconceptions. We have continually to hold before us the difference between the camera's vision and human perception. If we fail to do this we fail to understand the difference between naturalistic imitation and representational art.

There is a widespread notion that there is some intrinsic value in technique. My attitude to this notion will also be familiar to the reader of this inquiry. I hold that no work of any intrinsic value can be produced by an artist unless his hand obeys his mind; but that obedience cannot be held to have a value in itself; adequate technique is indispensable but it has no existence apart from the particular activity of which it is a part.

The intrinsic value of a work of original art or disinterested popular art derives from the artist's initial experience and the communication to himself of that experience in symbolic concrete form. Technique is called into being as a process in the achievement of that purpose. It is a mistake to credit it with intrinsic value of its own.

In the case of venal popular art which has, as I have submitted, no intrinsic value, technique is called into being as a process for the achievement of that contact with the spectator's familiar experience which is the purpose of the work. Here again it is impossible to credit the technique with intrinsic value of its own; it is here again merely part of a process and inseparable from it.

The notion of the intrinsic value of technique is the result, I think, of the assumption that naturalistic technique is difficult. But, as I have already explained, that technique is a mere trick which any flapper can be taught in a year or two at an art school. In the case of the original artist using *representational* technique to symbolize actual or imagined perception, the invention of an appropriate technique in each work is, in truth, difficult; nevertheless if the artist's mind is clear enough to give precise directions the hand's obedience is a relatively simple aspect of his task.

It should also be noted that most cases in our day of what is called precocious artistic talent are merely cases of facility in the naturalistic technique. Children normally do not employ this technique; because the ordinary child's mechanical vision is reinforced to perception by curiosity and various kinds of desire. Normally it is not till the child has acquired the habit of looking at pictures or photographs that it begins to record its purely mechanical vision; when it does this rather earlier than usual it is credited with precocious artistic talent and the career of an artist begins to be discussed at the family table; and as I have

205

mentioned earlier the absurd notion that facility in this trick is evidence of the qualities that make an artist is encouraged by art masters who live by its perpetuation.[1]

What I submit then in respect to the value of technique is:

(1) Technique has no intrinsic value.

(2) The acquired value of any particular technique is just the amount of value which the spectator may choose to present to it. This is a varying value. At one time 'artistic' people present acquired value to one technique, at another to another, just as at one time they present high acquired value to one type of art and at another to another.

N. VALUE OF GENIUS

In 'Genius and the critic' in Part I, I have suggested that the activity of the genius may be complex or simple. My view is that the genius is either a man who can reconcile conflicting attitudes and fuse them to a homogeneous whole or else a man of an unusual clarity of thought who can remain consistently in one attitude and evolve magnificent symbols of his enlargements of experience in one chosen field.

All works of genius have intrinsic value, because all such works are original art. In appropriate conditions they also always eventually have high acquired value because they are always eventually admired by spectators.[2]

The admiring spectators are generally in the first instance derivative popular artists who regard the works of genius as a storehouse to be plundered, though such artists generally miss the true character and purpose of those works. Eventually the large public which we call 'the world', in its study of the past, arrives via the imitators, to the fountain-head; and we then have the intrinsic value of the original works together with, but still separate from, the acquired value of the derivative artists' appreciation and the acquired value of 'the world's' appreciation.

Moreover it must be noted that complex works of genius present value to

[1] Childrens drawings seem to me to fall into two types: those which are secret communications of something to themselves and those which are records of their direct and immediate vision. I refer here to the first kind and in the 'Epilogue to the 1935 edition' to the second. Naturalistic photographic technique is not required for either procedure or used in either till after experience of photographs [1935 note.]

[2] If they are preserved. For that, appreciation by rich men or bodies is required. Cf. next section 'The question of survival'.

several kinds of spectators; also that when the artist is powerful enough to symbolize formal and descriptive, or formal and romantic, or religious and formal enlargements of experience in one original work, he enables people to secure a double or a triple or a fourfold value from his work. But when an artist is not powerful enough, any conscious attempt to combine enlargements of different kinds of experience in one work produces hybrid works of low intrinsic value; and the same thing happens when the artist is merely muddle-headed.

Thus works by a genius, though always the cause of thousands of intrinsically worthless works of derivative art, may themselves have the highest intrinsic value of their category or combine the high intrinsic values of several categories of art.

Also it must be noted that the genius may produce work of high intrinsic value in one category and include in the work elements that have less intrinsic value because those elements are less perfect of their kind. Such a genius often has intelligent original followers who can discriminate between the perfect aspects of the master's work and its less perfect aspects. Such intelligent followers are not tempted to imitate the perfect aspects of the master's work but are impelled to emulate the less perfect aspects and produce work of their own where those aspects shall be improved upon. Rubens, for example, as an original descriptive artist, was supreme, but as a formal artist, though brilliant he was not of the highest class; his intelligent original follower Jordaens developed the formal aspects of Rubens' art to much more subtle elaboration, as can be seen in Jordaens' pictures in the Brussels Museum.[1]

What I submit then on this point is:

(1) that the intrinsic value of the work of genius is always high of its class and may be multiple; and

(2) that its acquired value in appropriate conditions is bound eventually to be high also.

O. THE QUESTION OF SURVIVAL

It is commonly assumed that works of high intrinsic and acquired value survive and works of low value of both kinds disappear. This is an error. All

---

[1] I refer to the pictures called *The King drinks*, where the topers have obviously not interested the painter in any degree. These pictures are brilliant experiments in mountain-of-bricks Cubism; the architectural disposal of the volumes is different in each case and in some it is incredibly subtle and complicated.

forms of popular art, it is true, tend to disappear because they are often executed in perishable materials and because their acquired value is subject to fluctuation. But even when we get to works executed in relatively speaking permanent materials like stone or bronze or oil paints their survival depends on a number of factors.[1]

Many of the survivals from the past have survived through the accident of rediscovery. Much intrinsically valuable art may still be buried; much has perished utterly. Apart from accidents, a work of art, being an object, can only physically survive if it is owned by people capable of preserving it in their lifetime and of handing it on from generation to generation; such people are (*a*) rich men who can preserve their property in safe conditions and transmit it by testament and (*b*) rich public bodies, e.g. the Church, the civil authorities, museums, etc. which can place it in or on humanly speaking permanent buildings or in public places (streets, parks, etc.).

From the time of the Italian Renaissance rich men have had the habit of collecting works of art; when national galleries and museums were instituted such rich men acquired the habit of presenting or selling the whole of their collections to the nation. Our own National Gallery began with the Angerstein collection, and it has been continuously recruited in the same way since; and the British section of the Gallery received a hundred and fifty-seven pictures in one day when Robert Vernon, a horse-dealer, presented his collection in 1857.

The taste of rich collectors is not impeccable. They frequently buy popular art of no intrinsic value. But the public finding the works presented by rich men displayed in the national museums is led to assume that all the works have survived because they are intrinsically eminent as works of art.

It is important, I think, to realize that the presence of a work of art in a museum cannot be taken as a criterion of its value both for the reason I have just indicated and because, as I mentioned earlier, trustees and curators who esteem it their duty to flatter the public by displaying popular rather than original works are not unknown.

I have made no reference to money values because that, of course, is a separate inquiry in itself. But we must remember in this connection that there are in the world to-day two distinct factors which create the money values of works of art: the first is critical appreciation by people who specialize in art study and the second is the taste of exceedingly rich men; and that sometimes these factors work together and sometimes they are opposed. We must also remember

[1] I have referred to the almost total destruction of original works by the ancient Greek sculptors in *The Meaning of Modern Sculpture*. [1935 note.]

that the money values of works of art to-day are influenced by the dealers' knowledge of the financial resources of potential purchasers; and that for this reason both original works of genius of high intrinsic value, and popular works which have low or no intrinsic value, often have money values of an exaggerated kind when their possession is desired by exceedingly rich men or museums.

P. CONCLUSION

I have now done what I set out to do. I have described the character of the modern movement in the plastic arts, as I understand it; I have contrasted that character with the ideas of art and technique in the nineteenth century against which the modern artists have reacted; and I have made a sketch for a theory of values on the assumption that the original artist when he believes that his work has intrinsic value without reference to spectators other than himself has grounds for that faith which alone supports him and 'keeps him going'.

In other words I have set down what I hold the modern movement to be and what I hold to be its intrinsic value.

I know well that what I have set down in each section is only the beginning of each story. But I believe it in each case to be the right beginning, and that is why I have set it down.

Q. SUMMARY OF VALUES

(a) Original art

1. Original architectural art, honestly and competently passed as right by the artist as spectator of his own work (hereinafter referred to as the artist-spectator), has high intrinsic value as a successful symbol of a man's successful effort to enlarge his experience of formal order; such art if apprehended by another spectator performs for him a task which as a normal man with a normal urge towards greater comprehension and appreciation of normal order he desires to perform himself but cannot.

2. Original romantic art, honestly and competently passed as right by the artist-spectator, has high intrinsic value as a successful symbol of a man's successful effort to enlarge his experience of unusually emotive fragments; such

o   209

art if apprehended by another spectator performs for him a task which as a normal man with a normal urge towards greater comprehension and appreciation of unusually emotive fragments he desires to perform himself but cannot.

3. Original descriptive art, honestly and competently passed as right by the artist-spectator, has high intrinsic value as a successful symbol of a man's successful effort to enlarge his scientific, social historical or moral experience; such art if apprehended by another spectator performs for him a task which, as a normal man with a normal urge towards greater comprehension and appreciation of everyday life, he desires to perform himself but cannot.

4. All original art is produced without reference to the work's effects on spectators other than the artist.

5. In addition to its intrinsic value original art may have acquired value deriving from the spectator's appreciation. But that acquired value is another kind of value; it cannot contribute to the work's intrinsic value, or detract from it; it cannot be a criterion of the work's intrinsic value.

(b) Popular art

1. Disinterested popular art of any kind honestly and competently passed as right by the artist-spectator has a measure of intrinsic value as the fulfilment of the artist's purpose. But as that purpose does not include any enlargement of the artist's experience the intrinsic value of his work is much lower than the intrinsic value of the corresponding kind of original art.

2. Venal popular art cannot be honestly and competently passed as right by the artist-spectator because the rightness or wrongness depends on the incidence or non-incidence of the contact with other spectators' familiar experience which the artist set out to achieve. Venal popular art has therefore no intrinsic value.

3. The sole value of venal popular art is acquired value derived from the spectator's appreciation.

4. That acquired value is a variable factor; the value of venal popular art tends for that reason to go up and down and sometimes totally to disappear.

5. All derivative art is popular in kind.

(c) The value of technique

1. The intrinsic value of a work of original art or disinterested popular art derives from the artist's fulfilment of his purpose. Technique is called

into being in that process. It is a means to an end. It has no intrinsic value of its own.

2. In venal popular art technique is called into being as a process in the achievement of that contact with other people's familiar experience which was the artist's purpose. Here again it is a means to an end; and has no intrinsic value of its own.

3. Any particular technique may have an acquired value from spectators' appreciation. That value is variable; at one time one technique is given a high value, at another time another. But no amount of acquired value thus presented by spectators can give intrinsic value to any technique.

4. It is a fatal error to assume that any particular technique is a type of art.

(d) Value of genius

1. The work of genius is always original. It may be simple or complex.

2. If complex its intrinsic value may be multiple.

3. Such art if fully apprehended by the spectator may give him several kinds of satisfaction by enlarging his experience in several ways.

4. The acquired value of a work of genius cannot add to or detract from its intrinsic value. Also it cannot be the criterion of that intrinsic value.

5. The acquired value of a work of genius is variable. But eventually in appropriate conditions it is always high.

6. Muddle-headed art is easily mistaken for the complex work of genius.

(e) Value of survival

1. Some works of art survive on their intrinsic value, some on their acquired value; many survive as the result of accident, most as the result of appreciation by rich men or powerful bodies able to preserve them.

2. The presence of a work in a museum is no criterion of its intrinsic value.

3. High money values are determined partly by the critical appreciation of people who specialize in art study and partly (and mainly) by the taste of exceedingly rich men.

INDEX